Myths of Ethnicity and Nation

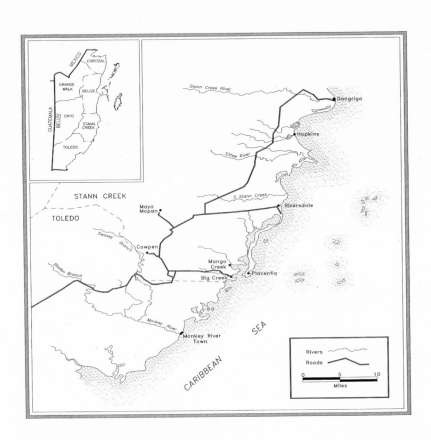

Mark Moberg

# *Myths of Ethnicity and Nation*

## IMMIGRATION, WORK, AND IDENTITY
## IN THE BELIZE BANANA INDUSTRY

The University of Tennessee Press / Knoxville

All photographs by the author.

*Frontispiece.* The Stann Creek and Toledo Districts of Belize. Map by Jody Badillo, U.S.A. Archaeological Lab.

Parts of chapters 6 and 7 have appeared as "Myths That Divide: Immigrant Labor and Class Segmentation in the Belizean Banana Industry" in *American Ethnologist,* copyright 1996 by the American Anthropological Association.

Parts of chapter 7 have appeared as "Transnational Labor and Refugee Enclaves in a Central American Banana Industry" in *Human Organization,* copyright 1996 by the Society for Applied Anthropology.

*Library of Congress Cataloging-in-Publication Data*

Moberg, Mark, 1959–
Myths of ethnicity and nation : immigration, work, and identity in the Belize banana industry / Mark Moberg. — 1st ed.
    p.  cm.
Includes bibliographical references and index.
ISBN 0-87049-970-x (cloth: alk. paper)
1. Banana trade—Belize—History. 2. Banana trade—Belize—Employees—History. 3. Agricultural laborers—Belize—History. 4. Alien labor—Belize—History. 5. Belize—Ethnic relations.
I. Title.
HD9259.B3B426 1997
338.1'74772'097282—dc21                                        96-51261
                                                                CIP

For my parents

The Fruit Company Incorporated
reserved for itself the most succulent,
the central coast of my own land,
the delicate waist of America.
It rechristened its territories
as the "Banana Republics"
and over the sleeping dead,
over the restless heroes
who brought about the greatness,
the flags and their freedoms,
it established a comic opera:
it ravished all enterprise,
awarded the laurels like Caesars,
unleashed all the covetous, and contrived
the tyranny of the Flies. . . .
Then from the bloody domain of tyrants
the Fruit Company Incorporated sailed off
with a booty of coffee and fruits
brimming its cargo boats, gliding
like trays with the spoils
of our drowning dominions.
—Pablo Neruda, "La United Fruit Co." (1950)

Neruda, Pablo. 1974. *Five Decades: A Selection
(Poems: 1925–1970)*. Edited and translated by Ben
Bellett. New York: Grove Press. Used by permission.

# Contents

# Illustrations

# Tables

# Acknowledgments

A great debt of gratitude is owed to all who made this book possible. I first wish to acknowledge the National Science Foundation, whose grant (DBS-9211573) funded most of the research on which the book is based. I also thank the University of South Alabama's Research Committee, which provided support for a pilot project in 1991. Finally, my return to the field and the Archives of Belize in 1995 was made possible by a Summer Stipend (FT-40792-95) from the National Endowment for the Humanities.

In less positive fashion, I also acknowledge those who attempted to impede the research, for they sharpened my resolve to bring it to completion. Shortly before I planned to leave for the field, a supermarket tabloid crudely caricatured the project as a wasteful government expenditure. Compounding geographical ignorance with slander, a congressman quoted in the paper questioned my motives for "visiting a country with beautiful beaches." He also requested that the NSF reconsider its support for the project. Congressional interference in peer-reviewed scholarship was still uncommon in 1992, but the experience foreshadowed a wave of imperious hostility to all forms of critical inquiry in the humanities and social sciences. NSF's Program for Cultural Anthropology deserves my deepest thanks for resolutely defending the project, and the procedure of peer reviewed scholarship, from such demagoguery. Unfortunately, the Summer Stipends Program of the National Endowment for the Humanities, to which I owe much of the first and second chapters of this book and its epilogue, may not survive recent congressional efforts to foreclose critical scholarship.

My friend and Dean, Steve Thomas, shared with me the long and eventful drive through Mexico with which the research began in 1993. To my colleagues David Gartman, Lynn Kwiatkowski, and Greg Waselkov I am also indebted for their friendship and editorial assistance in the process of research and writing. I especially wish to thank Jody Badillo of the USA Archaeology Lab for preparing the maps in this volume. I owe much as well to the Belizean scholars who assisted me at every step of this project, including Dr. Joseph

Palacio of the University of the West Indies, John Morris and the late Harriot Topsey of the Department of Archaeology, and Charles Gibson, Margaret Ventura, Marvin Pook, and Louis Avila of the Archives of Belize in Belmopan. Finally, Antonio Zabaneh and Zaid Flores of the Banana Growers' Association in Mango Creek provided much assistance in the early stages of field research.

In the course of this project, countless individuals facilitated my entrée and participant observation on nearly all of the region's commercial banana farms. Regrettably, to acknowledge by name the many people in the banana belt, and one family in particular, whose assistance was vital to this research would be impossible for reasons of both space and ethical considerations. I would, however, like to anonymously thank four residents of Cowpen and Mango Creek who helped to administer structured surveys among banana workers. The material that follows will not be well received by all participants in the industry, least of all those whose power places them in a position to act on their objections to it. Suffice it to say that the names of all informants in this book have been rendered as pseudonyms. Only elected officials at the national level and Misheck Mawema, a labor leader who no longer resides in the country, are identified by their actual names. The one exception to that rule is the activist discussed in the book's epilogue, for her identity and story are already nationally known and could not be effectively concealed. Fortunately, I am able to acknowledge by name the able assistant who accompanied me for part of the fieldwork. Ana Castillo Burgamy exhibited a profound empathy for immigrants in Belize and is responsible for many insights in the following pages. My only regret is that the rodent- and tarantula-infested housing that we shared was so far removed from the beautiful beaches that some might impute to ethnographers' itineraries.

The process of seeking an outlet for a scholarly work on Belize is seldom an encouraging one, given most publishers' fears that any such book will be consigned to a small readership. Consequently, I was elated by the prompt and professional review that the manuscript received from the University of Tennessee Press, and the extraordinary faith in the project shown by its acquisitions editor, Meredith Morris-Babb. I also thank the two outside reviewers of this book, one of whom is anonymous, for their insightful comments on the manuscript. I was especially gratified by the enthusiastic review of Professor O. Nigel Bolland, as it is his pioneering historiography that has provided the model for my own research on Belize.

Ultimately, I owe my greatest thanks to my wife Debra Moberg and daughters April and Angela for their patience and unwavering support during my prolonged absence from home, which made many emotional demands on all of us. Angela blessed us with her birth halfway through my research, and indirectly inspired this work as it slowly assumed the form of a book. To her generation we bequeath a world seething with myriad forms of injustice, some of which form the central themes of this book. If at times we despair of ever seeing the birth of a more humane world, we should never resign ourselves to economic structures in which work is routinely brutalized. For the sake of our children's world, we must seek ways to restore human dignity to human labor.

# Prefatory Notes on Central American Banana Industries

1. So that our great sacrifices and our numerous investments will not be in vain, we must acquire and control as much national and private land and as many resources as our purchasing and absorption capacity allows.
2. We must lean toward enriching our company and keep open all possibilities for new fields of exploitation. In short, we must obtain as much land as our strategic interests warrant and that will guarantee our future growth and agricultural development, increasing our economic power.
3. We must obtain rigid contracts that will thwart all other competition, even in the distant future; so that any other company that is established and develops will be controlled by us and adapt to our established principles.
4. We must obtain concessions, privileges, franchises, exemptions from customs duties and exoneration from all public charges, and mortgages and all taxes and obligations that reduce our profits and those of our associates. We must build ourselves a privileged position in order to impose our commercial philosophy and defend our economic interests.
5. It is indispensable that we cultivate the imagination of our local vassals, to attract them to the idea of our general aggrandizement, and do the same with politicians and leaders who we will need to use. By observation and careful study we are sure that the population, degraded by alcohol, is amenable for that which it is needed and destined.

—H. V. Rolston, vice-president of Cuyamel Fruit, to the company's lawyer in Honduras (20 July 1920)

It may seem incongruous that a fruit considered benignly nutritious should be grown nearly everywhere under conditions that abuse the health and human rights of those who labor in its production. From the founding of the empires of the United Fruit Company and its chief competitors nearly a century ago, the production of bananas for North American and European consumption has been marked by a level of mistreatment of human and natural resources that is scandalous even by the jaded standards of imperial history. The very act that initiated United Fruit's involvement in Central America, the construction of Minor Keith's railroad through the malarious hinterland of Puerto Limón, Costa Rica, cost the lives of five thousand migrant workers from Jamaica and the West Indies, Italy, China, and Central America. Of this number, an estimated 80 percent died in laying just the first twenty miles of track (Stewart 1964, 43). To this day, Costa Ricans of West Indian ancestry observe that "under every one of those *poleen* [railroad ties] is the body of a colored man" (Purcell 1993, 26).

Perhaps most striking to the observer of labor relations and living conditions on Central American banana plantations is the fact that muckraking exposés such as Charles Kepner's *Social Aspects of the Banana Industry,* first published in 1936, have lost none of their power or relevance with the passage of time. Despite the efforts of United Fruit to improve its decidedly negative image throughout Latin America, the company's euphemistic public relations campaigns merely underscore the most resented elements of corporate paternalism, from workers' "dormitories" to so-called break-even commissaries (cf. May and Plaza 1958).[1] During his fieldwork on a United Fruit plantation at Sixaola, Costa Rica, Philippe Bourgois measured a room for three workers in company housing at 2.3 by 3.3 meters (1989, 4). As for the company's claim that the it sells provisions to workers at cost, McCann (1976, 40) observes that in the 1950s such nominally nonprofit commissaries actually generated a surplus of $3 million on sales of $19 million to the company's Central American employees. McCann, a former United Fruit executive, explained that such operations are made to appear to "break even" by accounting procedures that charge losses by unrelated company operations to the commissaries: "In this way, the company store could take with one hand and still maintain the appearance of giving with the other" (ibid., 40).

Such miserly profiteering has been matched by a stunning waste of resources, the company at one time controlling well over twenty times the 139,000 acres under its cultivation simply to deny good banana-producing land to prospective competitors (ibid., 39–40). Prior to the advent of disease-resistant varieties in the 1950s, each time a United Fruit division fell prey to

Panama disease, once the bane of the Central American banana industry, or declining soil fertility, the company abandoned production in one region or nation for another uninfected and more fertile region. With each relocation, United Fruit "systematically destroyed the infrastructure it had constructed (railroads, bridges, telephone lines, etc.) in order to prevent competitors from being able to renew production on a smaller scale" (Bourgois 1989, 8).

Rather than remedying the conditions that generate often violent opposition to their operations from employees and citizens alike, the multinational fruit companies have historically resorted to intimidation and paternalism of the crudest sort. The corporate strategies enumerated in Rolston's 1920 letter have had counterparts among all of the banana multinationals throughout this century.[2] Since the 1940s, United Fruit (now known by its popular trademark Chiquita Brands) has maintained elaborate blacklists of "undesirable" workers, a practice that complements even older practices of spying on employees and defeating strikes by importing ethnically distinct workers as strikebreakers. Yet even these acts pale before its overt disregard of the sovereignty of Central American nations in protecting its interests. Samuel Zemurray, a colorful United Fruit president in the 1930s, openly acknowledged the company's use of petty bribery to obtain concessions with his offhand and much-quoted remark that "in Honduras, a mule costs more than a deputy" (Volk 1981, 5). With the passage of time, the scale of such practices changed, if their nature did not: in 1974, the company's president paid a $1.25 million bribe to the president of Honduras in exchange for a reduction of that country's banana export tax (ibid., 21). From its installation of the compliant Manuel Bonilla as president of Honduras in 1910 to its collaboration with the Central Intelligence Agency in overthrowing the reformist Arbenz government of Guatemala in 1954, the banana multinationals have recast the image of Central American governments as "banana republics" subject to their will and interests. Central Americans, seeing little that is humorous in the term, for their part refer to the banana companies and their pervasive influence as *el pulpo,* "the octopus."

Given the domination of world markets by Chiquita and a handful of competitors, it comes as little surprise that production processes, producer prices, and, by extension, wages and working conditions tend everywhere to be driven by the decisions taken in a few corporate boardrooms. In Belize, where banana growers are in most cases independent producers, fruit prices are nonetheless established by Fyffes Group Ltd., the largest European ba-nana importer and until 1986 a fully owned subsidiary of United Fruit. Consequently, the innovations of labor control devised on corporate-owned plantations elsewhere in Central America have been recreated on private farms in Belize. The overall similarity in banana production processes worldwide arises ostensibly from marketing strategies accommodating the tastes of North American and European consumers. Since the 1950s, when Panama disease–resistant varieties were introduced, most bananas produced for export have been of the Gran Nain or Valerie strains. Both varieties are much more susceptible to bruising in handling than types previously cultivated. Fyffes, like Chiquita, refuses to pay for fruit with any discoloration or other evidence of mishandling, claiming that consumers in developed countries are unwilling to buy such produce. Similarly, Fyffes refuses to purchase fruit that falls outside of a range between six and a half and ten inches in length, or fruit that has fewer than three "fingers" per "hand."[3] These requirements, justified by the company with reference to the tastes of North American and European consumers, lead to similar procedures for handling and packaging fruit throughout banana-producing regions of the Americas. They also account for the ubiquity of confrontational labor relations on banana farms, as workers attempt to maximize piece-rate earnings by handling fruit quickly, while supervisors try to slow the pace of fruit handling to improve quality. As will be seen, quality controls not only result in enormous waste of otherwise edible fruit but also provide Fyffes with a powerful mechanism for disciplining its often restive private suppliers.

Notwithstanding such similarities of production worldwide, in Belize production occurs on twenty-three farms of as few as eight acres and as many as seven hundred. What sets the Belizean industry apart from the massive United Fruit division documented in Bourgois's pioneering study is the diversity of farm operations and variety of local and imported populations put to work on them. Banana growers may rely on no more labor than that of their immediate families, or they may command a small army of three hundred workers or more. Consequently, just one ethnic group and gender may be represented in a farm's labor force, or as many as eight ethnic groups and four nationalities, men and women among them, may be employed on a farm. The largest farms in Belize recruit into their work forces men and women whose native languages include Spanish, Mopan Maya, Kekchi, Kachiquel, Quiché,

Creole English, and Garifuna. Hence, what emerges from this book is the multiplicity of experiences of labor control and resistance, a diversity that has not yet been homogenized through corporate directives or indirect control.

Despite the lack of direct corporate control over the Belizean banana industry, the conditions prevailing at the level of pricing and marketing closely influence the wage and working conditions on each farm. Hence, the abuses widely reported on banana plantations elsewhere in Central America have their local counterparts, probably because such practices are integral to the marketing and pricing policies of the banana multinationals. The authoritarian labor relations existing throughout the industry present the ethnographer with unique methodological difficulties. Farm owners are not unconscious of the appalling, often illegal, working and living conditions on their farms, and many appear uncomfortable or defensive in discussing them. It is indicative of such conditions that owners customarily deflect such questions by favorably comparing their own farms with those of a group of expatriate Europeans, whose ill treatment of workers is notorious even by industry standards. Similarly, workers have much to fear in describing the conditions under which they labor. Few are familiar with the practice and goals of ethnography, and probably all retain doubts that volunteered information will in fact remain confidential. Adding to the difficulty, if not peril, of research in this setting is the incorporation of the region and many of its inhabitants in hemispheric circuits of cocaine transhipment. While acutely observing the unmentioned aspects of life on banana farms, future ethnographers would be well advised to not directly inquire about the more conspicuous and profitable sidelines in which industry participants are involved.

Notwithstanding the reluctance of workers and growers to volunteer information about certain aspects of the industry, what one group reticently mentions in passing another details in torrents of indignation. Growers readily discuss the intransigence and disguised insubordination of their workers while avoiding mention of the working conditions to which they are subjected. For their part, workers denounce injustice suffered at the hands of managers and farm owners but sidestep questions of sabotage and destruction. Through this process of triangulation a mosaic portrait of the banana industry gradually emerges, a portrait that is, admittedly, viewed through the refractory lens of its participants.

If there is one area in which all participants agree to volunteer their opinions, it is the question of ethnicity and nationality. Growers view worker identity as a phenomenon closely related to the day-to-day operation of their farms, not unlike more prosaic matters of fertilizer applications or irrigation equipment. They volunteer information about their experiences "managing" their workers and discuss at length how loyalties of race, nationality, and ethnicity, as well as gender differences, affect their ability to produce a perishable crop with minimal disruption of the labor process. For workers, ethnicity and nationality are much less of a mundane matter and much more of an emotional one. They, after all, must live with one another and their often virulent prejudices. Immigrants, the large majority of banana workers, navigate the shoals of a host society that both relies on their labor and fears if not despises their culture. For Belizeans, national differences among immigrants are collapsed into the term *alien,* a convenient shorthand for new arrivals who take jobs at low wages and threaten to forever change the language and culture of an Anglophone Caribbean society.

Finally, a word of caution prefaces this ethnography of banana workers lest it be falsely seen to support the violent stereotypes that pervade Belizean discourse on immigration. It must be emphasized at the outset that the violence and predation of everyday life in the banana belt are attributable to no cause but the daily inhumanity to which immigrant workers are subjected. The consequences of poverty, racism, and marginalization are not pretty, and the poor are done no service when their lives are romanticized by otherwise well-intentioned ethnographers. Similarly, lest the chapters that follow suggest an unrelievedly hopeless account of oppression at the hands of a sovereign world market and grasping elites, the ongoing unionization drive discussed at the end of the book offers some solace. In the continuing efforts of immigrant workers to overcome the divisions in their midst, and of their allies in Belize and abroad to come to their aid, may yet be found some measure of triumph over inhumanity.

# Introduction

## CASTE AND CLASS IN SOUTHERN BELIZE

When approaching the villages of Mango Creek and Independence, twin settlements of about twelve hundred residents in southern Stann Creek District, visitors encounter a sign welcoming them to the Banana Capital of Belize. Although the nearest banana farms lie twelve miles away along a torturous dirt road, few Belizeans would dispute the sign's claim. The villages are home to most of the country's banana farmers and headquarters of the Belizean Banana Growers' Association (BGA). It is at the local port that Fyffes, the multinational corporation that markets Belizean bananas, maintains its offices, and from there that the nation's production is shipped to foreign markets. The export orientation of the region is so pronounced that, ironically, bananas are rarely found for sale in the villages' shops.

Mango Creek could serve as a textbook example of M. G. Smith's "plural society" (1965), for the segments of its population are brought together not by the bonds of kinship and natural community but by the industry's voracious demand for labor. For a variety of related reasons, a striking discontinuity if not tension pervades the town, in marked contrast to the more homogeneous settlements outside the banana belt. Although Mango Creek is inhabited by Belizean Creoles, Garifuna, Mestizos, and Maya, as well as Honduran, Salvadoran, and Guatemalan immigrants, its residents move in two discrete and mutually antagonistic spheres: worlds locals signify with the word *Belizean* and the more disparaging term *alien*. Divisions of color, language, and nationality are readily apparent to casual observers, but other, less overt sources of tension augment these. Most of the community's wealth and attendant political power are concentrated in the hands of a single family whose members, most residents agree, "run everything around here." A defiant graffito scrawled on an abandoned building attests to the family's pervasive dominance and the paralysis it engenders among poorer residents: "Who gives a damn when the Achmeds own the town?" An incipient epidemic of drug abuse adds to the strains of ethnic confrontation and extreme stratification. The use of crack cocaine by some of the village's youth has fueled a wave of burglary and prostitution discomforting for a community of its size.[1]

However distinct these sources of tension appear, they are all arguably situated in a regional economy whose object is the production of a perishable commodity for the world market. Driven by the high risk and costs of banana production and the low returns of export prices, banana growers struggle in myriad ways to survive stiff competition with producers in other countries. Against a shifting and unpredictable background of tariffs, market preferences, and foreign consumer demand, banana producers are obliged to seek ever cheaper sources of labor, and to discipline those workers that would resist these trends. In the process, growers recruit workers of different ethnicities, nationalities, and genders, now favoring one group, now abandoning another. Finally, labor markets are ideologically redefined by often elaborate "myths of ethnicity," whereby the composition of the work force is attributed to the supposed predisposition of ethnically distinct workers for different forms of work. Having provided most of the farm labor in the banana industry until the early 1980s, Mango Creek's Belizean residents are now largely abandoned by it. In accounting for their absence from the work force, growers invoke an ahistoric folk ethnology that asserts the "unwillingness" of Creoles and Garifuna to perform farm labor. Displaced from such employment, many Creole residents have turned to other, more precarious forms of livelihood, such as "hustling" and drug trafficking.

This book describes the evolution of an ethnically segmented labor market in response to the local and international constraints on banana production in Belize. It entails a detailed ethnography of the Belizean industry, yet the resulting analysis illustrates in microcosm processes of ethnic change and conflict characterizing many regions of the contemporary world. Economic and political constraints on banana growers are numerous and, to a large extent, beyond their control. Producer prices are determined by the vagaries of international agreements governing tariffs and protected markets, as well as the fickle tastes of European and North American consumers. They are, in addition, affected by the operations and priorities of multinational corporations that market fruit, one of which holds a monopoly on the purchase and export of bananas from Belize.

Such factors alone compel banana growers to reduce labor costs, but the means by which low-cost labor is recruited and deployed are highly volitional. No single form of labor recruitment exists, as the segmentation of work results from a continuous process of experimentation and control by growers on the one hand and resistance by workers on the other. And given the increasingly complex ethnic mosaic of southern Belize, growers can recruit workers from a variety of ethnic groups and nationalities and can deploy their labor in nearly infinite permutations. Yet workers are not faceless factors of production like land or farm implements, for they must work and live together cooperatively if a minimum of industrial and social peace is to be maintained. The segmentation of the work force in the Belizean banana belt is taking place against a background of increasing immigration from Central America and heightened ethnic tension between native-born Belizeans and the new Hispanic arrivals, and often among immigrants themselves. How growers and workers negotiate these tensions is the subject of this book.

As an ethnography of Central American banana workers, this book unequivocally asserts the material and class underpinnings of the ethnic conflict that divides them. By doing so, the analysis sharply breaks from, and implicitly challenges, many recent treatments of ethnic and national identity that remain at the discursive level. Poststructural theorists (e.g., Sollors 1989; Spillers 1991) generally regard national and ethnic conflict as a contest of meaning and discourse but fail to situate such struggles in the more fundamental political and economic processes that draw the members of ethnic groups into competition. Even some structuralists and political economists attain similar conclusions with respect to the autonomy of ethnic conflict from its material basis. Advocates of the New Social movements (Laclau and Mouffe 1985), for example, increasingly regard identities other than class, such as ethnicity, gender, and sexual orientation, as the primary effective basis for contemporary political action. Noting the strident reaction of whites in the United States against minority civil rights in the 1980s, Omi and Winant (1986) similarly assert the irreducibility of race as the fundamental "organizing principle" of social action. Yet the economic restructuring that spelled downward mobility for millions of U.S. citizens during that decade—and that brought white and minority workers into head-on competition for jobs in a dwindling manufacturing base—pass unmentioned by the same scholars. As David Harvey noted in his devastating assessment of postmodern social theory, by positing the autonomy of cultural categories in the present conjuncture of global capitalism, such inquiries preclude understanding of—and reasoned action against—"the political economic processes . . . that are becoming ever more universalizing in their depth, intensity, reach and power over daily life" (1989, 116–17).

While acknowledging that ethnic identities are culturally constructed and negotiated, this book is premised on the claim that such constructions acquire salience because of their relationship to class. Conversely, insofar as they inhibit recognition of class membership, ethnic and national identities diminish the ability of wage workers to challenge the social and material basis of power. In its incorporation of countless culturally distinct populations as wage labor, Eric Wolf observes, "capitalism did not create all the distinctions of ethnicity and race that function to set off categories of workers from one another. It is, nevertheless, the process of labor mobilization under capitalism that imparts these distinctions their effective values" (1982, 380). As will be seen in the following chapters, the conflicting ethnic and national sentiments so evident today in the Belizean banana industry did not originate with the relatively recent recruitment of immigrant labor. Indeed, these antagonisms have existed since the first years of the arduous Afro-Caribbean and Hispanic encounter in lower Central America—an encounter that, from its outset, has been governed by plantation agriculture's segmented labor recruitment.

## Class, Ethnicity, and Conflict within the Work Force

Despite predictions to the contrary among neoclassical economists as well as early political economists, the virulence of ethnic antagonism shows little sign of lessening either within developed nations or on the frontiers of capitalist development. Paradoxically, both bodies of theory concurred that the expansion of wage relations would diminish the appeal of nationalist and ethnic loyalties among working classes. Asserting that labor is allocated with maximum efficiency when hired by skill and cost rather than ethnicity, neoclassical economists continue to hold that racial segregation in the workplace will in the long term prove counterproductive (Friedman 1962; Cain 1976). Nineteenth-century radical political economy reached the same conclusion via an alternate route, Marx and Engels predicting that workers of differing backgrounds would develop class-based loyalties by virtue of common conditions experienced in the workplace (Marx and Engels 1977, 228). Compelled by price competition to replace skilled labor with machinery, firms would reduce the wages of all workers to minimal subsistence levels. Hence the compulsions of the market would lower living standards within an already impoverished working class, in the process incubating the class consciousness destined to overturn the capitalist mode of production. That such predictions have almost everywhere failed to be realized has provided political economy with one of its greatest explanatory challenges.

A resolution of this challenge was suggested by Marx's later writings, in which he observed that employers manipulated ethnicity in the workplace to retain control over the labor force as a whole. Noting the ways in which prejudices toward Irish workers were promoted among English workers by employers and the popular press, Marx claimed that the resulting "antagonism is the secret by which the capitalist class maintains its power" (Marx 1977c, 591). These observations represented a critical break from his earlier analyses, which viewed the labor process in particular industries as an inevitable consequence of the prevailing technical forces of production.[2] In contrast, Marx's later work recognized that the minute division of labor and deskilling of industrial work served the interests of employers not only by increasing the productivity of labor but also by facilitating its control. These observations became the basis of later neo-Marxist analyses demonstrating how employers' strategies of labor control have historically determined the character of industrial labor processes (Braverman 1974; Burawoy 1979; Gartman 1986). These approaches suggest that technical-bureaucratic forms of labor control, emphasizing the proliferation of job and wage categories and machine-pacing of labor, supplanted more direct coercion and paternalism with the growing scale of industry under monopoly capitalism. Marx's later views also anticipate the class segmentation and split labor market theories of ethnic antagonism developed by modern political economists.

In contrast to neoclassical economists, who assume that labor is hired on the basis of cost and skill, most political economists note that employers are far from "color blind" when making decisions about labor recruitment. Such decisions critically affect their overall ability to control the work force and maintain prevailing patterns of surplus value extraction. Many political economists attribute ethnic antagonism in workplaces to differing wage rates, working conditions, and competition for jobs among members of distinct ethnic groups and genders (Baron and Bielby 1980; Bonacich 1980; Fligstein and Fernandez 1988; Miller 1989). According to the earlier of these "competitive" models of ethnic relations, split labor market theory (Bonacich 1972, 1976), antagonism increases when one ethnic group is compelled to accept lower wages than the dominant group. Employers attempt to displace high-wage workers by hiring the less-expensive labor of impoverished or immigrant workers, who are often ethnically distinct.

Bonacich contends that such hiring practices simply reflect prior differences in the cost of labor and are not necessarily discriminatory in intent (1972, 553). Workers belonging to the dominant ethnic group may resort to racial violence to defend their jobs against inroads by cheaper labor. Alternately, they may seek the deportation of immigrants, attempt to confine minority workers to low-wage positions, or create unions that deny membership to minorities. The split labor market model thus views divisive ethnic loyalties as the outcome of conflicting economic interests among workers themselves. These ultimately originate in the differential costs of labor, which may reflect antecedent conditions such as poverty, place of origin, earlier discrimination, or tenuous residential status.

In contrast, class segmentation models (Reich, Edwards, and Gordon 1981; Gordon, Edwards, and Reich 1982; Bridges 1988; Miller 1989) maintain that ethnic antagonism among workers results from discriminatory practices intended to enhance divisions within the work force. Historically, these divisions have corresponded to primary labor markets comprised of relatively well paying jobs and secondary markets (often within the same industry or firm) in which employment is low-paying, seasonal, or lacking in mobility (Miller 1989, 405). Primary markets in North American industry have historically been dominated by white males, while minorities and women have usually been consigned to secondary markets of manual labor and service employment. The lowest rungs of secondary-market employment are generally occupied by immigrants. Because of their insecure residence status and exclusion from programs such as welfare and food stamps, which bolster social wages, immigrants are willing to accept conditions that citizens consider intolerable. Yet immigrant labor, or the threat of its employment, can also be used to discipline secondary-market workers who hold secure citizenship status:

> [Immigrants] can be brought into competition with negatively privileged citizen labor, most particularly blacks, Latinos, women, and youths. As competitors

for the same category of jobs (e.g., in service and retail trade), undocumented workers provide the equivalent of a decrease in the overall wage levels associated with those jobs or a diminution of minimum wage laws in that sector. The latter strategy provides the equivalent of a reduction in the guarantees of citizenship without directly expressing the battle in those terms. (Thomas 1985, 210)

When divisions of ethnicity, citizenship, and gender correspond to differences in wages and working conditions, the work force as a whole is left more malleable, because primary-market employees do not perceive common interests with workers in secondary markets. Segregation may be viewed by workers belonging to dominant ethnic groups and genders as a defense of their livelihoods, but it lessens the ability of all workers to win improvements in wages and working conditions (Barrera 1979, 224). Where ethnic hierarchies correspond to wage scales, workers occupying the lowest ranks suffer the brunt of class segmentation by being assigned work considered too dirty, dangerous, or undignified for members of dominant ethnic groups. For such workers, the result of labor segmentation is "conjugated oppression," in which racism compounds the indignities of low-wage work (Bourgois 1988).

The differences between split labor market and class segmentation perspectives appear subtle, but their theoretical and practical implications are distinct. The models differ fundamentally in identifying the agents and beneficiaries in work-force segregation, although some aspects of the theories are compatible and may be usefully synthesized. Split labor market models elucidate the political responses of workers to ethnic divisions in their ranks, for historically dominant groups have usually rejected common cause with minority or women workers in favor of their castelike segregation or expulsion from primary markets. Yet empirical tests also bear out the predictions of class segmentation theory: work-force segregation lowers overall wages for workers in both primary and secondary markets. In those U.S. industries with the widest earnings disparities between white and minority workers, average wages are lower than in those industries with fewer racial disparities (Reich 1981, 300).

Although class segmentation models have been developed with respect to highly industrialized economies, wherever wage relations are implanted in multiethnic societies comparable patterns of labor allocation often emerge. For centuries plantations throughout the non-Western world have drawn diverse populations into the production and processing of agricultural commodities for consumption by the industrialized West. Millions were transported to the far reaches of empires as slaves or indentured labor for such enterprises, colonial administrators frankly counting on the disorientation and diversity of unfree workers to temper their resistance to often fatal working conditions. Due to the low pay and adverse working conditions usually associated with seasonal agricultural employment, the potential for class resistance remains more pronounced in export agriculture than in any other rural employment sector (Paige 1975; Scott 1979). Much ethnographic evidence from Latin America indicates that the composition of agricultural work forces is manipulated to inhibit collective resistance to plantation work regimes. Guatemalan cotton plantations recruit Indian and Mestizo workers from dispersed highland villages, for example, "so that differences in ethnic identity, language, and status impede the realization of common interests" (Bossen 1982, 267) In Perú, full-time farm workers, who are unionized and earn relatively high wages, tend to be Mestizos, whereas their more numerous and poorly paid seasonal counterparts are almost invariably Quechua speakers (Stein 1984). Among the most compelling studies of plantation work-force recruitment and control has been Bourgois's (1988, 1989) account of a United Fruit Company banana "division" straddling the border of Costa Rica and Panama. From voluminous archival records of corporate memoranda and cable traffic, Bourgois demonstrates how United Fruit consciously employed West Indian, Mestizo, and indigenous labor in ways that disabled class-based resistance to its operations. Even more complex mosaics of ethnicity can be discerned in the banana fields of Belize, and compounding divisions in the work force is the banana industry's wholesale employment of women in the packing sheds adjoining every farm. Drawing on a deep pool of impoverished Belizean and immigrant female labor, the industry has employed women since its inception to complete the most tedious, unrewarding, and yet exacting labor in export agriculture: the sorting and packaging of perishable fruit.

Ethnicity is but one of many divisions impeding collective resistance within a banana work force that is now thoroughly internationalized. In the last two decades, paramilitary groups and armed forces have unleashed waves of terror against the rural poor throughout much of the region (see Manz 1988; Falla 1994). Tens of thousands of displaced Central Americans have fled to Belize since 1980 in pursuit of work and peace, but the absence of substantial political repression in their new home does not facilitate their involvement in class-based movements there. Because the large majority of

immigrants working in Belize enjoy no formal protection against deportation to the repressive conditions of their homelands, few are willing to
overtly challenge the conditions under which they work. Ironically, then, immigrants find an incomplete refuge from terror in Belize, for the prospect of
involuntary return compels their acquiescence in the workplace even in the
absence of local oppression. Nor does their common status as primarily Hispanic immigrants inspire much common sentiment, for national antagonisms divide the immigrant work force unto itself. Having fought a brief but
bloody war in 1969, Honduras and El Salvador have since then incited their
citizens against each other through both the popular press and government
pronouncements. The results of such sustained propaganda are measured
today in the profound distrust and occasional violence erupting among
Honduran and Salvadoran immigrants in Belize.

Immigration emerged as the most critical issue facing Belize by the late
the 1980s, when the country's population claimed the highest proportion of
foreign- to native-born residents in the hemisphere. Immigration also presents many paradoxes, for harsh policy rhetoric intended for public consumption is coupled with a near total neglect of enforcement. The failure to
enforce immigration policy results not from the ineptitude of policy makers
but from their conscious decision to promote the expansion of a low-wage
work force. Because many immigrant workers are undocumented or enjoy
minimal legal rights to residence in Belize, they are incapable of organizing
for higher wages. Immigration policy in practice, then, closely complements
the state's development and structural adjustment priorities. Yet the settlement of a sizable foreign work force in Belize also generates unintended political consequences, for it exacerbates longstanding uncertainties of Belizean
national identity.

Since the entry of Mexican refugees from the Caste War of the Yucatán in
the late 1840s, Belize has had a substantial Mestizo population. The large majority of residents of the northern districts of Orange Walk and Corozal are
Spanish-speaking Mestizos (Brockmann 1977). Yet in many respects Belize
has resembled less the neighboring countries of Central America than the
"plural societies" of the former British West Indies. M. G. Smith (1965) and
others viewed the nations of the Anglophone Caribbean as amalgams of
largely noninteracting ethnic groups that form unitary societies only by the
compulsions of an overarching colonial administration. Notwithstanding a
tenuous balance between Hispanics and Afro-Belizeans in its contemporary

population, the country's national identity remains firmly wedded to the Anglophone Caribbean. Officially known as British Honduras until 1973, Belize has long been regarded as a West Indian enclave in an otherwise Hispanic isthmus. Belizean identity thus reflects the ideology of nationhood in many plural societies, in which one culture is held to represent national identity and all others are politically marginalized or stigmatized as "liabilities" to the nation (Safa 1987; Williams 1989, 1991). Wherever states are composed of heterogeneous cultures, each marginalized group potentially represents a competing political entity and is thus seen as a threat to national unity. Given the emergence of Mestizos as the largest ethnic group in Belize, a shift corroborated by the 1990 census, the country's official identity is now flatly contradicted by its demography. Conflict between ethnic groups, which originated in many instances from the displacement of higher-paid Belizean workers by immigrants, has increasingly assumed a phenotypic, cultural, and linguistic dimension. Yet antagonisms between Afro-Caribbean and Hispanic populations also have deep historic roots along the entire Caribbean littoral.

To the volatile mix of ethnicity, gender, and nationality among banana workers must be added the less visible if equally venomous divisions of ideology. Political party or religious loyalties have spatially polarized many communities in southern Belize, their residents relocating from neighbors and kin who profess differing party or religious affiliations. Targeted by patronage-dispensing politicians for their votes, the rural poor in Belize often succumb to formidable and even violent factional loyalties that inhibit community cooperation (Moberg 1991a). Conflicts between traditional (albeit syncretic) Catholics and Protestant converts have also divided many Mopan and Kekchi Maya villages of the Stann Creek and Toledo Districts (Howard 1977). Comparable sentiments may be discerned among Central American immigrants in Belize, many of whom seek deliverance from their oppressive surroundings in a variety of charismatic but divisive fundamentalist sects.

Yet if the multiple and conflicting loyalties experienced by banana workers dilute their sense of class membership, they are not thereby converted into the willing pawns of their employers. If so little trust exists among workers that they are unable to collectively challenge the conditions under which they labor, their individual consent to those conditions is only grudgingly given. As demonstrated for a wide variety of contexts in which overt resistance would be easily detected and quickly crushed (Scott 1985; Stoler 1985; Ong 1987), resistance among banana workers is merely driven underground, where it becomes virtually impossible to eradicate. The impotent rage expressed by farm owners at the theft and destruction of their property, the apparent conspiracies of workers to drag their feet or willfully misunderstand instructions, and the occasional hit-and-run ambushes of payroll agents attest to this subterranean level of rebellion. In the long run, as Scott (1985) documents, such "everyday forms of peasant resistance" often prove as costly to elites as overt rebellion, for it eludes even the most determined efforts to uproot it.

## Labor Recruitment in Agricultural Export Sectors

In both the industrialized and developing worlds, "myths of ethnicity, gender, and nationality" (Griffith 1987, 839) often justify the assignment of people to their respective positions within the work force. Purporting to explain the concentration of particular ethnic groups in different employment sectors, such constructs account for segregated job markets as "the 'natural' outcome of differences in the intellectual capabilities of races" (Williams 1989, 437). In Belize, similar beliefs rationalize the employment of immigrant and indigenous women in packing fruit, Mayas and Mestizos in manual farm labor, and Creoles and Garifuna in supervisory roles. Myths of ethnicity closely complement the political economy of export agriculture by segmenting the labor force, justifying differential wages and working conditions, and ultimately lessening collective resistance to employers. In colonial economies, where members of different ethnic groups were often consciously assigned to differing occupational and status groups, these assignments were nonetheless justified by reference to the supposed cultural preferences or aptitudes of different ethnic groups (Stoler 1985). Having confined blacks to public-service jobs in urban areas and East Indians to semi-indentured status on rice plantations in the interior, colonial authorities in Guyana then viewed "geographical space and economic roles . . . as the natural provinces of different ethnic groups" (Williams 1991, 150). In the process, they created elaborate mythologies that rationalized these occupational differences.

Such beliefs are often most explicit when the work force is segmented by gender. In *maquiladoras* along the Mexican border, managers "invariably" justify their exclusive reliance on a female labor force with claims that men are "more restless and rebellious than women; less patient; more willing to unionize; and perhaps most importantly, less resigned to tolerate rigorous work paces and inadequate working conditions for a low wage" (Fernandez Kelly 1983, 219). Although such characteristics are represented as inherent  qualities of male and female workers, they are in actuality reflections of the differing positions that men and women occupy in the labor market. Lacking full-time employment alternatives, women *are* in many instances willing to accept working conditions that men find intolerable (Green 1983, 319). Patriarchal assumptions also play a role in devaluing women's work. Because "it is generally assumed that women have husbands to provide for them and their children, the value of [their] labor power can be lowered" (Beechey 1978, 186).

Such myths, essential to maintaining disparities in wages and working conditions, may, like other ideologies, change more slowly than the material conditions that gave rise to them. As classical economists have observed, discrimination based on ethnic stereotypes rigidifies labor allocation and inhibits its efficient deployment in production. The same rationales for employing women in export processing (i.e., that they tolerate repetitive work routines at low wages) also preclude their replacement by other workers, despite occasional scarcities of female labor. "Myths of ethnicity" may even prevent employers who are experiencing sudden labor shortages from hiring workers if their ethnic identity is considered unsuitable for a particular task.[3] Given the perishable nature of agro-export commodities, ensuring dependable supplies of "appropriate" labor for each step in production is often problematic.

Where temporary labor must be quickly mobilized, employers often resort to nonmarket mechanisms of recruitment. Recruiting techniques in low-wage agriculture in the United States rely heavily on prior social networks or kin-based systems of authority among workers (Griffith 1987; 1993). Agricultural employers may, for example, expect male workers to bring with them women and dependent children from their households during periods of peak production. Domestic authority patterned along kinship and patriarchal lines thus reinforces labor discipline in low-wage employment sectors (Nash 1985). Such patriarchal attributes of domestic organization are found among some, but not all, of the ethnic groups incorporated into the Belizean banana industry. Recognizing the advantages of, in their words, "a foreman in every family," some farm owners intentionally recruit Maya farm workers for this reason. Yet others resist the temptation to recruit Maya families, noting that a dissatisfied head of household is likely to withhold the labor of other family members as well. Hence, domestic organization that in one context assists the employer in obtaining labor elsewhere becomes the basis of resistance to employer authority.

In other ways as well household organization complements the recruitment of low-wage labor. Relying upon ancillary unpaid activities as diverse as small-scale farming, livestock keeping, or hunting and fishing, households supplement the meager returns of their wage-earning members. In developing economies, household production coupled with reliance on wage labor is the mark of people who are neither fully wage earners nor fully peasants but, instead, "semiproletarians" (de Janvry 1981; Painter 1985). The provision of food or use values by family labor, although not sufficient to fully support the household, significantly supplements the low wages prevailing in export agriculture. Although household production of this sort may be looked upon as a subsidy to capital, allowing employers to pay lower wages than would otherwise be necessary, it may also become a source of resistance to the workplace (Trimberger 1979). Viewing wage work as a supplement to household production, semiproletarians may consider their wage earnings to be less critical to their survival than those workers who exclusively rely on them. In Belize, for example, banana growers complain that absenteeism and turnover is considerably higher among Belizean workers than immigrants. In large part this is because the former often cultivate small farms in their home communities or enjoy other sources of livelihood.

In the process of their incorporation into the banana industry's work force, immigrants and Belizeans bring with them highly divergent experiences that dictate differing levels of acquiescence to plantation discipline. Today's production regimes are not monolithic, for banana farms vary greatly in size, work-force composition and ethnicity, and, according to the workers themselves, severity of discipline. In the long run the terms of pricing and marketing dictated by Fyffes may result in uniform systems of labor control throughout the industry. For the time being, however, farm owners experiment with myriad permutations of worker recruitment. As workers of some ethnicities and antecedent experiences "don't work out," that is, are insufficiently compliant in the eyes of farm owners, rationales for their exclusion and replacement by other ethnic groups are steadily devised. As in the case of Belizean Creoles and Garifuna, whose labor has already been largely abandoned by those who recruit field workers, such rationales stress the unsuitability of some ethnic groups for farm labor. Myth making of this sort proceeds apace despite the inconvenient historical memory of those workers whose labor established the industry only later to be abandoned by it.

## Organization of the Book

Southern Belize, particularly the southernmost district of Toledo, is regarded elsewhere in the country as a remote and forbidding place. In the imagination of urbane Belize City residents, the southern part of the country is peopled by exotic, semicivilized cultures whose isolated hamlets dot the region's coastlines and inland tropical forests. In a nation undergoing rapid cultural change (in large part the result of North American media and economic influence), Toledo and Stann Creek Districts are thought to be the last refuge of traditions that persist outside of time. The visitor to the region does not have to look hard to encounter evidence of this historical lag, even in the larger villages and towns.[4] In the Mango Creek police station, for example, the officer on duty sits beneath a mildewed portrait of a youthful British monarch, whose likeness was removed from public buildings elsewhere during a period of decolonization in the early 1960s.

It is tempting to misconstrue such colonial vestiges for a total absence of recent historical movement. As Wilk (1991) demonstrates, many of what others have viewed as timeless traditions of the Kekchi Maya, ostensibly the region's most "traditional" culture, are actually the result of their periodic involvement in wage and commodity markets. Contemporary banana growers and their immigrant workers similarly describe the banana industry in timeless terms, offering facile cultural explanations for the paucity of Belizean workers on banana farms. Yet the current configuration of labor and ethnicity in the banana industry arose only in the early 1980s, when Hispanic immigrant labor was consciously recruited to displace a much more assertive Belizean work force. Much of this book seeks to reconstruct a labor history enshrouded in myths that rationalize but do not explain why the industry's work force is today dominated by immigrants.

Chapter 1 examines the political and ideological concomitants of British colonialism on the Central American isthmus, which in part account for the vehement response that Central American immigration has elicited from many Afro-Belizeans. Chapter 2 reconstructs the cyclical, uneven history of commercial banana production in Belize, one in which the banana multinationals have continuously sought to influence state policy and dominate private growers for more than a century. The contemporary international context in which the Belizean industry operates is the subject of chapter 3. Conditions of price and quality are dictated to Belizean growers by the multinational corporation that purchases their fruit, creating an ever-present imperative to lower production costs. Fyffes' transfer of virtually all production risk to growers in turn heavily constrains the nature of wage and working conditions on farms. Chapter 4 reconstructs the history of confrontation between Belizean labor and capital until the mid-1980s. This history of labor struggle is almost entirely effaced by today's growers and lives on only in the accounts of displaced workers, newspapers of the period, and a few surviving annual reports of the government's Banana Control Board. By 1985, the struggles between industry unions and management had culminated in the near total exclusion of Belizean labor from banana work and set the stage for today's reliance on immigrant workers.

Chapter 5 examines Central American immigration to Belize within the context of the country's evolving model of export-led development. Although the immigrants who comprise the industry's work force are uniformly cheaper and more malleable than the Belizean workers they replaced, they are far from homogeneous in any national, ethnic, or ideological sense. Chapter 6 details the uses of ethnic and national identity in systems of labor control on banana farms, documenting the often explosive results of differential job assignments that exacerbate "primordial" divisions among immigrants.[5] The origins of the immigrant work force are identified in chapter 7, through analysis of survey data from 157 randomly selected banana worker households located on six farms in the Stann Creek and Toledo Districts. Finally, chapter 8 concludes with an alternative vision of development and nationhood that diverges from the prescribed austerity and ethnic polarization entailed in today's neoliberal development models.

The history of Belize is both remote from and conditioned by the histories of its neighbors. Notwithstanding the exploitation and bigotry of the colonial era, British colonialism also imparted to the country some institutions at odds with the authoritarian practices prevailing throughout much of Central America. The country's functioning democracy, respect for human rights, and relative availability of land for smallholders are in part responsible for its ability to avert the tumultuous conflict experienced by the rest of Central America during the 1980s. It is with this recent history in mind that the ethnic relations on banana farms should be viewed. Rival models of development entail not merely policy differences about how to generate economic growth, but competing views of how a society should constitute itself. The benefits of economic growth based on low-wage labor are real enough, at least for the elites who appropriate them. Less often mentioned are the costs of such strategies: growing ethnic polarization, stratification, and land consolidation by elites. Export-led growth with low-wage labor thus threatens to steer Belize's future in the direction of its neighbors—in a way that neither native-born Belizeans nor newcomers are likely to cherish.

Myths of Ethnicity and Nation

# 1 ❧ Culture and History in the Forgotten District

Occupying just under 8,800 square miles of territory on the Caribbean littoral of Central America, Belize is not the smallest country on the isthmus. That distinction belongs to El Salvador, whose population of 5.2 million occupies 8,292 square miles. Yet with only 189,000 inhabitants in 1991, Belize is by far the least densely settled of the Central American nations.

The country's small population is one of its many peculiar legacies as the only former British colony on the Central American mainland. For purposes of economic development, underpopulation is also one of the nation's greatest liabilities. Literally generations of colonial officials and development planners have attained the same conclusion: the country's small pool of skilled labor and attenuated local markets act as major barriers to sustainable economic growth (Dunlop n.d.; Evans 1948; Downie 1959; Development Finance Corporation 1977). Although the country's marshy coastline and seasonally flooded terrain long inhibited large-scale settlement by the major colonial powers, Belize's small population must be seen as more the result of historical than natural factors.

## Colonial Legacies of Land, Labor, and Class

Until the Central American republics won their independence in the early nineteenth century, Belize was officially a Spanish colonial holding. Having failed in repeated attempts to occupy the interior of the land and missionize its Maya inhabitants, however, the Spanish lacked either the resources or significant interest in defending the territory against rival colonial powers. Origins of European settlement in the territory are shrouded in considerable mythology, but it is probable that colonists from Britain, Spain's principal imperial rival, settled near the mouth of the Belize River in the mid-1600s. The Baymen, as the settlers were known, were in later centuries to become mythi-

1

cal progenitors of the Belizean nation and even immortalized in the country's national anthem. An early-eighteenth-century observer, however, rendered them in less than heroic proportions as "generally a rude drunken Crew, some of which have been Pirates, and most of them Sailors" (N. Uring 1726, cited in Bolland 1977, 28). This mixture of "ungovernable Wretches" (ibid.) was attracted to the site by the presence of logwood (*Haematoxlylum campechianum L.*), a low-growing tree found only on the Yucatán Peninsula and the Caribbean coast of Central America. Because it provided a fixing compound for clothing dyes, logwood was in great demand by the expanding textile industry of Britain in the seventeenth and eighteenth centuries. Indeed, by the mid-eighteenth century, an English report of the time regarded logwood as "absolutely essential to our Woolen Manufactures" (Burdon 1931, 77).

The fortunes of the English "Settlement at the Bay of Honduras," as it was known until 1862, varied according to the changing status of English-Spanish relations in Europe. In the early eighteenth century, the settlers were periodically expelled by Spanish forces, after the withdrawal of which they invariably returned to resume their woodcutting. Spain finally granted English timber cutters and their African slaves the right to occupy the territory under the Treaty of Paris in 1763. In exchange for the right to harvest logwood for export, the settlers were to recognize Spanish sovereignty over the territory. As further conditions they were not permitted to engage in agriculture or establish "fortifications and permanent settlements." Such terms, coupled with Britain's reluctance to antagonize Spain lest it lose its access to the region's valuable forest products, inhibited settlement and population growth well into the nineteenth century (Grant 1976).

Having failed to subdue the region's reclusive and occasionally rebellious Maya populations as a labor force, the Baymen turned elsewhere for timber workers. Throughout the seventeenth century, workers for logwood cutting were primarily recruited among the Miskito of coastal lower Central America. As the pace of woodcutting expanded and settlers turned to the more labor-intensive exploitation of mahogany, they found the available sources of labor within the region insufficient. Beginning in the early eighteenth century, settlers increasingly relied on the labor of enslaved Africans. Although there is no definite indication that Africans were employed in the colony's timber works prior to 1723, within a little over twenty years there were already two and a half times as many Africans as whites in the settlement (Burdon 1931, 72).

Slavery in the territory differed in notable ways from plantation slavery practiced in the West Indies, for Africans worked seasonally in timber camps, where they made daily use of axes and machetes. The fact that slaves worked without whip-wielding drivers and had access to potential weapons led some colonial-era historians to claim, after the slave owners themselves, that slavery in the colony "was much less oppressive than elsewhere" (Waddell 1961, 14). More recent scholarship (e.g., Bolland 1973, 1977) has refuted such claims by documenting the extreme punishments, even by West Indian standards, used to maintain control of scarce labor in the colony. In contrast to the sugar-producing West Indian islands, where escape in most instances was virtually impossible, an unexplored hinterland beckoned in Belize, as did nearby Spanish settlements offering freedom. Colonial documents evidence a continual hemorrhage of slave labor from the British settlement until the abolition of slavery in 1838. In part, this reflected imperial rivalries in the area, for Spain sought to undermine the British colonists economically by promising to free any slaves entering Spanish territory "under pretence of embracing the Holy Catholic Religion" (Burdon 1931, 79). While many fled to Guatemala or the Yucatán as a result of Spanish "enticements," others established Maroon colonies in the interior. Knowledge of such colonies probably contributed to a major slave uprising in 1820, when, according to the colony's English superintendent, "the Negroes who had first deserted . . . had excited others to join them" (Bolland 1988, 62). After the abolition of the slave trade in 1807, the slave population steadily declined from flight, disease, malnutrition, and the slaves' own practices of abortion and suicide. Finally, fairly high rates of manumission contributed to a diminishing slave population in the final decades of the institution, probably due to owners' fears that formally enslaved workers were more likely to flee to Mexico or Guatemala (Bolland 1977, 52–53). If manumission was adopted as a last, desperate effort to retain a timber-cutting work force, it nonetheless failed to stem a deepening and eventually chronic scarcity of labor in the nineteenth century. Nor did it mitigate the many overt forms of domination by which employers controlled scarce labor. In addition to recruiting nominally free populations, such as the Garifuna, to replace fugitive slaves, employers resorted to torture and mutilation of captured fugitives to deter others from escaping (see, e.g., Burdon 1931, 228).

A de facto suppression of agriculture continued long after Britain formally recognized British Honduras as a Crown colony in 1862, for a dominant class of timber companies and expatriate merchants viewed farming as a threat to the primary sources of their power (Bolland and Shoman 1977). These derived from their control of a profitable trade in imported foodstuffs and control of scarce labor for timber employment. Throughout most of the colonial period, timber interests and merchants acquired vast tracts of land not for cultivation but to deny its use to a prospective peasantry. By the late 1800s, a single forestry and import firm, the Belize Estate and Produce Company, had amassed half of the private land in the colony. Land consolidation conspired with debt peonage to ensure a steady flow of nominally free labor into the colony's timber camps (see Bolland 1981).

Although slavery was abolished in the colony in 1838, as it was throughout the British Empire, patterns of labor control changed little in the settlement following abolition. Employers devised an "advance-truck" system of labor recruitment that inhibited the growth of a free-holding peasantry and strengthened the dependence of most workers on the timber industry (Bolland 1988). Under this arrangement, workers received a wage advance prior to each season of forestry employment, and then purchased the balance of their needs on credit from camp stores. Charged prices that usually exceeded their ability to repay their debts, timber workers remained "virtually enslaved for life" by this pattern of labor contracting, according to the resident colonial secretary in 1890 (Ashcraft 1973, 36). By the end of the 1800s, nearly 40 percent of all criminal convictions in the colony were of men who failed to return to work for employers to whom they were indebted (PRO CO 123 165). Those so convicted under the colony's Masters' and Servants' Acts could be imprisoned with up to a year of hard labor, a sentence "easily enforced within the Settlement because the population was so small" (Bolland and Shoman 1977, 64).

A narrow reliance on mahogany and a few other forest exports, which still constituted 85 percent of the colony's economic output as late as the 1920s, subjected the colonial economy to increasingly volatile world markets in the twentieth century. This in turn greatly aggravated the economic uncertainty experienced by most working people. During the early 1930s, when the timber industry collapsed due to diminished export demand during the Great Depression, most of the working population was left destitute. Only after prolonged labor unrest and mounting sentiments for independence did the colonial government abolish the advance-truck system in 1943 (Ashdown 1978). Two years earlier, in response to widespread agitation on the part of idled forestry workers who organized the Labourers and Unemployed Association, the colonial government had finally granted workers the right to join trade unions (Bolland 1988, 181). As will be seen later, however, since their inception such reforms have actually accorded union members little protection from employers determined to exclude unions from their workplaces.

Efforts to diversify the economy and promote agriculture were deferred to the very end of the colonial era and were accepted by local elites only because of the exhaustion of the colony's last commercially useful mahogany stands by the 1950s.[1] By this time, the timber companies that once ruled Belize by fiat had ceased to operate profitably in a changing world economy. Yet attempts at agricultural development came far too late to reverse the concentration of the country's population in a few town settlements. The result to this day is a land stunningly sparse in human habitation, where many miles of unoccupied, and often unused, land separate villages of just a few hundred residents. When asking why so much of the country's land remains unoccupied, however, investigators may be easily deceived by appearances. Despite the promotion of agriculture in state policy, little has been done to distribute land to low-income households that might farm it. Rather, the large majority of land remains consolidated in the hands of a few owners, many of whom regard it as a speculative rather than productive investment. As of 1984, just 642 landowners, or 7.6 percent of the total, controlled 94.5 percent of the country's private land, a pattern of distribution even more inequitable than that when a few mahogany firms held the country in virtual thralldom (see Stone 1994, 26–27).

With more than one-quarter of the country's residents packed into the teeming former colonial capital of Belize City, Belize's hinterland is correspondingly unpopulated. Nowhere is this more the case than in the isolated southern districts of Stann Creek and Toledo, long neglected by the timber industry and colonial government alike. A region of scrub pine, palmetto, and savanna, alternating with dense broadleaf forests in alluvial areas, Stann Creek and Toledo lacked easy access to the valuable hardwoods harvested elsewhere in the country. As a result, both districts were generally overlooked by colonial timber interests and remained virtually roadless until the mid-1960s. Access to the South's few and widely dispersed settlements was gained only by sea or, in the case of Mango Creek, logging tractor. The region's only major road, the Southern Highway, grew from the ruts left by such vehicles. To the present day, it remains an unpaved and pockmarked roadbed that chokes travelers with dust in the dry season and mires them in mud during the wet.[2] Given its isolation and difficulty of access, it is no surprise that the far South is often termed the "forgotten district," a place Belize City residents visit reluctantly, if at all.

Despite the region's isolation, sporadic and short-term commercial activities drew residents to Mango Creek beginning in the late 1940s. At that time, the Belize Estate and Produce Company, then the largest of the country's timber firms, established a sawmill at the site to produce crude pine lumber for the domestic market. The promise of steady earnings attracted workers to Mango Creek from the settlement of Monkey River Town, ten miles to the south. Despite the "company town" atmosphere that Belize Estate established—the only local sources of goods were commissaries run by the company—a steady influx of workers attested to the lack of wage opportunities elsewhere in the region. The area experienced considerable population growth after 1961 when the Hercules Company, an American firm, established facilities to extract resin from the pine stumps left behind by Belize Estate's woodcutters. Just four years later, Hercules relocated to Guatemala, apparently to extricate itself from a unionized work force (*Amandala* 1978, 9). Within two years, Belize Estate shut down its operations as well, leaving the large majority of local residents with no means of livelihood. From a population of 881 residents recorded in the 1960 census, Mango Creek dwindled to just twelve families in 1968. Local sources of employment were confined to the Savanna Products Company, a farm producing winter fruit and vegetables for the U.S. market, but in 1969 this, too, closed down. "This town," one longtime resident recalls, "was as dead as a cemetery. Even a johncrow [vulture] would not pitch here after the companies pull out." The sawmill was dismantled and moved elsewhere, but two six-story rusting storage tanks were left behind by the resin operation, mutely attesting to the booms and busts that drew residents to the site and then stranded them.

## A Shifting Cultural Frontier

Both in the colonial era and today, the population in the vicinity of Mango Creek has been among the most diverse in a country of startling ethnic diversity. Southern Belize constitutes a shifting "frontier zone" (Helms 1976, 2) of intense interaction across ethnic and linguistic lines, coupled in recent years with dramatic population movements. Although the Yucatecan Maya established settlements and a few sizable towns in southern Belize during the pre-Columbian classic period, only the northern and central regions of the colony remained heavily populated at the beginning of the seventeenth century, when the first British arrived. Most settlements of the Mopan Maya, who had earlier occupied the Stann Creek and Toledo regions, were abandoned long before the arrival of the English. The few remaining Mopan were driven from southern Belize by timber cutters in the eighteenth and early nineteenth centuries (Wilk and Chapin 1990, 14). Beginning in the 1870s the region was re-populated from Guatemala by both the Mopan and another Maya-speaking people, the Kekchi (Gregory 1984; Wilk 1987). Both groups entered rural Toledo fleeing debt peonage on coffee plantations and economic "reforms" in Guatemala that alienated their lands in the bordering state of Alta Verapaz.

Long isolated in the mountainous hinterland of Toledo, the Mopan and Kekchi confined themselves to milpa (shifting) cultivation of maize and beans, the Mopan supplementing these with pork and rice production for town markets. Historically the Kekchi have remained more aloof from outsiders, earning a reputation for elusiveness, despite their periodic forays into wage and commodity markets (Wilk 1991). After the completion of the Southern Highway in 1966, many Mopan, and to a lesser extent Kekchi, began migrating northward in search of new arable lands (Wilk 1984). Most arrived to find that prime land close to the highway had already been claimed by the region's emergent agricultural elites. As a result, although the Mopan and Kekchi have established a number of hamlets and villages along the highway since the 1970s, they must trek four to seven miles inland to cut milpas in foothills beyond the grasp of commercial agriculture. Their migration has also brought them in proximity to the two primary export agro-industries of the South, so that some Maya settlers along the road now work for wages on the region's banana and citrus farms.

From its origins to the present day, the majority of Mango Creek's population has consisted of Creoles, the descendants of European settlers and the African slaves they imported as labor during the early colonial period. Reports of the importation of African slaves to Belize via Jamaica date to the 1730s, but it is likely that some slaves accompanied the first British settlers in the colony decades earlier. Other populations of African descent, including several hundred members of the British West India regiments, were settled in Belize as formally "free coloureds" in the early 1800s (Bolland 1988, 81). Through the mid-nineteenth century segments of the Belizean population continued to be known by their antecedent tribal and linguistic affiliations as "Congoes, Nangoes, Mongolas, Ashantees, Eboes, and other African tribes" (Crowe 1850, 50). Even maps of Belize Town from as late as the 1850s indicate a neighborhood known as "Ibo Town," apparently named after the ancestral tribal affiliation of its residents.

In the contemporary Belizean population, Creoles are varied in appearance, light skin color generally being associated with higher social status. Yet all Creoles are characterized by some common linguistic and cultural markers. Speaking a rich patois of English, African, Spanish, and Amerindian lexical elements (Dayley 1979, viii), most Creoles also command to varying degrees the standard West Indian English of primary school instruction. Following the abolition of slavery, many Creole workers remained bound to the timber industry through debt peonage. Others were excluded from agricultural pursuits by the consolidation of the country's land in the hands of a timber oligarchy (Bolland and Shoman 1977). With their reliance on imported foodstuffs and involvement in wage labor, Creoles in town became associated with a widely reported, if exaggerated, aversion to agriculture (Ashcraft 1973). Noting that lower-status Mayas and Mestizos were relegated to subsistence agriculture, an earlier observer wrote of Creole attitudes toward farming that "occupational prejudice was compounded by racial disdain; to be a farmer, thus, was not only socially inferior, it was also racially degrading" (Lewis 1969, 293). Although such attitudes may still be discerned among some town residents, Creole villages in the South have long agricultural traditions due to their isolation from the timber economy dominating the rest of the country during the colonial period. Such is the case in the Toledo settlement of Monkey River Town, whose residents began to cultivate bananas for export more than a century ago. After moving to Mango Creek in the 1970s, many of the same Creoles later provided field labor as large-scale commercial banana production got underway in that decade.

Members of a second Afro-Belizean ethnic group, the Garifuna, reside in the region as well. Often phenotypically indistinguishable from Creoles, the Garifuna are nonetheless highly distinct in culture, history, and language. Originating on the eastern Caribbean island of St. Vincent from the admixture of escaped African slaves and the indigenous Red Caribs, the Garifuna devised a syncretic culture based on Island Carib (actually an Arawakan language) and the fusion of Amerindian and African religious and kinship practices (Helms 1981; Kerns 1983). Following a generation of wars for colonial control of St. Vincent, all but several hundred Garifuna were defeated by the British in 1796. The survivors were then deported some thirteen hundred miles across the Caribbean to Roatán in the following year. From there the Garifuna migrated along the Caribbean coast, reaching southern Belize sometime around 1800 to establish a number of small fishing villages and later the town of Dangriga.

Upon their arrival in the colony, the Garifuna were regarded with great apprehension by English settlers because of their earlier fierce resistance to the British seizure of St. Vincent. Such perceptions fed upon the continual anxieties of slave owners that the introduction of "free colored" populations into the colony would induce their own laborers to rebel. In the case of the Garifuna, such concerns were heightened by the belief that they had been influenced by the revolutionary zeal that swept the Francophone Caribbean after 1789 (Gonzalez 1988, 20). In 1802, a Belize Town magistrate called for their wholesale expulsion from the colony due to "the danger of a [slave] insurrection led by these people" (Burdon 1931, 60). Yet in a settlement starved of labor from the defection of slaves and abolition of the slave trade, the colony's elites found they could ill afford to exclude a "a good and useful laboring population" (Kerns 1983, 32). Strategies turned instead to co-optation, as village headmen were converted to agents of British indirect rule (Moberg 1992c). By the time of abolition, Garifuna men were already supplementing their traditional fishing activities with seasonal work for wages in the mahogany camps of the interior.

Although many Garifuna men in southern Belize continue to pursue subsistence fishing and other local livelihoods, migratory labor has taken many men and women far from the villages, and country, in which they were raised. Substantial Garifuna communities now exist in New York, Chicago, and Los Angeles. In Belize, as well, the Garifuna have been increasingly incorporated as producers and workers in agricultural sectors geared to the world market. Residents of the Garifuna coastal village of Seine Bight, some ten miles from Mango Creek, continue to practice small-scale fishing, whereas those of the newer village of Georgetown, located ten miles inland, are primarily involved in subsistence and commercial farming. Both villages in the past and to the present day have supplied labor for the region's commercial banana farms.

The processes of exile and oppression that fueled settlement in the region continue to operate to the present day. Since 1980, untold numbers of Salvadoran, Guatemalan, and Honduran immigrants have flowed into southern

Belize, most fleeing either civil conflict or economic hardship in their native lands (Everitt 1984; Wouters 1983; Palacio 1987, 1988). This newest wave of immigration has generated anxiety among many Belizeans of African ancestry, in part because of the numbers of new immigrants (estimated by some to be as many as sixty thousand nationwide [Branigan 1989]) and because of their origin in the surrounding Hispanic countries. The magnitude and culture of this immigrant flow threaten what many Belizeans view as their country's implicit if not official national identity. Despite the diversity of cultures represented in the Belizean population, the sense of nationhood held by most Afro-Belizeans remains firmly fixed in the Anglophone Caribbean. With the arrival of the most recent immigrants to the country, Afro-Belizeans have become for the first time a minority in the land, making many realize that the country's "official" identity is now irrelevant to its actual composition.

## Nationhood and Ethnicity in Plural Societies

> An absolute national morality is inspired either to withdraw from "alien" things or to transform them: it cannot live in comfort constantly by their side.
>
> —Louis Hartz (1955)

In seeking to end domination of their lands by foreign monarchs, European nationalists during the eighteenth and nineteenth centuries argued that each "nation" (that is, ethnic or linguistic group) should control its own state (Worseley 1984, 235ff.). In practice, ethnic nationalism of this sort has been problematic where the rights of minorities are concerned. Despite the troubling history of minority oppression engendered by nationalist movements in Europe and the Third World, such ideologies continue to enjoy broad appeal in many regions. In the former colonies of Europe, ethnic nationalism has often been at its most virulent, in large part because "colonial policies, laws, and practices amounted to a kind of 'divide and rule' strategy by playing off one ethnic group against another" (Bolland 1988, 200). With the departure of the colonial power the resulting antagonisms seethed to the surface as various ethnic groups vied for control of the newly independent state. In some nations, such as India and Nigeria, this competition resulted in actual or attempted partition of the state along ethnic and geographical lines. Elsewhere, as in Guyana and Fiji, it has led to political polarization by ethnicity, as members of rival ethnic groups attempt to seize the state and wield its power to their exclusive advantage.

The relationship between nationality and ethnicity in Belize has been complicated historically by the colony's, and later the country's, uncertain sovereignty. Arguing that it "inherited" Spanish sovereignty over the region after independence, Guatemala has claimed Belize as part of its national territory since the mid-1800s. In part for domestic political purposes, Guatemalan military and political leaders have asserted this claim with increased vigor since the late 1950s. Yet it would be in error to conclude that Guatemalan threats to retake Belize are simply demagoguery intended to divert domestic opposition to military rule. In 1961, Guatemala collaborated with the United States in training Cuban exiles for the failed Bay of Pigs invasion in the hope that the United States would persuade Britain to relinquish control of Belize (Thorndike 1983, 97). Guatemalan troops threatened to invade Belize in 1972 and 1975, leading Britain to dispatch ground and naval forces as well as jet fighter bombers to the country (Calvert 1976). Alternating diplomacy with saber rattling, Guatemala offered "solutions" to the dilemma throughout the 1970s, at one time proposing that Britain cede to it all of Toledo District, including the town of Punta Gorda. In 1981 the Belizean and British governments negotiated a withdrawal of the Guatemalan claim in exchange for rights of access to Belizean waters, but domestic opposition in Belize doomed these arrangements, known as the Heads of Agreement. Not until 1992 did the civilian president of Guatemala, acting unilaterally, state his willingness to recognize the independence and territorial integrity of Belize, a move that incensed many of the country's military officials. Most Belizeans placed little faith in the president's reassurances and were not surprised when Guatemala rescinded its recognition two years later. Because Guatemala constitutes the primary direct threat to the nation's sovereignty, Guatemalans in particular, and Hispanic Central Americans in general, have long been regarded as suspect in the eyes of many Creole and Garifuna Belizeans.

During the colonial period, the Spanish and later Guatemalan claims to Belize intensified British efforts, notable throughout its colonies, to cultivate a sense of identity with the empire in the minds of its subjects. This process entailed a systematic neglect of those ethnic groups considered to be resistant to integration with colonial institutions and "national culture." By the late nineteenth century, a clear ethnic hierarchy had emerged in British Honduras, one in which Creoles were accorded particular privilege based on their command of English and association with mahogany cutting. British Honduran identity became implicitly associated with the Creole culture of Belize Town, the only major settlement in the country where English and its Creole derivation were exclusively spoken. The country's history was also mythologized in the process: in defiance of ethnohistorical evidence for a continuous Maya occupation of Belize, Creoles still regard themselves as the descendants of Europeans and Africans who settled a putatively uninhabited territory: "Anglophone Creoles came to consider 'British Honduras' as 'theirs,' defining it as black, Protestant, and English-speaking. In so doing . . . they sought to define all other ethnic groups as marginal, outsiders, or 'aliens,' as popularized in the Creole saying, 'We da fu ya, everybody else da come ya'" (Bolland and Moberg, 1995, 4).[3]

Higher status and tangible preferences in the colonial order, including the assignment of some Creoles to the civil service and constabulary, were ideologically rationalized in terms of the Creole's supposed attachment to the British Empire. As evidence of such, colonial authorities regularly invoked what became the colony's "creation myth" of the Battle of St. George's Caye. During the 1798 battle, which marked the last Spanish effort to seize the settlement by force, slaves were reported to have stood "shoulder to shoulder" with their English masters to repel the attackers (Burdon 1931, 272). Although originating as a defense of slavery,[4] the account of the battle attained legendary status in countless retellings to later generations of schoolchildren and undoubtedly strengthened the Anglophone orientation of Creoles. Lacking any comparable claim to defense of the colony, non-Creoles were deemed members of the colonial polity only to the extent that they exhibited fidelity to Anglo norms. As elsewhere in the British Caribbean, ethnic groups that refused to assimilate to such conventions or evince loyalty to empire were judged to be liabilities to national progress (see Williams 1991, 30).

As late as 1959, near the end of direct British administration of the colony, an authoritative government report on land use and development in British Honduras reiterated ethnic stereotypes in wide use a full century before. In reference to the colony's Creole population, authors of the report noted with some satisfaction that a "race of 'British Central Americans' seems to be in the making" (Wright et al. 1959, 35). The report was much less complementary in its portrayal of the colony's non-English speakers, who were thought to resist the officially Anglophone national identity. "The Carib" (Garifuna), the authors lament, is "the race which has made least attempt to merge with the rest of the country. . . . The indolent Carib has evolved a philosophy which allows him to spend the early part of the day line-fishing from a canoe, paddling back in time to sell his fish and spend the remainder of the day resting" (ibid., 35–36). In contrast to such constitutional lethargy, the "Spanish" are a "volatile" population "in closest affinity with that often inscrutable, rather reserved individual, the Maya Indian" (ibid., 37). Acknowledging the agricultural expertise of the colony's Amerindians, the report nonetheless imputes to them the childlike rationality common to all stereotypical characterizations of "primitives": "On a sudden impulse they may throw away the labour of weeks on something which has no use or meaning in their home life" (ibid., 38).

Notwithstanding the persistence of such ethnic stereotypes and the anti-Hispanic attitudes arising from the Guatemalan claim, ethnic strife until the early 1980s was considerably more subdued in Belize than in many colonial societies. Although the British established a status hierarchy based on race and ethnicity, the workings of the colonial color line were not entirely uniform in effect. As English speakers and Protestants, Creoles were favored over Mestizos for positions in the colonial civil service, but officials' color prejudices often worked to the advantage of light-skinned Mestizos who acquired fluency in English and a secondary education. At a more general level, patterns of ethnic interaction in the colonial economy conspired against pronounced antagonism within the work force: "Free Creole and Garifuna labourers worked alongside slaves in the mahogany camps, and in the early sugar plantations Creole, Garifuna, Mestizo, and Maya workers were subject to the same system of labour control, through a system of advance payments and truck practices at the company stores" (Bolland 1988, 200).[5] Such practices inclined colonial-era workers to a feeling, in Bolland's words, "of being in the same rotten boat" rather than overt rivalry (ibid.). By the eve of independence, the generally noncompetitive ethnic relations in Toledo District suggested to one observer that "within Belize as a whole social class may be becoming a more important determinant of social interaction than ethnicity" (Cosminsky 1976, 112). Hence, the adoption of a multicultural model of nationalism by the first independent government, led by Prime Minister George Price and the Peoples' United Party (PUP), was not a utopian gesture in the early 1980s. The PUP government's policy on national identity was set forth in a high school history text commissioned by the Ministry of Education in 1982:[6]

> For much of our history, the natural interaction of cultures which co-exist within one community was inhibited by the colonial policy of divide and rule, which ensured that our various cultures remained largely isolated from, and suspicious of, each other, and that the colonizer's culture remained dominant. An essential part of the decolonization process must therefore be the elimination of all colonially inherited prejudices about each other's cultures. (*History of Belize* 1983, 73)

For these reasons, as well as the fact that all of Belize's ethnic groups are minorities, decolonization seemed to pose little threat of overt strife. Although the state has historically been dominated by Creoles, until recently neither political party has been able to attain power without multiethnic support. The PUP tended to favor closer relations with Central America, whereas the opposition United Democratic Party (UDP) adopted much more of a Caribbean orientation. Nonetheless, both parties have been successful because they were not defined in ethnically exclusive terms. Several trends point to the polarization of Belizean society in the wake of Central American immigration, a polarization that may lead to party-based ethnic strife akin to the competition between blacks and East Indians in Guyana. If so, Belize may be standing on the brink of a hegemonic nationalism in which Belizeans of African ancestry attempt to explicitly attach their identity to the state.

Evidence for this claim is suggested by recent electoral results indicating a Creole defection to the UDP, which pointedly employs anti-immigrant rhetoric in electoral campaigns (Bolland 1991). Of equal note has been the emergence of a conscious pan-Afro-Belizean identity among some Creoles and Garifuna who see themselves as having common adversaries in Hispanic immigrants and "Spanish" Belizeans. An editorial in the country's most widely read newspaper, for example, claimed that "Creoles and *Garinagu* have not made common cause on anything in our lifetimes, but there is a common adversity now being faced by both groups. Blacks, and it does not matter to which tribe they belong, will be marginalized in Belize in the next ten years unless they develop conscious, common strategies for survival here" (*Amandala* 1991a, 2). A Creole writer for the same paper demanded "balance" in immigration policy, calling on the government to admit one Garifuna from Honduras for every Hispanic Central American, and one Haitian for every Chinese immigrant (*Amandala* 1991b, 5). Such sentiments underscore diminishing support for the model of pluralistic nationalism endorsed in the early days of independence.

## Historical Memories of Exclusion

Hostility toward Central American immigrants by Anglophone Belizeans is notably more pronounced in communities such as Belize City and Dangriga, where Hispanics comprise a small, albeit growing, minority. Yet anti-immigrant sentiments have their counterparts in even the smallest communities that have played host to Central American arrivals. Mango Creek, to which immigrants are attracted for employment in the banana industry, has been oddly bifurcated by the immigrant influx. Belizeans and Central American immigrants form seemingly separate populations in the same community, forced to interact yet divided by language and mutual suspicion. In local shops and restaurants, Central Americans transact in Spanish and are answered, often with minimal civility, in English. A Honduran Pentecostalist revival punctuated by shouts and cries in Spanish vies in volume with reggae played on a boom box. Members of either group freely volunteer their opinions of the other, often in their presence, and recount in detail the violence, dishonesty, or indolence to which they are allegedly inclined. Although such sentiments are played out in the few, but tense, daily interactions between groups, their origins have deeper historical roots. In Mango Creek, distrust of immigrants does not merely represent a revival of colonial-era ethnic prejudice but reflects the ways in which ethnic groups have been incorporated and abandoned as labor in the region's banana industry. The processes of labor recruitment and displacement that have characterized the industry since the early 1980s recapitulate the experience of ethnic conflict elsewhere in lower Central America.

The tide of overt ethnic antagonism that threatens to overtake Belize may be nationally unprecedented, but it is situated in a long regional history of segregation, competition, and conflict among Hispanic and Afro-Caribbean workers. Afro-Belizeans have both direct and historical knowledge of the marginalization of black workers in the agricultural sectors of Honduras, Costa Rica, and Guatemala. Throughout much of lower Central America, the Hispanic and Afro-Caribbean encounter has been an arduous one, in part due to labor-control strategies in plantation agriculture that consciously manipulated ethnicity and nationality. In United Fruit's Costa Rican operations, for example, "the company imported laborers from different West Indian islands to avoid labor solidarity. . . . When Blacks went on strike, the company used Hispanic strike breakers and vice versa. . . . To make matters worse, the

Company often paid Blacks more than Hispanics for the same type of work" (Purcell 1993, 32). Treating Anglophone Afro-Caribbean workers as a (comparatively) privileged labor aristocracy, plantation managers also cultivated many West Indians as spies and informers against a majority Hispanic work force.

These labor-control strategies made for extraordinarily volatile ethnic relations among agricultural workers in Costa Rica, Honduras, and Guatemala. Well into the 1940s, Hispanic banana workers in Honduras demanded the deportation of West Indian and immigrant Belizean co-workers on racial grounds, and regularly incited violence against them (Echeverri-Gent 1992, 302; Argueta 1992, 62). Similarly, racism may partly account for the persecution of some Honduran Garifuna communities following a military coup in the mid-1930s, which caused hundreds of refugees to flee to southern Belize (Moberg 1992a, 39). By the beginning of World War II, all of the Central American states had imposed restrictions on West Indian immigration and curtailed the civil rights and movements of existing Afro-Caribbean populations within their borders (Echeverri-Gent 1992). Finally, for many Belizeans, the racism encountered elsewhere in Central America is compounded by the bigotry they have experienced as Afro-Caribbean immigrants in the United States, where some seventy thousand Belizeans are now thought to reside.

Combined with the Guatemalan claim to Belize, such experiences lead many Afro-Belizeans to attribute virtually genocidal intentions to all "aliens," Central Americans in particular. In the words of the Creole scholar Ronald Clarke, Afro-Belizeans hold "a deep-seated ethnic fear, a fear of extinction" because "the history of the black man on this continent when he has been reduced to minority status is a sad, sad story" (Stone 1994, 189–90). Such suspicions are not unwarranted, given the bellicose and often racist statements of the Guatemalan government regarding Belize, especially during the precarious British-Guatemalan standoff in the mid-1970s. In a recent, masterful treatment of Belizean national identity, Stone (ibid., 189) reports that "Guatemalan leaders [have] crudely joked that Guatemala will take back *Belice,* but Britain can take back the *negritos.*" Such repartee may be confined to the private sphere, but the public pronouncements of Guatemalan leaders have done little to dispel Belizean anxieties about the future. In the mid-1970s, Kjell Laugerud, then Guatemalan president, stressed that his government specifically sought the land rather than the people of Belize. Guatemala's vice-president of the time, Mario Sandoval Alarcón, a right-wing paramilitary leader, more directly warned Belizeans who opposed annexation that they "could go where they pleased" (Calvert 1985, 167). Hence, Creole and Garifuna Belizeans fear that the Hispanic influx of recent decades will not only alter the country's demographic "balance" but also reproduce within Belize the marginalization that blacks have historically experienced elsewhere.

Ethnic polarization in Belize has reached ominous proportions since the early 1980s, but such tensions do not simply reflect the magnitude of the Hispanic influx. Rather, immigrants have been incorporated into the labor market in ways that imperil the livelihoods of many Belizean workers. For the first time in the country's history, ethnicity corresponds to sharp new socio-economic divisions among workers, divisions that are often accentuated by employers. In both the banana and citrus industries of Stann Creek and Toledo Districts, labor recruitment strategies are reminiscent of the mechanisms of labor control and domination common to the rest of Central America. In Belize, such strategies have been used to displace Afro-Belizean workers from entire categories of employment, to undermine unions, and to diminish wages and working conditions in agriculture. For workers displaced from agricultural jobs, employers' use of immigrants as cheap, docile, and ultimately disposable labor—and their abandonment of Belizean workers—summons up long-nascent fears of discrimination akin to the experiences of Afro-Caribbean populations throughout Central America. For many working Belizeans, the expulsion of Creole and Garifuna labor from commercial agriculture and increasingly from industry serves as a presentiment of marginalization to come.

# 2 ❦ *Boom, Bust, and Monopoly Control*

## CYCLES OF BANANA PRODUCTION IN BELIZE

In the early 1990s, representatives of the Belizean government and commercial agriculture hailed bananas as the nation's "new bonanza," an export crop that would provide the key to much-needed economic development in the far South. The latter claim remains to be demonstrated, but Belize has, in actuality, produced bananas for export nearly as long as any other Central American country. The assertion that bananas are a "new" industry finds a counterpart in an even more faulty historical memory, one that denies Belizeans' willingness to labor in banana fields. The first of these claims is readily negated by century-old photographs in the National Archives that depict stems of bananas in Belize City awaiting shipment to the United States. Photographs of a slightly later era, depicting United Fruit Company operations in the Stann Creek Valley during the 1910s, dispel the second notion, for they reveal a work force that was decidedly Afro-Caribbean in appearance.

As seen in the previous chapter, Belize exhibits a culture history and institutional legacy distinct from most of Central America. Contemporary Belize differs most strikingly from neighboring countries in its low levels of overt political repression and human rights abuse. Following colonial-era historians, many Anglophone Belizeans themselves proudly point out these contrasts with the rest of Central America. Often the intended effect of such comparisons is to portray British colonialism as a benign if not benevolent influence, one that resulted in an "island of democracy" in Central America. Scholarship that departs from the official historiography of the colonial era, however, reveals a history steeped in oligarchical control of land, debt servitude of the work force, and pervasive discrimination based on color and property ownership. It was not until the first stirrings of the independence movement in the 1930s, followed by the country's decolonization in the 1950s, that significant steps were taken to reverse some, but by no means all,

of these inequities. Hence, the tendency to regard Belize as a regional exception effaces a colonial political economy more akin to than unlike the rest of
Central America.

Nowhere is the convergence between Belize and Central America more
evident than the parallel experiences of the region's countries in the international banana trade. In the first two decades of the twentieth century, the
Boston-based United Fruit Company emerged as the largest North American
banana importer, in part through intimidating and underpricing its competitors throughout Central America. United Fruit's strategies of dominating, and even overthrowing, governments to secure its interests lent nations
of the region the unwanted sobriquet of "banana republics." Belize is conspicuously absent from the list of nations so designated, ostensibly because of
the "impartial" career diplomats appointed to administer the territory during the colonial period.[1] Yet it was during United Fruit's ascendancy to near
monopoly status in the Central American banana trade that the company's
presence was felt most strongly in the colony. Further, dispatches of the early
1900s from the colony's governor to the Colonial Office in London, as well as
official correspondence with the company, reveal that colonial officials were
no more assertive than governments of neighboring countries in dealing
with the banana multinational.

In contending with British colonial administrators, United Fruit had no
evident recourse to the bribery or threats that it employed with some success
in Honduras and Guatemala. Rather, the company's influence with colonial
officials coincided with the colony's growing orientation toward North
American markets, which left it particularly vulnerable to the demands of
U.S. capital. By 1903, Belize was sending the majority of its exports to the
United States, following a decade of declining trade with the United King-
dom. As the direction of the colony's trade shifted between 1890 and 1900,
bananas accounted for, on average, 71 percent of the value of all exports to the
United States (Government of British Honduras 1890–1903). During this period, then, Belize became more fully integrated with the circuits of trade that
had earlier tied the rest of Central America to North America. Yet although
the U.S. market became critical to the colonial economy at this time, the
colony's banana exports were, as the government itself admitted, "a minute
part" of the fruit trade as a whole (Hutson 1925, 176). Even at its peak, the
output of the colony's banana industry represented no more than 3 percent of

United Fruit's total banana imports to the United States (ibid.) This imbalance in trade points as well to an imbalance in power relationships. Whereas the economic well-being of Belize was increasingly tied to the banana trade, companies that controlled the marketing of bananas could dispense with the colony's contribution if need be. Hence, the colony's relatively minor role in the fruit trade, combined with United Fruit's monopoly over it, made the firm indispensable to the colony's economy and gave it considerable influence over its officials.

### Monopoly by Default and Design

The development of a rudimentary banana industry in southern Belize in the late nineteenth century was not the inevitable result of the region's favorable land and climatic endowments. For years, Belize Town merchants and the "forestocracy" had doggedly resisted the expansion of any agricultural activity that might compete with the timber industry's monopoly over land and labor. They were largely successful in blocking agricultural development until 1879, when a reform-minded governor, Frederick Barlee, lowered the price of Crown lands to one dollar per acre to promote their cultivation by would-be small-scale farmers (Cal 1991, 313). Further antagonizing the local oligarchy, the governor altered the government contract for mail and freight delivery from a shipping line based in Kingston to one based in New Orleans. This move was explicitly intended to promote the shipment of the colony's bananas to the growing U.S. market.

Barlee's reforms earned him the ire of the colony's timber companies as well as merchants, who relied on access to British goods through Jamaica. Led by the powerful Belize Estate and Produce Company, both groups aggressively lobbied the Colonial Office for his recall, a demand that it dutifully obliged in 1884. Land prices were subsequently raised to their earlier level of five dollars per acre, yet during the short-lived Barlee administration, reformed land-tenure laws induced thousands of Belize City residents—ostensibly the most "agriculturally averse" population in the country—to move south, where timber companies had not yet consolidated their hold on land. Most acquisitions by small-scale farmers were limited to the Stann Creek District, where only 12 percent of the land was under private control as late as 1890, compared to more than 90 percent in all of the northern districts

(Ashdown 1979, 25). There many of the new settlers established banana farms to take advantage of the growing export demand for fruit.

By the mid-1880s, colonial newspapers were recording a perceptible exodus of workers from the timber industry, "as many captains and labourers from mahogany gangs . . . have been able to invest their earnings on banana plantations instead of spending them in Belize [City] in riotous living" (*Colonial Guardian*, 1 Jan. 1887, 2). Soon the newspapers were lamenting that "the price of mahogany labour has gone up to $20 a month . . . partly due to the fact that a great many of the best labourers have become peasant proprietors of banana plantations" (Shoman 1994, 127). Census figures of 1880 and 1890 confirm this steady flow of Belize City residents to banana-producing areas of the South. More than 80 percent of the banana growers in 1888 at the newly established village of Mullins River in northern Stann Creek District had English surnames (Cal 1991, 315). The remainder bore Hispanic names, indicating that growers were Mestizo or possibly Garifuna. The overall population of the southern districts increased 5.7 percent between 1871 and 1891, a period in which the northern half of the country exhibited no net growth. The majority of the population growth in the South was centered in banana-producing areas such as Monkey River Town, whose size increased from 250 inhabitants in 1881 to nearly 700 ten years later. The colony's banana farms attracted a diverse work force, including Creoles from Belize City and Garifuna of nearby settlements, as well as Mestizos and Maya from the neighboring countries (ibid., 321). To satisfy the growing need for labor, one estate even imported Bahamians and black and East Indian Jamaicans during the 1880s.

The growing demand for fruit in North American markets stimulated expanding production in the colony and encouraged a few members of the colony's mercantile and timber elites to enter banana production for themselves. In 1890, five banana companies were chartered in the colony, as both fruit producers and shipping agents for bananas grown on independent farms. By mid-decade, a few comparatively large-scale growers had emerged among the colony's producers. The average farm at Mullins River, for example, encompassed more than 75 acres under cultivation by 1895 (ibid., 316). The largest fruit company in the colony, the British Honduras Syndicate, cultivated bananas on a 14,301-acre estate nine miles inland from Stann Creek (now Dangriga) Town and operated a mule-driven tramway to convey its fruit to port.

By 1897, about six thousand bunches of bananas were being shipped weekly from Stann Creek and further south at Monkey River. At both locales, bananas were transhipped in paddled dugout dories and rowboats to steamers docked offshore. Although the colonial government paid subsidies to two steamship lines to carry mails and the colony's fruit, frequently the New Orleans–bound steamers had filled their holds with Honduran and Guatemalan bananas before calling at the colony. When this happened, the harvests of local farms were simply dumped into the sea, resulting in "an enormous waste of fruit" (PRO CO 123 300). In part because of the occasional inability of growers to market their fruit, and because banana producers now included in their ranks some of the colony's more powerful private landowners, the colonial government sought more reliable arrangements with North American shipping firms to transport locally produced fruit. Such agreements were to bring the government into a close embrace with United Fruit, which would become the exclusive exporter of the colony's bananas until a virtual collapse of the industry in the late 1920s.

Within one year of its incorporation in 1899, United Fruit had begun to quietly purchase majority ownership of six steamship lines operating along the Caribbean coast of Central America. These acquisitions gave it immediate majority control of the region's export banana trade (Kepner 1967, 42). Among the shipping lines purchased by the company was the Belize Royal Mail and Central American Steamship Company, a firm that held the colony's subsidized mail contract. Within several months of United Fruit's acquisition of this line, the shipping branch of the Vaccaro Brothers Fruit Company[2] began calling along the southern coast to purchase fruit. The new line was welcomed by both banana growers and merchants, for with renewed competition United Fruit reduced freight charges and began accepting "eight hand" stems of fruit that it had formerly rejected (*Colonial Guardian*, 22 Dec. 1900, 2). Soon, however, United Fruit lowered its freight charges far below those of the Vaccaros, a tactic one newspaper termed a "ridiculously transparent stratagem" (*Colonial Guardian*, 1 Jan. 1902, 3).[3] The company quickly garnered the majority of the colony's banana and freight business, and within a year forced the Vaccaro line to withdraw its steamers from the colony. Having become the settlement's only carrier of mail and bananas, the company immediately exercised its monopoly by raising charges for freight and lowering the price of bananas that it procured in the colony (ibid.). Soon thereafter, when United Fruit's mail contract expired in 1902, the company informed the government that it would suspend steamship service to the colony unless granted an annual subsidy of $14,500. This amount was nearly 50 percent greater than the subsidy previously provided under the Belize Royal Mail line's contract with the government (PRO CO 123 240).

The colony's governor, Sir David Wilson, responded with the offer of a $12,000 annual subsidy, which United Fruit accepted. In an unanticipated act of defiance, however, the unofficial members of the colony's legislative council, who were appointed from the expatriate and Creole elite, refused to approve the governor's proposal. By a majority vote, the council proposed an alternative contract that would lower the annual subsidy to $10,000. United Fruit immediately announced a suspension of steamship service to Belize, a decision that, in the governor's words, represented "a great calamity to the Colony" (PRO CO 123 240). Henry Keith, the manager of United Fruit's Honduras Division, imperiously informed Wilson of the company's position in these terms: "I am now instructed to withdraw all previous offers relating to the Mail Contract, and I now beg to advise you that the Company will only accept a Mail Contract on the conditions of the one that has just been proposed—namely—$14,500, subsidy per annum. . . . I am also instructed to inform you that these terms are final with my Company and if not accepted, all negotiation may be considered closed" (ibid.)

After the colony had gone a month without scheduled mail, freight, or passenger service to New Orleans, the governor reopened negotiations with Keith while looking for a renewed opportunity to secure passage of his proposed twelve-thousand-dollar contract. When one unofficial member failed to appear at a council meeting, Wilson suspended the rules of order requiring prior notification of legislative items and cast the deciding vote himself on the subsidy (*Colonial Guardian*, 8 March 1902, 3). Unofficial members and the press were outraged by the governor's "high-handed and undignified maneuvering" (ibid.) to pass the contract, and a fruit grower in Stann Creek charged that Wilson had "cringed to the Trust and betrayed the fruit industry of the Colony to [its] tender mercies" (*Colonial Guardian*, 26 July 1902, 3).

In a subsequent protest to the Colonial Office, the unofficials cited a litany of abuses suffered by the colony since United Fruit had acquired the contract in 1900: "Consignees were notified that in future all goods must be taken from alongside instead of being landed as formerly: The freight rates were increased: Discrimination was introduced against supporters of other [shipping] lines: Fruit was rejected without reasonable cause in large quantities, on more than one occasion because the subsidized mail steamers had filled up with fruit from the Southern Republics" (PRO CO 123 240). Finally, the council's only "coloured" member condemned the racial segregation that already permeated all aspects of United Fruit operations in Central America: "Black passengers though paying first class fares were prevented from sitting at table with the other passengers and were otherwise treated as a class apart" (ibid.) To be humiliated by the company was galling enough, but to subsidize such treatment was intolerable for the dissenters: "We feel that too many sacrifices have been made and the Government has gone too much out of its way to retain the Services of the United Fruit Company" (ibid.). Responding to both the governor's anxious dispatches detailing his negotiations with United Fruit, and the councilors' protest of his actions in securing the subsidy, Colonial Office staff in London penned comments for internal circulation. Perhaps the last, anonymous notation on the Colonial Office minute paper from 1902 best expresses the colony's new-found predicament in dealing with the United Fruit Company: "Nothing else to be done, but the Govt. has been completely bluffed by these sharp Yankees" (ibid.).

### Crown Colony as Banana Republic

From the outset, United Fruit established its presence in Belize on its terms and extracted concessions more favorable than those granted it by other Central American governments. Following the precedent of the company's founder, Minor Keith, United Fruit was granted many of its Costa Rican and Honduran landholdings for token sums or entirely free of charge, albeit in exchange for the construction of railroads. Company-built railroads remained under long-term corporate control but were encouraged by national governments lacking the resources or expertise to extend track beds and rolling stock into the tropical lowlands (Kepner and Soothill 1935, 154ff.). Established in exchange for vast holdings of virgin land on which to cultivate bananas, railroads provided United Fruit with a transportation monopoly needed to foreclose competition.

In Belize, however, United Fruit secured such a monopoly without having to assume the immense costs of railroad construction. In an 1899 dispatch to the Colonial Office, Governor Wilson first proposed that the government itself construct and operate a railway in order to promote banana production and, specifically, encourage United Fruit's investment in the colony: "The future action of [United Fruit] . . . will be greatly influenced by the decision whether there is, or is not to be a railway to the interior . . . with a pier for loading fruit direct from the railway trucks. If a railway is decided upon, they may introduce much capital here to grow fruit for themselves, or buy it from producers here. If on the contrary there is to be no railway, they will probably devote their energies and their capital to obtaining their supplies of fruit from the Honduras Republic and further South" (PRO CO 123 233). The governor's next sentence indicates that his support for the project had been secured through the sort of manipulation for which United Fruit was soon to become famous: "As an instance of the possibilities in this direction, Mr. Walsh, the future manager in Central America of the United Fruit Company, informed me at an interview which I had with him . . . that he was at the present moment in doubt whether he would establish his head-quarters at Belize or at Puerto Cortés [Honduras]" (ibid.) Such "doubt" implied that the company's decision would hinge on the government's provision of railroads and land for its use. Notwithstanding the colony's willingness to extend such concessions, all company operations in British Honduras were soon to be directed from its Bananera Division headquarters in Guatemala.

In 1906, the colony's governor received a pledge of financial support from the Colonial Office for the construction of a narrow-gauge railroad in the Stann Creek Valley to improve market access for the region's banana producers. The railroad was to extend from a pier at Commerce Bight, a harbor south of Stann Creek, to a parcel of land then under consideration by the United Fruit Company at Middlesex, twenty miles up the Stann Creek Valley. Although the railway would transport the produce of all growers along its right of way, the project was primarily intended as a concession to United Fruit for the development of a plantation. Rhetorically, colonial officials rationalized public concessions to the company as investments that would one day generate larger freight and tax revenues from a flourishing industry. Such expectations proved unrealistic, due to severe underestimates of railroad construction costs and a naïve belief that the company would adhere to its contract with the government when it was no longer profitable to do so.

After receiving assurances of a government-operated railroad linking Middlesex with the coast, United Fruit negotiated with the colonial government for the purchase of seventy-five hundred acres at the site. Correspondence regarding the sale between the Colonial Office and Governor Sir Eric Swayne reveal that the latter had become a virtual agent for the company in conveying its interests to London. The Colonial Office had originally directed Swayne to price the Middlesex estate at rates comparable to banana-producing land in Jamaica, or about $7.50 per acre. In response, Swayne argued that the company was unlikely to pay more than $1.00 per acre, in addition to the cost of the land survey, due to the presence of abundant inexpensive land in the neighboring republics. Failing the prompt offer of an attractive sale price, Swayne warned, the company would probably take its investments elsewhere:

> Comparing British Honduras with Guatemala, I find that the United Fruit Company paid nothing for their large plantations in Guatemala. . . . [If higher prices are asked] the large companies referred to, will, I anticipate, prefer to extend their operations in Guatemala, where they already work large blocks of land, and have invested money in local railways and tramways, and where conditions are in so many respects more favourable; and having once given up their idea of establishing themselves in the Colony, their interests in the future are not likely to coincide with ours. (PRO CO 123 255)

Swayne's argument apparently won the day, for his proposed valuation of the Middlesex estate was accepted by the Colonial Office in July, 1907.

A final agreement setting forth the conditions of United Fruit operations in British Honduras was signed between the company's president, Minor Keith, and the colonial government in July 1909. The company received the 7,549-acre estate for one dollar per acre, plus fifteen hundred dollars in surveying costs. It also provided that United Fruit would plant out bananas "or other agricultural produce" over 250 acres per year. In exchange, the contract limited the land tax on United Fruit holdings to ten cents per acre per year, exempted bananas from export taxes, and excused the company's agricultural implements and machinery from import duties (PRO CO 123 261). To recoup the government's costs of railroad construction, the agreement committed United Fruit to operate in the colony for twenty-five years. During that time, railroad freight rates were to be limited to only five cents per stem of fruit, and no provision was made for renegotiation of fruit prices paid to private growers (PRO CO 123 295a). These terms entailed lavish concessions to the company, at least when compared to the conditions under which other would-be agriculturalists acquired land in the Stann Creek Valley. Much to the governor's embarrassment, an issue of the official *Government Gazette* juxtaposed the United Fruit contract with an advertisement for Crown lands available to residents of the colony wishing to settle along the railway. Smallholders who purchased land in the area were required to pay between three and eight dollars per acre and held to stricter cultivation standards than the company (*Clarion,* 22 July 1909, 94). Further, unlike the company, smallhold-ers were not exempted from duties or the standard land tax rate of fifty cents per acre.

The colony's newspapers reacted to this double standard with populist in-dignation, notwithstanding the generally elite interests that they repre-sented.[4] The *Clarion* sarcastically "congratulate[d] the Trust on its easy vic-tory over a weak Government ready to respond to the wishes of the rich and powerful" (ibid., 98). The *Colonial Guardian* went even further in denounc-ing the government as "amongst the worst we have had. . . . Just think of the contrast this policy presents—a wealthy foreign trust . . . is granted land at one eighth the price that taxpayers of the Colony . . . are allowed to purchase it at, although the profits made by the latter would remain in this country to the benefit of the Colony generally—No wonder people living in the Stann Creek District believe that the Government have [*sic*] constructed the railway for the United Fruit Co." (*Colonial Guardian,* 11 Dec. 1910, 3). In the face of such criticism, and its inability to sell more than ten acres of land to small-holders at its advertised rates, the government was forced to withdraw its ear-lier terms and put land up for sale along the railway for one dollar per acre (*Clarion,* 16 March 1911, 329).[5]

Over time, the colony's greatest subsidy to the company—and loss to its treasury—was the construction and operation of the Stann Creek Railway. When the railroad was approved by the Colonial Office, and negotiations begun with United Fruit, a narrow-gauge line twenty miles long was envi-sioned at a cost of $280,000. By the time the railroad was completed in 1909, its gauge had been widened to accommodate heavier rolling stock and its length increased by five miles due to an initial surveying error. So, too, had its cost to the treasury nearly tripled, to more than $841,000. In 1911, the project's cost overruns came to the attention of several members of the House of Com-mons, who demanded to know from the Colonial Office why such conspicu-ous expenditures were being made on behalf of a non-British firm (PRO CO 123 271). Members of Parliament were puzzled by the colonial gov-ernment's compliant relationship with United Fruit, but the railroad's over-runs and operating losses only strengthened the company's hand in dealing with the colony. Colonial authorities realized early on that the railroad's financial success was contingent on United Fruit's willingness to supply it with freight. Because of the government's overriding, if futile, desire to recoup the railroad's costs, the company was able to wring further demands from colonial authorities. Overcoming even parliamentary opposition, the company soon acquired a monopoly on the colony's international communications, as well as its only scheduled passenger steamship service.

No sooner was the railroad completed than the company sought permission to establish a radio telegraph station in Belize, the colony's first, to communicate with its ships and other divisions in Central America. A parliamentary committee in London objected on the grounds that a private foreign company should not control the colony's only radio communication links abroad. The Colonial Office pleaded with the committee that it accede to the company, foreseeing possible retaliation if United Fruit's request were declined:

> The United Fruit Company is very important to British Honduras as a buyer and exporter of fruit, and it would be a serious thing for the Colony if the Company's operations were discouraged. . . . It is not too much to say that if the United Fruit Company were to suspend its operations in and about Stann Creek, the [rail]line would be . . . a hopeless failure. For this reason, therefore, it is important to maintain good relations with the United Fruit Company. . . . This appears to be a justification for the unusual proposal to place telegraphic communication in the hands of a foreign company. (PRO CO 123 267)

The parliamentary committee was resolute before such pleas and denied the company's request. United Fruit lost little time in responding to the decision. In January 1911, the company withdrew its passenger steamers from service to the colony, substituting smaller vessels that carried exclusively mail and fruit. The suspension of the colony's only passenger service to the United States caused, in the governor's words, "a good deal of dissatisfaction in the Colony" (PRO CO 123 268). In response to the governor's request for a resumption of the service, C. H. Ellis, United Fruit's New Orleans manager, wrote: "It would greatly assist me if I could be assured that we could get our Wireless Station established there, and a small increase in the passenger rate there on the large steamers. . . . I need not tell you that our experience with operating the large steamers to Belize was very unprofitable and unsatisfactory" (ibid.). The governor forwarded Ellis's correspondence to the Colonial Office with an added plea on behalf of the company: "A wireless station is peculiarly necessary for a large Fruit Company, and I am convinced that without one we cannot hope to have the 5,000 ton steamers calling here. . . . I trust, therefore, that you will be able to see your way to permit the station to be established" (ibid.). In May 1911, Parliament relented, granting United Fruit permission to operate a radio station in the colony. Not coincidentally, passenger steamship service to Belize resumed the following month.

## Fluorescence and Collapse

From its promising start in the 1880s, banana cultivation rapidly expanded along the Stann Creek Valley in the first two decades of this century. Some 140,000 stems of fruit were exported from the entire colony in 1893, increasing to 621,000 from Stann Creek alone in 1917. Besides offering an inducement for United Fruit's investment in the colony, the railway was intended to boost banana exports by making new farmlands accessible. After 1910, both small- and large-scale producers in the Stann Creek Valley took advantage of the railroad's presence to expand their scale of cultivation. By 1920, an estimated ten thousand acres of land in the colony were under banana cultivation, mostly in the Stann Creek region. Yet a series of natural and climatic disasters following the construction of the railway were soon to prevent these newly opened lands from realizing their potential.

Heavy rains in June 1911 flooded most of the valley's tributaries, washing out two bridges on the line and completely isolating the United Fruit plantation (PRO CO 123 268). Restoration of the rail link took the remainder of the year, but by 1914 United Fruit's operations had expanded to more than eighteen hundred acres under cultivation at Middlesex. In the following year, a hurricane struck Stann Creek District, with "a most disastrous effect on the banana plantations," according to that year's railway report (PRO CO 123 284). More than 75 percent of the Middlesex plantation was leveled, and an estimated 300,000 stems of fruit lost throughout the valley. Bad weather returned in 1917, when heavy flooding caused an additional loss of 115,000 stems on the region's farms. As the colony's acting governor noted in a dispatch explaining the railway's continuing losses, "The volume of business with Middlesex is reduced owing to blow-downs, floods, etc. This farm has had much misfortune" (PRO CO 123 291).

The industry's decline was much in evidence by the end of the decade, but bad weather was not to prove its coup de grace. As early as 1914, United Fruit workers had detected Panama disease on some portions of the Middlesex plantation. The disease is highly infectious, being transmitted from plant to plant during periods of flooding, or even through contact with workers, livestock, or tools that have been exposed to *Fusarium* spores. The colony's agricultural officer, W. R. Dunlop, inferred that Middlesex had probably been infected by a contingent of United Fruit workers sent to the plantation from the company's Guatemalan division. Initially, the disease was limited to the United Fruit holdings, and for a time expansion of independent farms along the railroad more than compensated for declining production at Middlesex. In 1918, the disease made its appearance on farms throughout the Stann Creek Valley, apparently borne downstream from Middlesex by the floods of the previous year. Soon production was declining regionwide as infected plants succumbed to the disease. As Dunlop's 1920 report on the Stann Creek Valley grimly observed, the ambitious expectations that had inaugurated the railroad had all but evaporated by decade's end:

> Travelling up the railway one passes small banana fields separated by secondary or else virgin bush, until one comes to 14 miles [from Stann Creek Town] after which banana cultivations are almost continuous. But many of these fields present a dismal sight. Some of the fields have "played out" . . . through soil exhaustion and have been abandoned to the weeds and bush. Other sections have succumbed to the Panama disease, and the brown headless trunks still standing as they died lend to the fields a ghostly, grave-yard appearance. (PRO CO 123 300)

In 1918, United Fruit ceased clearing new land at Middlesex, and it completely abandoned production there in 1920.

Postmortems of the banana industry claimed that its demise was only partly the result of contingent factors, such as disease and adverse weather, for the effects of natural disasters were greatly amplified by poor cultivation techniques. Even the harshest colonial critics of United Fruit generally exonerated the company from any blame for the banana industry's decline. Instead, observers of the time condemned the "primitive . . . milpa-style" methods (Sampson 1929, 23) and "fugitive crop-taking" (PRO CO 123 329 2) under which the colony's bananas were grown for export. A 1919 dispatch by Governor Sir Eyre Hutson explained the impending collapse of the industry in terms of such land-extensive techniques: "The neglect of weeding, cultivation, and manuring . . . bring with it the usual results. The bananas become played out, . . . the fields are abandoned, and new virgin forest land is cleared and planted" (PRO CO 123 295a). The colony's agricultural officer largely concurred in his assessment about a year later: "Banana growing as a stable industry was doomed from the very start by the methods of production in a valley where the available land is strictly limited. . . . The only system that would have rendered the industry stable, apart from the disease, would have been the Jamaican system of intensive culture. If that had been adopted from the first, if a proper quarantine against the disease had been introduced also from the very first, then the industry today might have been a flourishing concern" (PRO CO 123 300). Yet where other observers had attributed land-extensive techniques to either the ignorance or indolence of the colony's banana growers, Dunlop went on to observe that cultivation practices on local farms were predictable responses to the conditions under which banana growers marketed their fruit: "It all comes back to the agreement with the United Fruit Company. The Jamaican system of [intensive] production should have been insisted upon in the agreement, and the price paid for fruit should have been higher . . . to meet the increased cost of production under the intensive methods. It is highly probable, in fact certain, that the United Fruit Company would never have signed such an agreement" (ibid.).

Belatedly, colonial officials realized that the contract with United Fruit had been, as one dispatch noted with characteristic understatement, "a very one-sided one" (PRO CO 123 292). Prices specified in the contract enabled the company to pay the colony's growers significantly less than it paid for fruit in its other areas of operation, and even less than its accountants valued its own fruit from Middlesex. Similarly, the railway's chronic operating deficit, which reached $77,320 by 1920, was attributed—only after United Fruit abandoned Middlesex—to freight charges that "are and always have been ridiculously low for the service rendered," according to the railroad's superintendent in 1920 (PRO CO 123 300). Low producer prices aggravated the industry's crisis after 1918, brought on by war-related inflation in the cost of labor and raw materials and declining production from disease. United Fruit's response to an urgent petition by its suppliers in British Honduras was to raise prices by just two cents per stem in June 1919. On behalf of Governor Hutson, the colonial secretary called upon the company's Boston headquarters for a greater increase in the prices paid to independent growers:

> Your Company has never failed to bring to this Government's notice the increased cost of conducting the service of the fruit ships, a representation which has been recognised by this Government, but His Excellency . . . urg[es] your Company to offer a larger increase in the price paid for bananas throughout the Colony than that offered in June last, in order to save this important industry to

the Colony. . . . His Excellency has never understood why the price offered by the Company for bananas in British Honduras should not be more in accordance than it has with the prices offered and paid in Jamaica. (PRO CO 123 300)

The company, whose role in the colony was now reduced to that of a marketing outlet for independent growers, responded to the governor's appeal with a set of revised marketing procedures. Although growers in theory could earn more under these revisions, the governor noted that "the conditions imposed by the Company provide for strict grading of the bunches, and if they carry out thorough inspection the gain to the planters is questionable" (ibid.). Indeed, for stems of seven hands (bunches) or less, the growers would receive just twenty-five cents, or ten cents less than they had previously. Further, while introducing much more uncertainty about producer prices, the new contracts protected United Fruit's monopoly control over the colony's banana industry by prohibiting independent growers from selling their fruit to any other buyer.

United Fruit's withdrawal from the colony as a producer did not heighten the government's resolve in dealing with the company, despite some indignation in official circles at its practices. The company's decision to abandon Middlesex flaunted its contract with the government, which mandated that it cultivate "bananas *or other agricultural produce*" there for not less than twenty-five years (PRO CO 123 295a). In 1919, with the impending cessation of banana production at Middlesex, Governor Hutson noted in his dispatch to the Colonial Office that "I am not aware that [United Fruit managers] . . . think of substituting any product for bananas in the Stann Creek District. I have recently addressed an inquiry to the Company on the subject, inviting them to state definitely what they propose to do in the matter, with a view to meeting their moral obligations under their agreement with the government" (PRO CO 123 295b). The government's suggestions of alternative crops were not greeted with enthusiasm by the company's division manager, who noted simply that United Fruit had already "lost a considerable amount of money on the plantation" (PRO CO 123 295b). Yet even as United Fruit completed its withdrawal from the colony the government continued to scrupulously observe its own obligations. A recommendation to raise freight rates on the railroad in 1920 was vetoed, for example, because it "would be construed as an invitation to [United Fruit] to vary the Agreement" (PRO CO 123 300). The government did not insist that the company comply with its contract, and even offered to refund the purchase price of Middlesex when United Fruit ceased operations there (ibid.). The company rejected this largesse, instead placing the estate up for sale in 1921 for fifteen thousand dollars, or nearly twice its purchase price (PRO CO 123 316). Incredibly, colonial officials not only accepted the company's attempt to profit from breach of contract, but recommended that the government itself buy back the estate on these terms two years later (ibid.).

If the colonial government's stance toward the company in the early 1920s seemed to border on self-abasement, its unwillingness to confront United Fruit also reflected the company's continued, albeit indirect, control of the colony's banana industry. Governor Hutson had debated whether to hold the company to its obligations in 1921 but opted against confrontation after meeting with several influential Stann Creek banana growers:[6] "I was considering whether the government should take any action in the matter [but] I hesitated to do so, at present, because I wished to do nothing which may prejudice the position of banana planters in the District" (PRO CO 123 302). Recognizing that United Fruit remained the sole buyer of bananas in the colony, the governor understood that legal action would only bring price or marketing retaliation that would destroy those producers who remained, including members of the colony's nascent agricultural elite.

Banana production in the Stann Creek Valley continued to decline through the 1920s as farm after farm was abandoned to Panama disease and the disincentives of United Fruit's prices. From 1917 to the 1931 closure of the region's last remaining large estate, the Riversdale Farm at South Stann Creek, annual production fell from a peak of 886,881 stems to just 78,867 (AB M.C. 1056; AB 318–33a). Some producers remained along the railroad, and United Fruit steamers continued to periodically call for their fruit at Stann Creek. The fate of these growers was sealed in 1937 when the government, computing the railroad's cumulative losses at $2 million, declared it an intolerable burden on the colony's finances. The tracks were dismantled and all rolling stock sold off to the Jamaican government, closing export markets to many small-scale producers in the Stann Creek Valley who had remained unscathed by the disease.

Although banana production on large plantations ceased in 1931, the end of the first boom in banana production did not signal a complete cessation. Along the southern coast of the colony, small-scale farmers continued to cultivate the fruit for export through the 1940s. Now-elderly Monkey River residents note that banana farming under milpa cultivation remained the pri-

mary local livelihood at least until World War II. With the termination of
United Fruit's shipments from the country, Monkey River farmers turned to
other marketing outlets. These they readily found among former "rum run-
ners," operators of fast boats who smuggled liquor into the United States
during Prohibition. Having been put out of the contraband business by the
repeal of the Eighteenth Amendment, they turned to shipping bananas from
Belize across the Caribbean and Gulf of Mexico to Tampa, Florida.

## Revitalization

Following the collapse of plantation production, the colonial government repeatedly encouraged banana farming on a scale larger than that of milpa cultivation. Colonial officials apparently hoped that the availability of an experienced English-speaking labor force would lure foreign investment in
agriculture, perceived as critical following the sharp contraction of the timber industry and rising labor unrest during the 1930s. In a memorandum
courting potential investors, the government noted that "many of the people
of British Honduras are already familiar with [banana cultivation], having
worked on banana plantations in the Stann Creek valley or the [neighboring]
Republics" (AB 318–33b). Yet such appeals induced neither investment in
plantation agriculture nor more regular shipping arrangements, undoubtedly due to the Depression and diminished market demand in the industrialized nations. Indeed, during the 1930s the multinationals that marketed fruit
in the developed countries found themselves with a glut of produce, leading
them to slash retail banana prices by as much as 80 percent (Davies 1990,
154).

Following World War II, the Colonial Development Corporation, a British
agency providing financing for development projects in the colonies, promoted the reestablishment of plantation production in Stann Creek District.
In response to these incentives, M. D. Greene and Jack Atkins, two investors
from Mobile, Alabama, formed the Waha Leaf Banana Company with an investment of $2 million. Situated on fourteen hundred acres at a site that the
partners named Alabama (now the location of Maya Mopan Village), the
Waha Leaf farm introduced disease-resistant varieties, the heavy reliance on
chemical inputs, and aerial spraying, now commonplace in banana production. One of the longest continuously farming growers in the region recalled
that "at least 95 percent" of the labor on the Waha Leaf farm was obtained

locally: "Labor was not hard to get in those days, especially after all the industries that had left the area here. People had to leave [Mango Creek] because of unemployment. When they heard about the banana business at Alabama, they went to work for the Greene and Atkins people." By 1960, Greene and Atkins employed eighty-two Creole and Garifuna workers from Mango Creek, Monkey River, and Seine Bight, as well as twenty Mayas from Toledo District. In 1962, when the government created the nearby Garifuna village of Georgetown to relocate displaced residents of hurricane-damaged Seine Bight, many male residents of the new village went to work at Waha Leaf as well (*Belize Times* 1964). Three times monthly about fourteen thousand boxes of fruit were loaded on ships for the eight-to-ten-day passage to Mobile. In 1967, Greene and Atkins sold the farm to a pair of European investors who, according to a longtime participant in the industry, "run it right down to the ground. . . . All they did was squeeze it dry." When the farm closed in 1970 due to disease and management problems, an experienced labor force was left behind. Many of these workers were subsequently hired onto state-run banana farms when the Belizean government sought to reestablish the industry for a second time in the early 1970s.

While the banana industry is in resurgence in the 1990s, it remains at less than half of the acreage established in the first boom eighty years ago. Much as the promoters of the "new" industry are unaware of its phases of expansion and collapse in the past, so they hold a particularly ahistoric perception of the present. Few of the large-scale growers who dominate the industry today resided in the region during the industry's infancy, and nearly half of the farms are owned by relatively recently arrived North American, Danish, or Jamaican expatriates. Perhaps for that reason, many growers describe the utilization of labor on today's farms in essentially timeless terms, as if contemporary patterns of labor recruitment in the industry are little changed from the past. Most rationalize their reliance on immigrant labor with the pointed assertion that local residents are unwilling to work in banana fields. "Our main problem in this industry," one farm owner stated in 1993, "is that our local people don't want to do the machete work. Once its machete, hauling fruit, harvesting, they won't do it. You will hardly find a Creole or Carib willing to work in the fields." Another expressed it in pseudo-anthropological terms that, as seen above, are historically inaccurate for the region's Creole and Garifuna residents: "You know, it is not a part of the culture of these people to work in farming. Their fathers and grandfathers were woodcutters, not farmers." A recently arrived American grower put it more bluntly: "Belizeans are lazy. They are happy to have a soft job, like driving or supervising. But you won't find them behind a machete."

To a casual observer, such claims may seem to be corroborated by the distribution of field workers encountered on today's banana farms, few of whom are Creole or Garifuna. Yet as the foregoing suggests, the residents of the region were extensively involved as workers and growers in the industry in the past; indeed, the modern banana sector was created almost entirely by their labor. This suggests that the current configuration of the banana work force is less the result of longstanding cultural preferences among workers than the hiring preferences of employers. The reason for these preferences will be explored in the following chapter.

### The State Creates a Banana Industry: 1969–1985

As with its colonial counterpart, the contemporary banana industry in southern Belize owes much to various forms of state subsidy. Today's industry is an outgrowth of the state's attempt to directly manage and finance banana production on government land in the early 1970s. In a country the size of Belize, the "state" does not appear as a faceless monolith but is experienced by residents in the actions of the prime minister and local representatives, who are personally well known to many of their constituents. It was not uncommon, for example, to see former prime minister George Price chatting with a street vendor in Belize City, or dropping in to talk with a small farmer on his visits to the countryside. Such populist touches do not, however, usually translate into policy formation, an area in which some confidants have much more influence than the average constituent. Having married into then-premier Price's family, Gregorio Achmed, an aspiring businessman in Mango Creek, was particularly well positioned to influence the government's priorities for development in the region. When Belize Estate, Hercules, and Savanna Products closed their operations in the late 1960s, leaving most local residents without earnings, Gregorio and his older brother, Samuel, realized that their own shops and other commercial ventures, built laboriously over the previous sixteen years, were threatened as well. "When Savanna closed down," Samuel remembered, "I turned to my brother and I said, 'Well, we are dead here now.'"

In 1969, the Price government invited Fyffes, United Fruit's British-based marketing subsidiary, to consider developing banana plantations in southern Stann Creek District, a move intended to relieve unemployment in the region. Fyffes sent a delegation at government expense, but declined the invitation to establish production in the region, stating that the proposed lands were too dispersed and too limited in area to warrant direct investment (Alonso 1987, 1). A later consulting team from the British Ministry of Overseas Development similarly advised against the government's reliance on banana production as a mechanism of development, noting that plantation production on the proposed four thousand acres of land would be successful "only at high cost (of inputs) and without maximizing productivity per unit of labour, which should be a major aim of such developments in Belize" (ULG Consultants 1975, iii). Yet another delegation invited from United Fruit in Honduras by Samuel Achmed, himself a medium-scale banana grower since the 1960s, attained the same conclusion. Although roundly ignored by prospective industry participants, the conclusions of such delegations offered some remarkably prescient predictions. If the banana industry came to rely on immigrant labor, the British consultants warned, "the addition of a large Spanish element may upset the overall balance of ethnic groups within Belize. . . . Social conditions in such an unbalanced community may lead to an undesirable amount of tension and even violence" (ibid., 78–79).

Notwithstanding such advice, and the reluctance of the multinationals to invest directly in the area, the Achmed brothers invited Price to Mango Creek to discuss the prospects for a direct government role in revitalizing the industry. During two days of meetings with the premier in 1970, the brothers presented a plan in which the government would make land and credit available to thirty growers at a project site known as Cowpen, twelve miles west of Mango Creek. After touring the area with Price and unveiling their proposal, Samuel Achmed recalled, "Price said to us, 'We will give the banana business the support it needs because of you; you know what the banana industry can do.'" That the brothers' suasion outweighed the advice of all previous industry consultants is one indicator of the clientelistic nature of the Belizean state.

The Price government proceeded to negotiate credit for the operation and marketing contracts for Belizean bananas. A multilateral lending agency, the Commonwealth Development Bank, was reluctant to provide financing directly to the farmers at Cowpen, obliging the government to take responsibility for repaying their loans in the event of default. In 1973, the government finalized a contract with Fyffes, which gained exclusive marketing rights in

Britain for Belizean bananas. Fyffes's parent company, United Fruit (then known as United Brands and now as Chiquita), was to sell planting materials of the wind- and Panama disease–resistant Gran Nain variety to local farmers. With the government in effect assuming all risks of production, Fyffes and United Fruit overcame their earlier reluctance to collaborate in the redevelopment of the industry. As will be seen, the banana companies' relationship to their Belizean suppliers has changed little since the early 1970s, or, for that matter, from their earlier involvement in the colony's banana trade between 1900 and the 1920s. Throughout this century, and until the present day, the multinationals have attempted wherever possible to shift risk from themselves to growers. Until the construction of a $6.5-million deep-water shipping facility at Big Creek in 1989, of which Fyffes is minority owner, the banana companies refused to make any direct investments in the Belizean industry at all.

Two parallel forms of production were envisioned during the period of state management. The original proposal drafted in 1972 was that thirty "tenant farmers" would lease land from the government. These growers were allocated between thirty and sixty acres of land each in the zones known as Farms 2, 3, and 4 at Cowpen. Depending upon the amount of acreage they requested, the tenant farmers were allotted loans of between thirty thousand and sixty-two thousand dollars to commence production. The loans were to be repaid automatically through deductions from crop receipts once fruit shipments began. Farm 1, a single block of four hundred acres, was to be run directly by the government as a demonstration farm, and to get production immediately established for export. Together with the privately owned farms of Bladen-Trio, located twelve miles south of Mango Creek, and Caribbean Empire, located eighteen miles to the north, the industry was intended to encompass close to four thousand acres under cultivation by the mid-1970s (Commonwealth Development Corporation 1983).

In the period of state management, the industry's development was ostensibly overseen by the Belize Banana Control Board (BCB), a government agency that managed the state-run Farm 1, provided infrastructure such as roads, cableways, and packing sheds on all of the Cowpen farms, and coordinated fruit shipments with Fyffes. The Banana Board, as it came to be known, was managed by a board of directors consisting of the chairman and vice-chairman of the Banana Growers' Association (to which all growers belonged), the ministers of agriculture and finance, representatives of the Commonwealth Development Bank, and a chairman appointed by the government. Notably absent was any representation of banana industry workers, whose inclusion industry unions later tried to obtain without success. Whereas tenant farmers hired their own labor, workers on Farm 1 were directly employed by the board. By the mid-1970s, tenant farmers employed around 200 workers, and another 125 were employed on the government's Farm 1. According to Banana Board reports of the time, nearly all of this labor was derived from the surrounding villages of Georgetown, Mango Creek, and Seine Bight, as well as from the Toledo District (Banana Control Board 1974, 5).

Almost from the outset, the state-managed banana industry encountered serious financial and production problems. In part, climatic factors were responsible for early losses suffered by the industry, for within a year of the establishment of farms at Cowpen, nearly half the acreage there was destroyed by Hurricane Fifi in 1974. During the following year, the banana-growing region of the country again suffered losses from wind damage as well as its worst drought in thirty-five years.[7] Government mismanagement also played a major role, for the board failed to provide adequate infrastructure to pack and ship fruit from the tenant farms. Only two packing sheds were constructed to service all of the tenants and the state-run farm, obliging the board to impose packing quotas on each grower. These quotas fell short by as much as 60 percent of the harvesting capacity of each farm, making it impossible for farmers to recoup their labor and input costs from their meager sales. One grower claims that his production costs at shipment rose to twenty-four dollars per box by the late 1970s, or nearly six times the producer price obtained from Fyffes. Unable to service their debts, tenant farmers were soon dropping out of the scheme, their land being taken over directly by the Banana Board. By 1984, the last full year of government management of the industry, only ten tenant farmers were left, all seriously indebted to the government.

Yet despite its mismanagement and climatic setbacks, the collapse of the state-run industry was not solely the result of local factors. Even with appropriate management and infrastructure, the industry would have been hard-pressed to survive in the face of contract conditions and shipping arrangements imposed by Fyffes and its parent company. Following the decision to promote banana industry development on its own, the government was never able to challenge the contract terms dictated by its buying partner. Having made no physical investment in Belize, and viewing the Belizean industry as at best a minor supplier of fruit, Fyffes could negotiate from an unassailable position. The company gradually increased its producer prices through the early 1980s, yet because of its lack of direct investment in Belize, the company generated nearly 100 percent profits on each box of fruit purchased from Belize by the mid-1980s.[8] Even more injurious to the industry, if not humiliating to its producers, were the shipping conditions contained in the contract with Fyffes. Contending that an insufficient volume of fruit would be produced to warrant port calls in Belize itself, Fyffes specified that the Banana Board would, at its expense, barge all Belizean fruit to Puerto Cortés, Honduras. There it would be combined with other United Fruit produce for shipment to Europe. This arrangement, which continued until 1989, added four to five days to the shipment time for Belizean bananas to Europe, greatly increasing spoilage rates and damage due to additional handling. It also resulted in lowered net prices to the producer, which are determined by quality inspections upon landing.

Under these unfavorable conditions, the state-run industry accumulated ever-increasing annual deficits. By 1985, the board had accrued more than $29 million in total losses (Alonso 1987, 2). Like the rest of Central America, Belize at that time was experiencing long-term declines in the terms of trade for its primary exports, forcing the newly independent government to negotiate a standby agreement with the International Monetary Fund (IMF) in 1984. Obliged by the IMF to reduce public expenditures and adopt an austerity budget, the Banana Board's losses represented a burden that the state could no longer afford.

Independent banana growers of that time, like their contemporary counterparts, tended to view the banana multinationals as unscrupulous adversaries. Former participants often claim that the collapse of the state-run industry was no accident. Throughout the period of state management, Fyffes's and United Fruit's visiting advisors encouraged the government to take over insolvent farms and manage them directly. Although ostensibly intended to maintain a stable volume of fruit arriving at Puerto Cortés, the government's management of indebted and often neglected farms only heightened its own financial deficits. Some former tenant farmers hint darkly that the multinationals wished to see the government saddled with a huge debt, so that it would eventually be forced to sell the entire industry at bargain prices to foreign corporations willing to reinvigorate it. If managers of Fyffes and United Fruit believed that their companies would be beneficiaries of the Banana

Control Board's misfortunes, they were to be disappointed. In 1984, the Price government, again with the advice of the Achmeds, developed a plan to sell banana farms in parcels to private growers rather than the banana multinationals.[9] Thus began the contemporary phase of the industry's development. As will be seen in the following chapter, this strategy denied the banana multinationals direct control over Belizean farms but did little to mitigate the monopoly power that Fyffes continues to assert over its suppliers in Belize.

# 3 ❧ *Local and International Contexts of Production*

> How can man secure his position in the verdant but overwhelming
> tropics? In the world at large, moral and social codes are more clearly
> defined . . . than they were a century ago. But along the banana frontier
> the trade is often forced to administer justice, provide for the general
> welfare, and promote social reform, in addition to managing the most
> difficult of the world's agricultures.
>
> —Charles Morrow Wilson (1947)

> One begins properly to appreciate the great civilizing influence of a
> much-maligned American corporation—the United Fruit Company—
> that spells the economic salvation of these countries and promises an
> honest wage to the laboring classes.
>
> —William James Showalter (1913)

Given their ubiquity in both a wild and domesticated state in low-
land Central America, bananas may be thought a relatively simple crop to
cultivate. To do so profitably for the modern world market, however, requires
the mobilization of resources and labor on an industrial scale. It is no coincidence that the commercial success of banana farms closely correlates with
their scale and degree of capitalization. "Bananas," the former chairman of
the BCB once observed, "require a large fortune to make a small fortune. As
far as the small man is concerned, he would be better off planting cassava."

## The Production Process

The nutrient and climatic needs of the banana plant are straightforward
enough. Requiring abundant moisture and year-round temperatures in excess of fifty degrees Fahrenheit, banana production is confined to the low-

land humid tropics. Although Belize lies to the north of all other banana-exporting regions of the Americas, and is therefore more at risk for periodic chills, the southern part of the country is well suited to growing the fruit. With daytime temperatures ranging between 80 and 96 degrees throughout the year, and an average annual rainfall of 120 inches, the damp, heavy atmosphere of the Stann Creek and Toledo Districts resembles a sauna to visitors from northern latitudes. Bananas flourish under such conditions, notwithstanding the oppressiveness experienced by the region's human inhabitants.

To profitably produce commercial quantities of fruit, farmers require considerable knowledge of the plant's peculiarities. While a banana "mat," or root bed, may be in continuous production for more than ninety years, as in some Honduran plantations, the plant must be constantly coaxed and cajoled to yield the kind of fruit that consumers in the developed countries take for granted. The large bud, or "navel," that forms at the end of a banana stem, for example, is cut off the stem soon after it forms so that the plant puts energy into fruit, rather than flower, production. Every year a "mother" trunk (the part of the plant that produces fruit) sends up from its base several shoots, or suckers. After fruit is harvested from a plant, the mother and all but one of its "daughter" suckers are cut back to allow a fruit-bearing trunk to regenerate. Knowing which of these suckers to retain is critical to the plant's productivity, yet by no means obvious to the novice. One North American investor told his field laborers to simply remove all but the largest sucker, discovering too late from an experienced Belizean grower that suckers facing east yield nearly twice as much fruit when they mature, due to their greater exposure to sunlight.

Of equal importance to such esoteric knowledge is the formidable mix of chemicals used to protect the plant and its fruit from an array of tropical pests and diseases. In addition to four different fertilizers and lime used on farms throughout the year, farm workers regularly apply the potent nematicide Mocap (ethoprop) to banana plants. To combat an epidemic of black sigatoka, an airborne fungus that causes prematurely ripened fruit, all farms are crop-dusted weekly with a variety of fungicides, including Tilt (propiconazole), Bravo (chlorothalonil), and Calixin (tridemorph). Secondary growth that constantly threatens to overtake farms in the tropics is cleared with the highly toxic herbicide Gramoxone (paraquat), administered by farm workers carrying backpack sprayers. Approaching a banana farm by road, visitors smell the lingering chemical cocktail that hangs over the fields even before the first banana plants come into view. Should they contact the fruit directly, several farm chemicals are so caustic that they immediately blemish and ruin it for sale. To protect their crops from exposure to aerial and surface spraying, as well as predatory insects, each farm employs some workers (known as *plastiqueros*) exclusively to tie plastic sacks over the fruit as soon as it appears on the plant. For their part, farm workers are provided with no protection from the toxic substances they handle.[1]

For all its capital intensity, banana production is unique in its intensive use of labor as well. Because they bear fruit throughout the year, banana farms are not characterized by seasonal fluctuations in labor demand: unlike the region's citrus farms, for example, there is no "off season" during which laborers leave the area in search of work elsewhere. In contrast to other agro-industries as well, banana farms employ labor in as hierarchical and segmented a fashion as that of any manufacturing industry. A five-hundred-acre farm will employ between eighty-five and one hundred full-time field workers in a wide variety of tasks. During three harvest days per week, the farm will also employ a part-time labor force of equal size to pack bananas for shipment. Most unskilled field labor is deployed flexibly, the same worker conceivably assigned to four or five different tasks throughout the week. Such is the case for workers applying fertilizer and lime, spraying herbicide or nematicide, bagging fruit, propping banana plants, or deleafing, in which dead or diseased leaves are cut from the plant. Each of these tasks is paid at a different piece rate; indeed, few field workers on any farm are paid an hourly wage. Although the elaborate pay scales that result greatly complicate record keeping, farm managers prefer piece rates as a means of ensuring labor discipline and guaranteeing completion of tasks. More-skilled tasks, such as digging drains or pruning plants, are paid at higher rates and are usually assigned to a few specialized workers with more experience.

Large farms are subdivided into blocks to which the same group of workers and supervisors is assigned on a daily basis. Farm 4 at Cowpen, for example, encompasses 543 acres over four blocks, each of which employs a team of eighteen to twenty-two workers (see fig. 1). The subdivision of the farm and its labor force allows for closer supervision of workers and pay rates. For purposes of production, it also ensures that workers and their supervisors are well acquainted with the characteristics and problems of the area under their control, something that would be impossible were workers assigned to different parts of the farm every day. One captain is assigned to

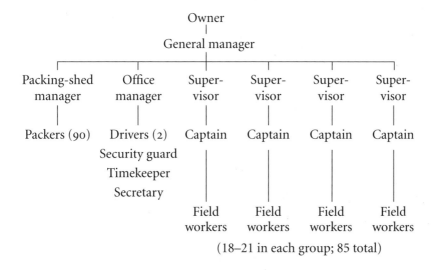

Fig. 1. Organization of management and labor on a 450-acre banana farm.

directly supervise work on each block. He remains in the fields in close proximity to the workers under his supervision, ensuring that tasks are completed correctly and on time. Finally, a supervisor is employed over each captain to determine the tasks to be completed on each block and to relay directives from office management to the fields.

On Sunday afternoons, the beginning of the week's harvest signals a shift in activity from the maintenance work completed over the previous four days to the work of cutting fruit and conveying it to the packing shed. Both the tempo and intensity of labor increase between Sunday and Tuesday as field workers cut and haul fruit for as much as twelve-hour shifts. Some thirteen weeks elapse from the appearance of fruit on a banana plant to its readiness for harvest. A colored plastic ribbon is tied to each stem of fruit during the week that it appears on the plant, the color for that week having been earlier established for all farms by the BGA. By counting the ribbons of each color, managers can estimate the amount of fruit to be harvested during a particular week. The aggregate estimate from all farms is then used by Fyffes to determine the size of the vessel required for each shipment to Europe. In turn, this figure provides each farm with a quota for shipment, which it must neither exceed nor fall significantly short of. For field workers, the ribbons also provide an indication of what fruit is to be harvested during any one shipment period.

Harvest work is among the most arduous of any labor to be found on banana farms. Given the susceptibility of Panama disease–resistant varieties to bruising, hauling banana stems is not only heavy work but also, paradoxically, exceedingly delicate. Captains constantly remonstrate their harvesters to handle the fruit with care and scold them pitilessly should a stem fall to the ground: "When you back [carry] a stem to the cable," an uncomprehending Honduran was warned in Creole, "you must handle it like fu yu own pikni [child]. If you make it drop, we'll find somebody who won't." Although the piece rates associated with harvesting are significantly higher than maintenance work, the duration and intensity of harvest labor prove physically exhausting for most workers. It is strictly the domain of young men, generally those seeking to accumulate some savings so that they can leave the banana fields altogether. Workers report that after just two or three years of harvest labor, most men are "used up" (*agotado*) and no longer able to continue as harvesters.

On harvest days, banana farms resonate with the sound of fruit being moved along cableways, a metallic reverberation resembling a train over distant rails. Large farms are arrayed with miles of cable, suspended by braces at a height of about seven feet. On Farm 4, ten cables converge from all parts of the farm on the packing shed, not unlike a railway freight depot. When fruit is harvested, two cutters (*corteros*) lift each harvestable stem onto the shoulder of a hauler (*juntero*). The hauler steadies the bagged fruit, which weighs sixty to eighty pounds, on a doubled truck inner tube strapped to his shoulder. Once the stem is cut, the hauler staggers under its weight to the cableway while negotiating mud that is often ankle deep. At the cable, the hauler will hang the stem from a hook suspended from rollers. He will repeat this process four hundred or more times a day. *Plastiqueros* move among the suspended stems, removing bags and weaving the plastic around the hands of fruit to cushion them on their way to the shed.

Once a "train" of thirty or more stems is assembled, the heaviest work of all falls to the *cablero,* or cableman. With a leather harness strapped around his waist, the cableman pulls the banana train hundreds of yards from the harvest site into the packing shed. Each train will have a ton or more of fruit suspended from it. En route to the shed, cablemen carefully negotiate six-inch-wide planks that span drainage ditches ten feet deep. Walking on the slick

Fig. 2. Creole field supervisor and ripening fruit.

irrigated clay soils of local farms is treacherous in itself, but under their load, cablemen usually slip and fall several times on each trip to the shed. Yet cablemen are under tremendous pressure to complete each round trip quickly, not only from a captain anxious to meet production schedules but also from the urging of their co-workers. Because fruit cannot be cut until cablemen return to the farm with rollers and hooks for suspending the stems from the cable, the pace of their work establishes the extent of the others' earnings as well as their own.

Once it has been removed from the fields, the fruit proceeds through a series of assembly-line-like steps for packing. In contrast to field labor, most of these steps in packing are paid at the prevailing minimum wage of two dollars per hour. The use of wage rather than piece rates is possible in part because several packing-shed supervisors move constantly among workers to reinforce discipline. Because workers are hired only for the two-day packing period, with no guarantee that they will be rehired the following week, the consequences of a single instance of poor performance are far greater for shed workers than for field employees. Those seeking employment in packing arrive at the shed every Sunday afternoon, creating a labor pool considerably in excess of the work available. From this group the shed supervisor selects, in the words of one Creole captain, "the ones who didn't give no trouble in the past. We go with the best, we let go the rest."

At the entrance to the packing shed, workers "deflower" the fruit, removing by hand the small blackened buds that form at the end of each banana. The stems are then conveyed to a crew of male workers who cut the hand, or cluster, of fruit from the stem. They toss each cluster into a three-foot-deep sorting trough filled with water and detergent. A line of up to forty predominately female workers then sorts through the floating hands, removing fruit that is blemished, bruised, cut, fused, too large or too small, or otherwise unacceptable for shipment. Although most of this fruit would be perfectly edible once ripened, none of it makes the "grade," the criteria that Fyffes specifies for fruit salable to its European customers. Rejects are flung onto a conveyor belt and from there deposited into the back of a truck. Rejected fruit, making up around 18 percent of each harvest, is simply dumped by the roadside outside of Cowpen, creating a sickly sweet smell that lingers heavily over the entrance into the village. Most of the fruit rots in immense piles, but a portion of it feeds scavenging pigs that some residents keep to supplement their earnings.

Fig. 3. Packing-shed workers sorting fruit.

Having sorted out hands of acceptable fruit, the women transfer them
into yet another set of water-filled bins, where a much smaller work crew
again evaluates the fruit by size and quality. The smallest acceptable fruit
ranges in length between six and a half and seven and a half inches and is
placed on plastic pallets for packing in small (twenty-eight-pound) boxes.
The largest salable fruit ranges between eight and ten inches and is packed in
larger (forty-pound) boxes. All fruit falling outside these dimensions is dis-
carded at this final point of sorting. Once on the pallets, the fruit is sprayed
with Fungiflor, a chemical that inhibits fungus growth during shipment. The
pallets then roll on a conveyor to packing stations, where women line boxes
with plastic and arrange the hands of fruit inside each box. The box is then
rolled to the next station, where a man uses a vacuum hose to remove air
from each plastic liner. He closes the box and lifts it onto a final conveyor,
which takes it to a truck for loading. From the farm, the fruit is then driven
thirteen miles to the port at Big Creek, where it is loaded onto a freighter
eventually destined for Europe.

## *The Small Man Feeds the Big Man: The Making of Latifundia*

The capital and labor intensity of the process outlined above is characteristic of all the large farms in the banana belt. Although they lack cableways and irrigation, and may have packing sheds that are no more than open-sided thatched huts, even farms of ten acres must apply the same array of inputs and follow the same specifications for quality control as the largest farms. To some degree, these procedures are the result of natural exigencies, for monocrop production of any perishable produce in the humid tropics entails huge agronomic risks. Yet the complexity of banana production is also dictated by factors exogenous to the region. Primary among these are the way bananas are retailed to consumers in the supermarkets of developed countries, where the appearance and size of fruit often determine whether it can be sold at all.

On even small farms, the input expenses of banana production are astonishing. Many of these expenses are deducted automatically from the box price, so that growers see only a small fraction of the producer price when they are paid for a shipment. From the prevailing base price of $13.08 per forty-pound box, $4.22 is deducted in mandatory levies for the Banana Growers' Association, the government, port use, a disaster insurance fund, and the purchase of boxes from Fyffes at $2.00 each. An additional $1.30 is deducted from each box by the BGA for aerial spraying to control black sigatoka, which has threatened the country's banana production since 1979, when spores of the fungus were blown to Belize by a tropical storm.

Growers estimate that chemical inputs and labor amount to about 75 percent of their production costs, many citing the high cost of inputs as the single greatest factor limiting profitability. One U.S. expatriate noted that comparable products could be purchased in the United States for up to 50 percent less than their price in Belize, attributing high local prices to the fact that three Belizean firms hold the marketing rights to farm chemicals and set prices among them. When wages and farmer-supplied inputs are taken into account, what appears initially to be a profitable crop generates a slim profit of just $1.55 per box, according to the BGA's best-case scenario. As will be seen, current contracts with Fyffes specify numerous penalties for low quality or box weight, the result being that farmers not infrequently owe money to the company after selling their fruit to it.

The profitability of farms increases with their productivity, yet the irrigation, cableways, and complex systems of drains that contribute to the volume of production present daunting expenses for even large-scale investors. To establish a 400-acre farm similar to the operation described above would entail an investment of close to $3 million, or $7,800 (U.S.$3,900) per acre. For the growers able to make investments of this scale, these expenditures quickly translate into much higher earnings per acre. According to BGA records, the region's four smallest farms encompassed an average of 12.3 acres under cultivation in 1992. Lacking cableways or irrigation, these farms produced on average 236 boxes per acre in that year. The four largest farms, all of which have irrigation and cableways, averaged 397.5 acres under cultivation and produced 556 boxes per acre in 1992. Such economies of scale have contributed significantly to the concentration of acreage under banana cultivation in the hands of an ever-smaller number of growers.

On the eve of privatization in 1984, just ten tenant farmers remained in production on government lands in Cowpen. Although the government had always articulated a policy encouraging the coexistence of both large and small farms in the industry, it was evident that small-scale farmers found it difficult to survive on their own. When state-run farms were sold to private investors in the following year, assets were sold to the highest bidder, excluding most prospective small-scale growers. Five of the former tenant farmers, augmented by five partners seeking to enter banana production, were nonetheless able to retain a foothold in the industry. This they did by forming the Belize Banana Growers' Cooperative, a group that collectively bid for the purchase of Farm 4 when it went up for sale in 1985. The fate of the co-op in the years that followed provides a clear illustration of the difficulties facing small-scale banana growers.

The co-op was organized in 1985 after some debate among the members whether to form a share-holding company or a cooperative. They opted for the latter because of the availability of grants and loans from development agencies that specifically targeted co-ops and credit unions for assistance. "If we didn't form that group," former co-op member Eustus Williams recalled, "then the bigger growers would have taken over the whole industry. We were the only small growers here. Government policy at that time was to have small growers, which was why they started off with tenant farmers. So when they started selling the farms, we got together the ten of us at Farm 4."

The co-op members cultivated a total of 560 acres, each member farming blocks ranging in size between 30 and 90 acres. Much-needed rehabilitation of the farm was achieved through a grant of fifty thousand U.S. dollars from a United States government agency assisting "grassroots development" projects in the Americas. With this infusion of cash, the cooperative rapidly entered into production and, for a short time, turned a profit. The co-op's initial promise led its foreign sponsor to hail it, prematurely, as "a resounding success story" (Shaw 1988, 26), proving "that small farmers can also be aggressive businessmen with a significant role to play in their country's economic and social development" (ibid., 20). As if on cue, officials of the Belizean government's Department of Cooperatives, who enjoyed a close relationship with the U.S. development agency, effused that the farm was "the most successful agricultural co-op in the history of the cooperative movement in Belize" (ibid., 26). Yet even as such praise was being published in the development agency's slick quarterly magazine, the cooperative was encountering daunting financial problems.

Having purchased separate parcels of Farm 4, each individual initially was responsible for his own area of the farm. As a result, coordinating labor, packing, and shipment quickly became intractable problems given the widely varying conditions and levels of input use on each member's farm. Several members held substantial acreage but failed to apply inputs at recommended levels. Because the co-op received loans collectively, the more productive members ended up bearing most of the costs, while any benefits were distributed equally. To remedy this situation, the co-op hired a general manager and staff in 1988 to supervise the farms as a single unit. Co-op members became in essence nonfarming directors, with day-to-day decisions concerning farm operations reverting to the general manager. This alleviated input application and coordination problems for a time, yet it also contributed to administrative costs. To maintain production and even to meet payrolls, the co-op continued to take out loans from the government's Development Finance Corporation, at the much higher interest of commercial banks, and debts to the BGA for input application continued to climb.

In 1990, the farm was irrigated at great cost in a last, desperate effort to boost production. By 1992, the co-op could not make its interest payments, much less repay any of the principal of its debts. In April of that year, the Banana Growers' Association informed the group that it could no longer provide inputs on credit without repayment of past debts, leaving members no alternative but to liquidate the co-op. Shortly thereafter, Farm 4 was purchased by the wealthiest member of the Achmed family, Phillip, for a total price of

$847,500. In addition, he assumed the co-op's debts, which stood at $2.9 million. Most of the staff, including several of the co-op members themselves, were retained as supervisors for the newly renamed Achmed Farms Ltd.

From this experience, Eustus Williams envisions no possibility for small farmers to survive for long in banana farming as the industry is constituted at present: "The inputs are too costly, and one little natural disaster and you have a total loss. Then the small man is out. The big man has reserves that can see him through difficult times, but the small man has to sell out." Another former member, one who clings to just eight acres of his own on the margin of Farm 4, put it similarly: "What we are seeing now in Belize is that the big money men are taking over. It is always the small man who feeds the big man, like the fry feed the shark."

Statistics on land distribution and ownership of banana farms bear out such patterns regionally. When the BGA began collecting data on land distribution on banana farms in 1989, twenty-seven growers cultivated bananas for export in the Stann Creek and Toledo Districts on nineteen farms, including the cooperative-owned Farm 4. By 1993, twenty-three banana farms were in operation, but the number of growers had declined to seventeen as a number of large growers acquired more than one farm, generally following the decision of small growers to sell out. During this same period, each grower's average landholdings increased from 144 acres to 245.6 acres. Much, but not all, of this attrition reflected the collapse of the cooperative and the acquisition of its lands by one large grower. Yet data on farm acquisition and expansion among growers suggest a continuing pattern of small farmer attrition and land consolidation by elites (see table 1).

In 1993, of the twenty-three operational banana farms, four were owned by a Danish firm and four by a Jamaican expatriate. In addition, four Achmed brothers each owned farms, among them the nation's three largest banana estates. Since 1990, three farms previously owned by small- or medium-scale Belizean growers had been acquired and greatly expanded by investors from the United States (a fourth small farm was acquired by Americans in 1992). Hence, nine corporations or individuals owned fifteen of the region's farms, which among them accounted for 3,993 acres, or 87.5 percent of all land under banana cultivation. The average landholding of these nine large growers was 462.9 acres. The remaining seven growers had among them just 575 acres on farms ranging from 8 to 165 acres in size, with an average of 82.1 acres. By late 1993, three of these smaller farms were heavily indebted and, as

*[margin annotation:]* foreign ownership

Table 1. Land Distribution among Banana Growers, 1989 and 1993

| Grower (1989 Rank) | 1989 Acreage | 1993 Acreage |
|---|---|---|
| 1 | 1,821 | 836.8 |
| 2 | 854.4 | 927.6 |
| 3 | 431.9 | 490.7 |
| 4 | 332.6 | 446 |
| 5 | 330 | — |
| 6 | 270 | 180 |
| 7 | 270 | — |
| 8 | 264 | 803.3 |
| 9 | 205 | 215 |
| 10 | 170 | — |
| 11 | 140 | 235 |
| 12 | 103 | — |
| 13 (co-op) | 90 | — |
| 14 (co-op) | 75 | — |
| 15 (co-op) | 70 | — |
| 16 (co-op) | 70 | — |
| 17 (co-op) | 50 | — |
| 18 (co-op) | 45 | — |
| 19 (co-op) | 45 | — |
| 20 (co-op) | 40 | — |
| 21 (co-op) | 30 | — |
| 22 (co-op) | 30 | — |
| 23 | 25 | 65 |
| 24 | 25 | 48 |
| 25 | 25 | 35 |
| 26 | 10 | — |

*Source:* adapted from growers' surveys by the Banana Control Board and the Banana Growers' Association.

*Note:* Grower 5 sold farm to a North American investor, grower 7 sold farm to grower 2, grower 10 closed farm without resale, grower 12 sold farm to a new Belizean grower, co-op members (growers 13 to 22) sold farms to grower 8, and grower 26 sold farm to two North American investors.

they were adjacent to much larger farms undergoing expansion, faced probable acquisition by their large-scale neighbors.

If the banana growers of the country appear to be radically divided between nearly equal numbers of small farmers and the owners of much larger estates, their producers' group, the Banana Growers' Association, seems remarkably impervious to polarization by landholdings. Small and large growers stress equally that all have a common stake in the industry and common interests as producers. Many, but by no means all, emphasize that growers' common interests stem from their dealings with their marketing partner, Fyffes. All growers are theoretically subject to the same contract conditions in the sale of their fruit to Fyffes, conditions that many, in private, vehemently denounce as exploitative and humiliating. Yet, growers are unable to unify to address these issues, leaving the BGA in most cases little more than a coordinating body and extension agency for the industry rather than a forceful negotiator with the multinational. The divisions among banana growers, then, relate not to the size of their landholdings, but to their relationship, as a group, to Fyffes.

### We Have to Punish You: Fyffes and the Growers

> Private planters are controlled by the fruit company through banana purchase contracts, which prevent them from selling fruit to competing exporters who might better the low prices they are receiving, but which do not prevent the company from increasing the rigidity of its inspections when it desires less fruit. . . . If [contracts] are not renewed the planters' investments are lost, as no other purchaser has been able to establish itself in the company's spheres of influence.
>
> —Charles Kepner (1936)

In Great Britain, where most Belizean bananas are consumed, the oval blue label attached to Fyffes fruit enjoys the same brand recognition that Chiquita does in the United States. This is probably no coincidence, as Fyffes was for nearly eighty years a wholly owned subsidiary of the United Fruit Company, the holder of the Chiquita trademark and the world's largest banana corporation. That relationship lasted until 1986, when, after a series of costly corporate acquisitions, the American multinational sold its Fyffes subsidiary to raise badly needed cash (Davies 1990, 230).

Throughout the twentieth century, the banana business has been among the most oligopolistic of all food industries: three firms control virtually all of the American market and European trade is dominated by the giants Chiquita, Fyffes, and Geest of Holland (Trouillot 1988, 164). Such market dominance has been associated with a tremendous concentration of assets in a few corporations: with fewer than a thousand employees worldwide, Fyffes has cash reserves of more than £100 million sterling and generated profits of more than £9 million in 1988 alone (Davies 1990, 225). Notwithstanding the oligopolistic nature of the industry, each of these corporations is engaged in fierce and often extralegal competition over markets and sources of fruit.[2] As will be seen, in theory this competition could allow suppliers, such as the banana growers of Belize, to negotiate more favorable marketing arrangements with Fyffes's competitors. That the growers fail to do so is in large part due to Fyffes's efforts to prevent such alternatives from being realized. Kepner's description of the relationship between banana companies and their independent suppliers is as valid for Belize in the 1990s as it was for United Fruit in the rest of Central America during the early 1930s.

The marketing of bananas in the European Union (EU) is governed by a succession of treaties first negotiated in Togo in 1975 and known as the Lomé Convention. Under its terms, bananas from forty-six ACP (African, Caribbean, and Pacific) states that were former European colonies could be imported into the EU free of duty, while all other fruit, notably from the "dollar" sources of Latin America, would be subject to a 20 percent *ad valorum* levy. These tariffs have not excluded Latin American fruit from Europe, as production costs throughout dollar areas are generally lower than costs for ACP producers. They have, however, acted as market preferences, ensuring that producers in countries such as Belize are able to remain competitive with their counterparts in the neighboring countries. Subsequent modifications of the Lomé Convention permitted fruit companies to import one box of dollar-area fruit free of duty for every box they import of ACP fruit. In the most recent set of conditions governing banana imports to Europe, those negotiated by the EU in 1993, imports from each ACP and dollar source were assigned quotas, beyond which duties would be imposed. For its part, Belize was assigned an annual quota of thirty-five thousand tons, which has caused considerable apprehension among growers as it effectively limits development of the industry at present levels. Producers from dollar areas, however, were dealt a much more severe blow in the form of a two-million-ton quota for the region, representing a 25 percent reduction of European banana imports from Latin America from their 1992 level (James 1993, 23).[3]

Corporate competition for supplies of fruit is played out against the background of such marketing agreements. Since the sale of its Fyffes subsidiary in 1986, Chiquita has lacked suppliers of fruit from the ACP countries. As a result, it has been severely affected by recent European Union agreements favoring ACP sources. For its part, since 1988 Fyffes has attempted to maintain sources in both ACP and dollar areas in order to import as much fruit as possible free of duty. In that year, it began importing bananas to Europe from Guatemala and Honduras in addition to its more established sources of Belize, Suriname, and the Dominican Republic. The multinationals jealously guard their sources to restrain producer price competition, with the result that Fyffes's entry into Honduras was systematically blocked by its former parent company, Chiquita. Similarly, Del Monte strenuously opposed Fyffes's entry into Guatemala. There resulted a series of extralegal corporate skirmishes that Graham Pritchard, Fyffes's representative in Belize, referred to as "the banana wars."

In 1988, the first freight train carrying Fyffes bananas to port in Honduras was mysteriously stopped and sidelined, railway officials explaining to frantic representatives of the company that it had been "lost." With some cajoling and bribery, Fyffes was able to get the bananas to port, only to confront other obstacles. After the bananas were loaded onto a freighter, Chiquita's lawyers obtained a restraining order forcing the ship to unload. With its bananas ripening on the dock, Fyffes sought to override the order. Pritchard explained, "They've got their judges and we've got ours. We had ours issue orders countermanding theirs so that the boats could be loaded again." While such maneuvers failed in the end to stop the shipment, the added transport time and handling of that first cargo left it a near total loss by the time it reached England. According to Fyffes, its operations in Honduras continue to be entangled in legal obstacles erected by its former parent company.

Such proprietary if extralegal control of sources is by no means limited to Honduras and Guatemala. In Belize, Fyffes is particularly concerned that other corporations dealing in dollar-area fruit may be casting a covetous eye on its suppliers to obtain preferential access to the European market. A ruddy-faced and usually genial Englishman, Pritchard visibly stiffened when asked to discuss specific aspects of Fyffes's contract with Belizean growers ("How do I know you won't go to work for Dole next year after I provide this information?"). As it turned out, growers readily volunteered the contract information that Fyffes was reluctant to release, together with running commentary on its conditions. When discussing relations between the company and its private suppliers, Pritchard asserted that if growers object to conditions specified in the contract, they are free to seek other buyers: "After all, they are independent parties. They don't have to sell to us." Legally, there is no barrier to the entry of Fyffes's corporate rivals, and many growers privately state that they would welcome the competition provided by Chiquita or Dole. At present, however, Fyffes holds a monopoly on banana exports from Belize, and it is likely to do all in its power to retain that monopoly.

The current contract with Fyffes is an intricate document setting forth in large part the obligations of growers to their marketing partner. Of primary concern to most growers is the determination of fruit prices, for although a base price of $13.08 per forty-pound box is specified in the contract, actual prices paid by Fyffes fluctuate according to the quality rating assigned to each farm's shipment. Fyffes imposes penalties on growers for short box weights, over-ripened fruit, and low quality. All fruit supplied by growers must be free of blemishes, scars more than one inch in length, and discoloration, and no more than two hands per box may consist of three fingers (all other hands must have four or more). Despite the fact that growers are not paid for any fruit that fails to meet these criteria, Fyffes reportedly finds markets for all the fruit that it receives in edible condition, either among retail outlets or institutional buyers.

Scoring is an involved process that directly determines fruit prices, yet to many growers it is a mysterious if not arbitrary factor affecting their operations. Upon the arrival of each Fyffes shipment in England, the company's quality scorers open a sample of boxes from each farm and evaluate the fruit along thirteen criteria relating to ripeness, scarring, blemishes, rot, width, and length. Each box is scored for the percentage of unblemished fruit, and these percentages are then averaged for the entire sample from each farm. This sample average constitutes the Percent Mean Score (PCMS) of that farm's shipment, which directly determines the price paid to the grower.

In what it describes as an incentive to produce the highest quality fruit, Fyffes pays growers quality bonuses of up to $6 per box above the contract price if fruit is scored at 85 or above. Should the score fall below 60, however, Fyffes imposes penalties, which may result in up to $6 deducted per box (table 2). As a result, growers not infrequently owe money to the company after it has ostensibly "purchased" their fruit. On one farm, an inexperienced packing crew inadvertently packed shorter (six and a half to seven and a half inches) fruit in forty-pound boxes, instead of the twenty-eight-pound boxes in which such fruit is supposed to be shipped. The shipment of seventy-seven boxes was scored at a PCMS of just 30, almost entirely because of the error. While the fruit was otherwise acceptable and undoubtedly sold by Fyffes to its retailers, the grower was levied a penalty of $980 for the shipment. While one-time losses for low scores can be substantial, of even greater concern to growers is the company's punitive response to consecutively low scores. The contract specifies that if two shipments from a farm in thirty days fall below a PCMS of 60, Fyffes will refuse to accept a third shipment from the same farm.

Under these contract conditions, growers assume all the risk of the twenty-one- to twenty-three-day transatlantic passage, for their scores and farm receipts suffer if ships are delayed or fruit is damaged in handling. Con-

Table 2. Quality Bonuses and Penalties
for Forty-Pound Boxes of Bananas

| Percent Mean Score | Bonus/Penalty |
|---|---|
| 85+ | +6.00[a] |
| 80–84 | +$5.60 |
| 75–79 | +$5.20 |
| 70–74 | +$4.10 |
| 65–69 | +$1.90 |
| 60–64 | +$ .70 |
| 55–59 | -$1.90 |
| 50–54 | -$4.10 |
| 45–49 | -$5.20 |
| 40–44 | -$5.60 |
| 35–39 | -$6.00 |

Note: Bonuses and penalties are expressed in Belizean dollars ($Bze 2.00 = $US 1.00).

[a]Figures in this column represent bonuses in addition to, or penalties deducted from, the base producer price of $13.08 for each box of fruit purchased by Fyffes.

cerns about fruit quality are particularly acute for Belizean growers, as Fyffes ships make three to four additional port calls after leaving Big Creek. During each of these, the ships' refrigerated holds are opened, exposing fruit to high temperature and humidity levels that hasten ripening. Although the issue of quality scoring is raised annually in negotiations with the company, Fyffes has been steadfast in its refusal to consider any other system. Growers attempted to have quality assessed in Belize before ships are loaded, and, failing that, to have BGA representatives stationed in England to observe the scoring process. Neither alternative was acceptable to Fyffes, and growers ultimately signed the contract without changes. One representative of the BGA claims that scorers have an incentive to grade hard because they are rewarded by the company for low scores. Fyffes saves money when fruit receives low grades, and scorers receive bonuses for such savings. More outspoken growers contend that the scoring system is used in a punitive fashion, to retaliate against those growers Fyffes's local representatives see as too assertive, and to scare others into acquiescence.

Brian Seals, one outspoken North American grower, claims that most small farms get good marks because that enables Fyffes to maintain a high overall quality rating without paying for it (quality ratings for an entire shipment are averaged for all farms, but not weighted for the size of each farm's harvest). As a result, the company enjoys generally better relations with small growers than with the owners of most large operations. This in turn critically affects BGA policies toward the company because all BGA decisions are ostensibly decided on a one-person, one-vote basis. Over five to six shipments, he asserts, any large farm "will take a hit," suffering a substantial drop in quality assessment. "That way, Fyffes ensures that only a couple of growers are mad at any one time, and most are satisfied enough that they won't unite to challenge them."

Even the method of selecting small, odd-numbered samples works to the company's favor, Seals contends. For small farms, three boxes are sampled to measure PCMS (that is, length and quality) and five are selected for weight. The current contract provides that 90 percent of the boxes weighed are within 10 percent of specified packing weight. If five boxes are sampled and just one is short by more than 10 percent, however, the shipment's average falls to 80 percent and a penalty of fifty cents per box is levied against that farm. Some growers allege that these sampling and quality scoring procedures are the means by which Fyffes guarantees high profits for its shareholders and bonuses for its CEOs. To its British retailers, Fyffes offers annual wholesale price contracts at a fixed price (about twelve pounds sterling, or twenty-five U.S. dollars per forty-pound box). "Now how can they offer fixed annual contracts to retailers on the basis of fluctuating producer prices and production levels?" Seals asked. "I'll tell you how; they set the price to us by manipulating quality measures. The way they have it arranged now, it is al-most literally impossible for Fyffes not to generate a profit."

In addition to quality scoring provisions and penalties, the contract speci-fies growers' obligations concerning the size and weight of shipments. The current contract requires growers to deliver fruit within thirty-six hours of harvest. Collectively, the growers must supply Fyffes with at least sixty thou-sand boxes of bananas every two weeks or Fyffes will suspend purchases until the level of local production improves. The BGA is required to provide Fyffes with an estimate of the number of boxes to be shipped eight weeks before the fruit is actually harvested, so that the company can procure a ship of appro-priate capacity. According to Graham Pritchard, this enables the company to hire vessels whose cargo holds will be filled to capacity on each shipment so as to minimize transport costs per box. If the growers fall short of this estimate by more than 5 percent, they will be charged $7.65 per box for each shortfall, the penalty being levied against those farms that fail to meet their estimates. Finally, the contract provides contingencies that insulate Fyffes against un-foreseen changes in world market conditions. In the event of devaluation of the Belizean currency with respect to the U.S. dollar, for example, Fyffes will consider renegotiation of prices no sooner than two months after the devalu-ation, and then only at its option. Finally, Fyffes retains the right to renegoti-ate in the event of any changed world trade or banana marketing agreements. "Do you see any way," an incredulous BGA official asked after describing these contract conditions, "that Fyffes failed to cover their ass?"

Apart from acting as a purchaser of Belizean bananas, Fyffes has increas-ingly become involved in their production. It has purchased an 85 percent share of one of the largest grower's farms, which it operates in partnership with him. Fyffes has also taken over management of two of the Danish-owned farms, for which it was paid a management fee plus 25 percent of their quality bonuses. Finally, it has established a fertilizer and nematicide scheme, in which it makes these inputs available to growers on interest-free credit. On shipment days, Pritchard and another Fyffes employee visit each of the region's farms to evaluate fruit and make suggestions for farm maintenance.

It is in this latter respect that Fyffes's involvement in production is often resented. Brian Seals recalled one such farm visit, which set the pattern for his subsequent strained relations with the company: "Once I refused to acquiesce when [Pritchard] 'suggested' that we follow some procedures and new input usage on the farm. Now these are supposed to only be suggestions, and I told him, no, we won't do it because it will cost us money and I don't believe we'll see any benefits. That guy actually said to me, 'Well then, we're going to have to punish you.' I told him if I ever hear him say those words again when he's on my farm, I will physically throw him off."

Indicative of Fyffes's relationship with its Belizean suppliers was a clause added to its 1993 contract, in which it succeeded in imposing new penalties against growers for peel rot, caused by the fungus anthrincnose. A study jointly commissioned in the previous year by the BGA and Fyffes and conducted by the Fundación Hondureña de Investigación Agrícola identified the sources of this problem in Belizean bananas. The study recommended that boxes be better ventilated and deepened in order to better accommodate Belizean fruit, which is more curved than other Central American bananas (Fyffes employs boxes of the same dimensions for all of its fruit, regardless of source). Finally, the report found that the incidence of peel rot increased with shipping time and the period of time during which bananas are cooled to fifty-seven degrees Fahrenheit during shipping. While all of these issues are under the company's control, company officials responded to the report by attributing peel rot to the transport of fruit over bad roads and called on the BGA to demand that the government better maintain roads from banana farms to port.

Seals recalled that growers learned of the new penalties for peel rot at a BGA meeting, during which all the growers, except himself, remained silent as Pritchard announced the company's decision:

> Right now, Pritchard can't stand me, because I'm the only one who will come out and ask him why we should pay for Fyffes' mistakes. At that meeting, he came out and told us about the new penalties. So I said to him, "Graham, I have a few questions for you. You say we have a box problem. Well, who designs the boxes we use? Fyffes does. Who sells us the boxes we use? Fyffes does." So I asked him, "When are you going to get off your ass and do something about 'our' box problem?" He just slammed his briefcase shut and walked out. The growers were too scared to say anything, but when he went out the door, they applauded.

If the contract conditions specified by Fyffes have angered most growers, a few have, at their own initiative, sought alternative contracts and more favorable terms from other corporations. Two of the Achmed brothers have made overtures to Chiquita, which is reportedly eager to gain access to an ACP source of fruit. It indicated a willingness to pay Belizean suppliers up to nineteen dollars per box as a base price, with up to four dollars per box as a quality bonus. When Phillip Achmed announced the results of his discussions with Chiquita at a BGA meeting, and urged its members to terminate their contract with Fyffes, the association nonetheless refused to do so, albeit by a narrow vote. That a majority of the association's members acquiesced to Fyffes may seem astonishing, given the vehement sentiments detailed above. The vote surprised few members of the association, however.

What prevents growers from uniting against Fyffes is the fact that, having offered partnerships, credit, and employment to some growers, the company can readily count on allies within the BGA. It is common knowledge among growers that some within their ranks enjoy preferential relationships with the company, relationships that vastly diminish the perceived common interests of banana producers. When asked why growers don't seek other marketing arrangements, Brian Seals replied simply,

> They're scared. Look, [the Jamaican] Smithson is in with Fyffes. The Danes owe their ass to Fyffes. [The growers] Castillo and Nuñez have jobs with Fyffes. So anything that's discussed in the BGA immediately gets back to Pritchard. If you go to one of those meetings, its a farce. Maybe four or five guys do all the talking. Everybody else is scared stiff. What are they scared of? Imagine this. How hard would it be for Pritchard to call London or send a confidential memo that says "grade hard"? Not that they would make anything up, but that they would look for every single possible defect they can detect. We have no control or appeal of the process. And you know, it only takes two bad reports for you to lose a third shipment. That could literally put somebody out of business. Now we don't know that this happens, but everybody knows that it could. They have that much power over us.[4]

In more succinct if colorful terms, a Belizean grower described the relationship between the company and its allies in the BGA in this way: "Fyffes and these men are the ass and the chamber pot. They are so stupid and selfish, they don't know when they've been shit on."

Growers who are unaffiliated with Fyffes tend to share such fears of company retaliation, one claiming that the scenario described by Seals has already come to pass. A BGA official observes that "Fyffes has already run two producers out of business, and a third is on the way out." The first two farmers referred to were cut off of the fertilizer loan scheme and received a series of devastating quality scores after attempting to organize a growers' boycott of the company. The third refers to Seals himself, for his outspoken criticism of Fyffes in association meetings and during contract negotiations. Although many growers feel that contracts with Fyffes's adversaries would improve their earnings, a BGA official is pessimistic. Were a contract negotiated with anyone but Fyffes, the contract conditions might initially appear favorable but would eventually converge with Fyffes's specifications: "All these multinationals treat growers in basically the same way, as servants."

The strategies of control and manipulation by which multinationals maintain supplies of fruit may appear remote from the farms on which the fruit itself is produced. Yet such strategies are inextricably linked to the conditions on those farms. Banana production is a costly and risky undertaking, one that is more likely to yield a loss than a profit. This is all the more true given the multinational's efforts to safeguard its own economic position and divest itself of risk, which is assumed instead by the grower. To examine how growers, in the recruitment and deployment of farm labor, have responded to the ecological, economic, and all-important political constraints under which they operate, we turn next to the populations that have been successively incorporated into the industry.

# 4 🌿 *Out of Work in the Fields of Gold*

## BELIZEAN LABOR IN THE BANANA INDUSTRY

[A] strike took place from 29th August to 2nd September. Members of the office staff also struck on 1st September, claiming to be Union members and in sympathy with other strikers. . . . A negotiating team, composed of management and members of the Growers Association met several times in an effort to find a solution, but no satisfactory settlement had been reached by year end. Government agreed to a policy of the employment of non-national workers on a one for one basis with Belizeans.

—Banana Control Board, *Annual Report* (1975)

In the B.C.B. office the manager is recruiting office staff from Honduras when there are a lot of graduates in the country of Belize without a job. Now that Mr. Rosa is the new manager, he have [*sic*] given all the privileges to the Honduraneans. . . . Today the banana industry marks the beginning of a banana republic.

—Letter to editor of *Amandala,* signed "employee of the B.C.B.,"
9 July 1982

A small item in the *Belize Beacon* of 7 June 1975 announced the signing of a collective bargaining agreement in Mango Creek between the Democratic Independent Union (DIU) and the Banana Control Board. Three months earlier, the union had won representation rights covering all workers on the area's banana farms, rights it was to hold until 1979.

In a photograph accompanying the article, negotiators for the union posed with representatives of the Banana Board, one of whom remains a grower to this day. If the faces of management are familiar to contemporary readers, those of the workers surely are not. All of the union members in the photograph are Afro-Belizean, either Creole or Garifuna, and none currently remain in the industry. The recollections of such individuals and a few photographs from local newspapers in the 1970s offer some of the only evidence that the composition of the banana industry's labor force was once substantially different from what it is today. As accounts of the period indicate, the militancy of labor at that time also was in marked contrast to conditions prevailing in the industry today, providing a key to understanding the transformation of the labor force that occurred in the following decade.

### Unions and Management in the Time of State Ownership

Promoted by the Price government in the early 1970s in part to alleviate the region's unemployment, the banana industry at Cowpen soon absorbed a great deal of all locally available labor. In the mid-1970s, the estimated male population of working age in Mango Creek, Georgetown, and Seine Bight was only about 350 (ULG Consultants 1975, 13), with the employable adult female population put at 189 (Alonso 1987, 5). Reports of the period repeatedly refer to a "shortage of labor" on local banana farms and stress the likelihood that workers will have to be imported in the future (ULG Consultants 1975; Banana Control Board 1974). Yet employment records indicate that if shortages existed, they were not because of any disinclination of Creoles and Garifuna to engage in farm work. Banana Control Board records from October 1975 put the total banana industry work force at 325, of whom 289 were Belizean, 28 were Honduran, seven were Guatemalan, and one was Salvadoran (Alonso 1987, 4). Despite the fact that a majority of the male and female residents of Mango Creek were employed either full or part time in the industry, the Banana Board in its first annual report announced that "an intensive campaign has been mounted to attract workers" from other regions and countries (Banana Control Board 1974, 5).

The reason for the Banana Board's preoccupation with labor shortages in the area may be inferred from a number of newspaper articles and the board's annual report of the following year. Management's anxieties about farm labor may also be gleaned from the photograph mentioned above, for the triumphant smiles of shop stewards and dour expressions of managers suggest that the latter had not fared well in their first negotiations with a unionized work force. Indeed, it was a moment that employers had attempted to postpone as long as possible. The Democratic Independent Union had first sought a collective bargaining agreement with the tenant farmers and the Banana Board in August 1974. The DIU's efforts to have workers polled on the question of union representation were repeatedly rebuffed by management, leading the union to call a one-day sit-down strike on banana farms in November of that year (*Beacon* 1975a, 3). With still no response on the part of management, during the following February the union threatened to strike indefinitely unless a poll was held. At this point, a group of employees widely regarded as promanagement announced that they had formed the Independence Labour Movement (ILM), a rival union that sought to challenge the DIU in representation elections. With a company union as a possible alternative to the DIU, the board's management finally consented to the poll. Yet at the end of that month the rival union was soundly defeated by the DIU, 270 to 43 votes, among farm workers (*Beacon* 1975b, 1).

In part, the Banana Board's protracted resistance to the vote may have been because the DIU was affiliated with the opposition United Democratic Party (*Beacon* 1975a, 3). More than likely, however, the board's management would have resisted any effort to organize the industry's work force by any union other than its own creation, the ILM. In contrast to industry claims that banana farms were hobbled by a shortage of labor, production records indicate that the small size of the local work force actually had little effect on the productivity of farms through the 1970s and early 1980s. Rather, their output was more directly affected by climatic factors and inadequate infrastructural investment on the part of the Banana Board. As the subsequent history of union-management relations reveals, however, the industry's demand for labor and the relatively small size of the local population permitted unions to forcefully negotiate wage and working conditions, negotiations that more often than not resulted in union victories. Hence, if there existed a shortage of labor from the standpoint of management, it was a shortage of low-paid, docile workers unrepresented by unions. More than any other factor, this accounts for management's initial refusal to countenance a unionized work force and later efforts to weaken and expel those unions that gained a foothold in the industry.

Prior to the unionization of the banana industry, farm workers at Cowpen were among the lowest paid workers in the country, earning an hourly wage of sixty-five cents. In 1974, at the union's request, a government Labor Department representative visited Cowpen to investigate the status of labor in the industry. His report indicates that living and working conditions were difficult at best for workers who stayed at the farms during the three-day shipment period:

The transport provided [part-time workers] was not even fit for cattle. All casual workers were to find housing for themselves. Since most of them were women they were subjected to immoral conditions so that they could have somewhere to sleep. Those who refused to grant favours were forced to sleep on the floor and to cook in the open. They overcrowded little shacks or they sought protection in numbers. . . . Drinking water was obtained from drinking holes next to pit latrines. When they used cardboard paper for sleeping mats, management took them away and burned them, telling workers to sleep on the hard floor. . . . As far as pay was concerned no worker knew at any one time how much he would receive. Sometimes, after a three day shipment, they got $26 after working some forty five hours. (Alonso 1987, 9)

Once the union won representation rights, two issues emerged that were to remain the focus of union and management struggles over the next ten years: pay rates and housing. In its first contract with the Banana Board, the union obtained a 12 percent pay increase through January 1976, followed by a 3 percent raise through October of that year (Banana Control Board 1975, 3). The contract also specified that workers were entitled to twenty-eight days of annual sick leave with pay, death and unemployment benefits, and vacation leave (*Beacon* 1975c, 1). Over the five-year period that the DIU represented the industry's work force, it negotiated wage increases totaling 27 percent for farm labor (Alonso 1987, 9).

From the outset, housing proved to be a more intractable issue. To this day, growers fault members of the local work force of the 1970s for their purported unwillingness to reside at the farms, obliging the board to transport workers twelve miles daily from Mango Creek to Cowpen. By the 1980s, transportation of packing-shed workers cost the board more than thirty-one thousand dollars annually (Banana Control Board 1984, 1).[1] Many present-day growers assert that Belizeans are simply averse to leaving the amenities of town, making them a less than suitable farm labor force. In the words of one, "You can't get Belizeans, ordinary Creoles, to live on the farm. You can't go into a village and offer a job to one of the Creoles and tell him he has to live out there. He would prefer not to work. He'd want transport there, to go and come everyday. No farm can afford that." Another quipped, "Sure, you can get Creoles to harvest bananas. But you have to move the banana trees to town to do it."

In actuality, the settlement of the banana industry work force at Mango

Creek, and the board's subsequent reliance on daily transportation, were the result of a conscious board policy rather than any cultural propensity of the work force itself. The oldest portion of Mango Creek today, known in the 1970s as the Banana Zone, consists of three blocks of weathered, two-room wooden houses. These were constructed in the early 1960s by the Hercules Company to house its work force. When that firm left Belize in 1965, it sold the houses to Greene and Atkins, who moved them to the village of Alabama to house their workers for the Waha Leaf banana farm.[2] Subsequently, when the Waha Leaf farm went bankrupt, the houses were in turn purchased by the Banana Board and moved once again to Independence, where farm workers were expected to reside in the newly established Banana Zone. "That was the biggest mistake," according to Samuel Achmed. "Those houses should have been all put out there at Cowpen. With proper everything, light, water and everything, they would have had no trouble getting people to live at the farm. It was the Banana Board's own mistake that it had to transport people everyday."

Housing for farm workers had been the subject of lengthy discussion in the first collective agreement between the union and the Banana Board. Housing was also one of the more glaring inequities in the industry, for managers wanted to charge rent for the spartan houses that workers occupied in the Banana Zone. Meanwhile, they themselves lived rent-free in screened spacious homes at Big Creek two miles away, and enjoyed electricity, running water, and indoor plumbing at board expense. In contract negotiations, the union argued that workers' housing in the Banana Zone should also be rent-free and provided with water and electricity. The union failed, however, to secure any agreement on these issues in its first contract. By August 1975 the Banana Board began without prior notice to charge workers twenty dollars per month for their houses, or about a fifth of their monthly earnings. The union protested, claiming that the issue of rent payments was not specified in the existing contract and that rent was being collected in an arbitrary manner to punish union activists. After the board rejected the union's request for a refund of rents and reopening of contract negotiations on housing, a spontaneous work stoppage occurred on Farm 4 during the morning of 29 August. Within a matter of hours, all work came to a halt on the other farms and in the packing sheds as well. Although they had not obtained recognition for collective bargaining, members of the office staff soon went on a sympathy strike with the striking farm workers. Management immediately fired the striking office workers, informing them that they had violated the terms of their employment by joining the farm workers' walkout.

As the general strike extended into a second week, causing the loss of at least one shipment of fruit, both sides hardened their positions. The Banana Board claimed that because the union had failed to follow the grievance procedure specified in the prevailing contract, its strike was illegal. The board agreed to negotiate with the union on the housing issue only after a general return to work. Only three members of the office staff were to be reinstated, however. After the labor commissioner in Belmopan sided with management in ruling the strike illegal, the union returned to work but refused to return to negotiations until the board reinstated the person designated as the shop steward for the office staff. Management refused to do so, prompting the union in turn to request formal intervention by the commissioner, a process expected to take several months. In the meantime, the union returned to negotiate the issue of rent collection on housing. The board agreed to refund rents to workers who had paid them only if they immediately vacated company houses. Management still refused to discuss the status of the dismissed office shop steward. The union refused to accept either of these conditions.

In December, with no apparent resolution in sight, a mediator (the harbor inspector for Belize City) was called in at the behest of the labor commissioner. He ruled that the dismissal of the proposed shop steward was unjustified, but nonetheless the board refused to reinstate him. A compromise solution was found, in which the dismissed worker would be offered a substantial severance package but would not be rehired. The union agreed to this, as well as a company offer to reduce rents to ten dollars a month.

Neither side could claim an outright victory in the dispute, but it is notable that the union accepted the dismissal of its office shop steward despite the mediator's decision in its favor. The outcome of a subsequent confrontation with management over union representation of the office staff left little doubt that the DIU's leadership, which was based entirely in Belize City, was quickly succumbing to manipulation by the Banana Board. A secretary in the board office was fired in 1976 after having passed information on management salaries to the union. As in the previous dispute, it was subsequently learned that she was the union's proposed shop steward for the office workers. The union filed a protest with the Labor Department and threatened farmwide strikes if she was not reinstated. Again the case went to arbitration in Belize City, where the board eventually found an accommodation with

Cecil Lewis, the union president. "We called him one side after the arbitration broke down," former board member Martin Davis recalled. "We said, 'Now this is nonsense. We've met three times and still everything come to deadlock. Now,' I said to Mr. Cecil, 'now you have to show that you are the leader we picked to lead the workers. We know that you are a good man, and that we can talk with you.' We try to build him up, you know, to make him easier to deal with. So finally he agreed, and he was satisfied with our [severance] package for her. We gave her a good amount of money just to get rid of her so we didn't have to deal with the union in the office. Mr. Cecil was a reasonable man. We could handle him."

If it was apparent to the Banana Board that working conditions could be manipulated by striking private deals with the union's leadership, workers themselves apparently came to the same realization by the late 1970s. In 1979, farm workers attempted to strike when contract negotiations broke down over wages and benefits. Union members apparently expected that the dues they had paid over the previous five years would provide some form of strike pay, but instead they received a rude awakening when the union announced that its strike fund was depleted. Only four days into the strike, workers began returning to the farms en masse. Former industry workers speculate that the union leadership had squandered or perhaps even embezzled members' dues. In that year, the DIU was forced back to the table to sign a collective agreement in which, for the first time since it had earned representation rights, no wage increase was provided for banana workers. Workers were outraged at the union's inability to win a wage increase, particularly as retail inflation for the year approached 20 percent in Belize.

If the Banana Board's management congratulated itself on the union's capitulation, it was soon to view the workers' response to the new contract with considerable alarm. Shortly after the signing of the 1979 contract with the DIU, as disillusionment with the union peaked among industry workers, some workers began demanding a new representational poll. Their choice to succeed the DIU was the United General Workers' Union (UGWU). The union had earlier resulted from a merger between the General Workers' Development Union (GWDU), which had been organized in the cane fields of northern Belize, and the Southern Christian Union (SCU), which represented dock workers in Belize City and Dangriga, citrus workers in the Stann Creek Valley, and employees of Belize Estate and Produce and the Development Finance Corporation. With the merger of the GWDU and the SCU in

1979, the United General Workers' Union became the largest labor organization in Belize. The union continued to expand its membership after the
merger, winning representation rights among electricity and public-works
employees in 1980. Moreover, its leadership under Misheck Chigayo Mawema, a schoolteacher who had been exiled in 1966 from what was then Rhode-
sia, was profoundly radical in outlook and uncompromising in negotiations
with employers. Mawema's political views, together with his nearly messianic
appeal to workers, terrified business leaders accustomed to dealing with conservative trade unions such as the DIU. On the eve of the amalgamation that
made the UGWU the country's largest union, Mawema taunted employers at
a rally in Dangriga: "One time the SCU used to be alone and they could
chance we [take advantage of us]. But now, I want them to try to chance we,
because we have we brothers together now—up north, out west, down south,
all kind a way! When a Dangrigan goes up north, he goes with his head high,
because he is going to his brother's home. When a Corozaleño comes here, he
is coming home. All Belize must be a home to all Belizean workers" (*Gombay*
1979, 2).[3] As Martin Davis of the Banana Board described the leadership of the
new union, "Yes, we could handle the DIU. But that new group that came in
later, with Mawema? Man, I'm telling you, there was no working with those
people. They were always after us about something. You just couldn't manage
Mawema like the DIU people."

### Contexts of Labor Militancy: Local, National, and International

Demands for a new representational poll began to be heard on banana farms
in May 1979, only one month after the DIU had signed a contract little
changed from the previous year. Although the Banana Board and Ministry of
Labor refused to hold a poll as long as the contract with the DIU remained in
effect, when the contract expired in 1980 new reasons were found for delay-
ing the balloting. Management first insisted on a list of workers eligible to
vote, then attempted to have some names struck by claiming that they were
in fact supervisory personnel. Throughout this time, Mawema and Leonard
Castillo, general secretary of the Dangriga branch of the UGWU, held meetings in workers' communities in preparation for the vote. After more than a
month passed without a contract, the union called on banana industry workers to strike to demand a poll. Castillo recalls how the union was able to establish contract rights in the industry even as management refused to meet
with its representatives:

In Belize you have to give the employer twenty-one days' notice before a strike. And we tell them you have twenty-one days to make up your mind. We had our people out in the fields and spread the word that something would happen on that day. That twenty-first day, we were there at five o'clock in the morning. We assembled at the gate. There were security officers, policemen, and hundreds of workers. The police even tried to rough us up. I told the policeman, "Look, we have nothing with you. We are dealing now with people and their lives. The people are saying they are not making enough to live on. And here we are now, while they are sitting in the office, taking us for puppetshow,[4] taking you for puppetshow, and they send you to talk with us. So you go back to them and tell them we are waiting for them to discuss with us."

Finally, at one o'clock that day, they come out of the office. I told the manager, I said, "We have been here waiting all this time. The workers are here with their tools, they are ready to work. Are you ready to discuss?" And that day, for the first time, we were able to bend their arm. They agreed. They said, "Yes, yes, yes, we'll sign a contract with you." But we remember what happen to their agreements in the past. So I said, "Get your paper, get your pen, and write it down. We have plenty of workers here who will witness what you say here." That was the only general strike we had here, and so we got into the industry without even calling a poll.

Subsequent contract negotiations between the board and the UGWU were protracted and bitter. After seven months of negotiation, the union won a 47 percent pay increase for farm workers in 1981, raising starting wages from 87 cents to $1.38 per hour. The union also obtained improvements in workman's compensation, vacation and overtime pay, and the provision of protective clothing for workers who handled farm chemicals. Yet the UGWU's attainments were to prove short-lived, as management devised new strategies to circumscribe the union's power. In 1982, it was able to obtain a raise of only 10 cents per hour. Thereafter contracts negotiated with the board in 1983 and 1984 contained no provisions for pay increases.

The rapid decline of the union's effectiveness in the banana industry, and its eventual expulsion in 1985, were the result of management strategies designed to neutralize the labor movement on banana farms. Yet the local collapse of the union also reflected and was abetted by processes at work in the larger national and international arenas. In 1980, when the UGWU entered the banana industry, it was at the peak of its power nationally and represented an estimated six thousand workers in eight workplaces or industries. The union had reached the point that, in the words of Oliver Ordoñez, its former director for international relations, "we could shut this country down with a general strike if we wanted to." Yet it was less the size of the union's membership that concerned business and government leaders than its ideological orientation. Although the UGWU was customarily derided by the conservative opposition party as "Marxist-Leninist" or "communist-inspired," the union's former leaders deny that the union entered into any alliance with Eastern Bloc countries.[5] Nonetheless, its ideological direction, as described by Ordoñez, differed radically from more conservative trade unions such as the DIU: "We called on workers not to see themselves in terms of their isolated interests. Sure, improving wages and working conditions are important, but they are not enough. We called on our members to identify as members of a working class with common interests. This was the kind of message that really began to scare the government and big employers." The message of working-class solidarity that Mawema and Ordoñez promoted was reinforced by the use of sympathy strikes, by which a strike at one workplace organized by the UGWU would quickly trigger work stoppages at other firms throughout the country. Indeed, it was through such actions that the UGWU attained such rapid expansion in membership in the late 1970s.

If the UGWU's ideological orientation was perceived as threatening among conservative political circles in Belize, such perceptions did not escape the notice of powerful international actors. As the Price government negotiated its way toward independence from Great Britain in 1981, it sought both political and economic support from the United States. Having traditionally sided with Guatemala's territorial claims against Belize, the United States remained the only nation—other than Guatemala itself—unwilling to support Belizean independence in the United Nations. Preoccupied with growing left-wing insurgencies in Central America, the Reagan administration was unlikely to provide such support to Belize if the Price government and ruling People's United Party were thought to tolerate leftist labor unions. Like the conservative opposition within Belize, U.S. consular officials viewed with some alarm the movements and pronouncements of UGWU leaders. For such officials, the participation of union leaders in trade-union seminars held in Eastern European countries and Cuba provided de facto evidence of their communist sympathies. As Leonard Castillo recalled, "As far as the U.S. government was concerned, our union was subversive. We were all in their red books. We go to Cuba, we go to Russia, we go to Czechoslovakia, we go all about. We believed in a socialist way of life, where people must get their fair share. And to them, that's subversive action. I believe [the United States] had a hand in what happened." Ordoñez offers a similar assessment, one that indicates a degree of Belizean complicity in assaults on the labor movement: "This was a time when the PUP needed the support of the U.S. for its independence. And there is no question that that support came with strings attached. The government could count on nothing from the Reagan administration until it showed that it was willing to domesticate the unions."

Such international considerations formed the backdrop to growing civil unrest in the months leading to independence. The opposition United Democratic Party and its trade unions had attempted to scuttle the recently negotiated Heads of Agreement with Guatemala, by which Belize made largely token concessions of access to territorial waters in exchange for Guatemalan recognition of its independence. The Public Service Union, which was allied with the UDP and represented most government employees, went on strike in April 1981 to demonstrate its opposition to the Heads of Agreement. In response, the government declared a state of emergency and dispatched troops to quell rioting and looting that had broken out in Belize City. Included in a flurry of emergency legislation passed during this time were provisions banning sympathy strikes and prohibiting picketing. The UGWU had supported the government's attempts to negotiate independence and resisted opposition calls for a general strike. Ironically, the government's emergency measures more directly affected the UGWU than the opposition unions because of its reliance on sympathy strikes to secure agreements. Finally, the Essential Services Act, also passed during the state of emergency, prohibited strikes by workers employed in public services deemed essential to the general welfare.[6] These initially included electricity, health, police, fire, water, and sanitary services, but were later broadened to include most government employees.

While the state of emergency legislation weakened the labor movement as whole, the UGWU soon found itself directly attacked by other trade unions. In the early 1980s, advisors from the American Institute for Free Labor Development (AIFLD)[7] worked closely with the more conservative unions and urged them, successfully, to isolate the UGWU from the national Trade Union Council (Shoman 1987b, 86). The union's leadership was then targeted by the government and employers, beginning with Mawema himself. D. L. McKoy, Price's minister of labor in the early 1980s, lived in Dangriga and considered Mawema "not only as a foreign agitator, a dangerous radical and communist, but also simply as a competitor for power in his constituency" (ibid., 99). McKoy and other cabinet members clamored for his deportation as an "undesirable alien," a move that had gathered much support in the Price government. Sensing the inevitable, and finding it at last safe to return home to Zimbabwe, Mawema left Belize with his family in January 1982.

In the year following Mawema's departure, all of the union's national leaders were fired from their jobs at the Development Finance Corporation, in the sugar industry, and at Belize Estate within several weeks of one another. Ordoñez himself received a letter of immediate termination one morning as he was walking to work: "To add to the shock, the very next morning my son was born. It wasn't just that I was fired and had a family to support. All of us who lost our jobs soon discovered we·were blacklisted. Our names had been sent throughout the government and every major employer as troublemakers and subversives. Their hope was that we would be forced to emigrate. That way they could be rid of us to do what they wanted to the labor movement." After several years of unsuccessfully seeking work, all but two of the union's former national leaders were indeed forced to leave the country to find employment.

If the persecution of labor leaders initiated the containment of the UGWU on the national level, the process was completed at each workplace by assaults on the membership of the union itself. This was attained through a systematic replacement of unionized workers by a new, often desperately impoverished work force. Prior to the 1980s, such measures would not have been possible in Mango Creek, given the aforementioned scarcity of labor in the region. In the following years, however, labor in southern Stann Creek District was to become not only abundant but also dispensable. Initially weakened by Banana Board strategies to import low-cost and docile labor from the neighboring countries, the union was fatally undermined in the mid-1980s as civil conflict and economic crisis in those nations fueled a massive stream of refugees into southern Belize.

### Internationalization of the Labor Force

> The opposing interests that divide the working class are . . . reinforced through appeals to "racial" and "ethnic" distinctions. Such appeals serve to allocate different categories of workers to rungs on the scale of labor markets, relegating the stigmatized populations to the lower levels and insulating the higher echelons from competition from below.
>
> —Eric Wolf, 1982

In early 1982, indignant letters from banana workers in Mango Creek began to appear in the pages of several Belize City newspapers. The letters hinted at systematic changes taking place in the work force of the banana industry, changes that were soon to undermine the union's effectiveness in dealing with management. It was in that year that the Banana Board hired two new managers from United Brands in Honduras in an attempt to revitalize the state-run industry, which was incurring heavy losses. Once in Mango Creek, the new managers apparently had more in mind that simply improving agronomic practices, as the following letter suggests:

> I am an employee of the Banana Control Board and have checked on many things that are going wrong in the banana industry. . . . Mr. R. who is promoted to manager of the Banana Control Board, has been in charge of all the farms in Cow Pen. This same manager Mr. R. from Honduras has so many powers over the Belizeans because Minister [of Agriculture Florencio] Marin give it to him. Belizeans are being pressured by this same manager so that he can bring in people from Honduras.
>
> If an employee goes into the manager's office to talk for his rights what he tells that person, if you don't like what is going on you can go. . . . Bananas have been shipping out of this country before Fyffes came here, and it is our Belizean people who in the past were managing, were supervising in the fields and packing houses. . . . The manager, if he wants to employ somebody he travels to Corozal[8] to recruit men; if he doesn't find any men in Corozal to recruit, he then recruits men from Honduras as if Corozal is the only place in the country of Belize. There are men arrived at Big Creek in the morning from Honduras and by midafternoon they are a chorehand at Cow Pen. Belizeans who have suffered from the beginning of the farm are now holding the bitter end of the stick. (*Amandala* 1982b, 3)

Most residents of the banana belt today describe the replacement of Belizean labor by immigrants as a process in which Belizeans voluntarily surrendered undesirable, low-paying work to the newcomers.  As one Creole manager on Farm 4 put it in 1993, "When this industry started out, it was lone Belizeans. Then afterwards, these people came in. That's the way it goes, because you find out that the natives after a while they just haul out and other people have to come in and do the work." Such accounts accord nicely with the widespread assertion that Belizeans are averse to agricultural labor. The managers who were hired in 1982, as well as the displaced former workers themselves, tell this story differently, however. "Most of the Hondurans that have been here for years were sent for," one of the managers recounts. "The growers themselves sent out feelers to Honduras that we need men good with a shovel, men good with a machete." At the same time that immigrant labor was being imported and put to work at Cowpen beginning in 1982, the new board managers were laying off members of the local work force. By the following year, 210 farm workers at Cowpen, or nearly half of the total work force at the four farms, had been laid off (Alonso 1987, 10). Virtually all those laid off were Belizean workers, many of whom had been with the industry since its inception ten years earlier.

"Of course we caught hell with the union when we reduced the work force," former board manager Alfred Winston recalls:

> The union in those days was the single biggest problem we had. If you see a worker doing something wrong and you scold him, whew, he run to the union and they all stop. All the leaders were guys who went to Patricio Lamumba University in Russia. They come back with weird ideas. That workers are all being screwed by capitalists. But after a while I learned how to deal with these guys. You just had to agree with whatever they said. Castillo used to come down every Friday to meet with us. He would sit there and cuss us out, "You're doing this and you're doing that," and I would say, "Yes, that's true. You're absolutely right. Don't worry, we'll take care of it." He would go home satisfied and that's the last we heard of him for a week.

Castillo's own account of the termination of Belizean workers parallels Winston's and reveals the union's inability to halt the displacement of its members by imported labor:

> [Management] would agree to something today, we tell the workers, this is the agreement we reach with the industry and these are the things they agree to. By the following day, that agreement has been forgotten by either one foreman or another. It was clear that the foreman was getting instructions to drop off the Belizeans one by one and start packing the sheds with aliens. You see, if the shed has forty women packing bananas, . . . the next thing unu [you] know, next shipment, there are thirty-five Belizeans, five new people. And these new people are never Belizeans. Next shipment, five more new people. We complain to the government about it. We ask the government to get Immigration involved. They sent down some officials and deported quite a number, only to find out that the same people were back in a week. You can't patrol the border with Guatemala, and I don't think they really want to keep them out in the first place.

After the layoffs of 1983, the Banana Board informed the union that no further wage increases would be considered for industry workers due to the board's severe indebtedness. The board then unilaterally began to override provisions in the existing contract. Initially, management suspended transportation for female packing-shed workers from the Garifuna village of Hopkins, some thirty-five miles to the north. Shortly thereafter the board ended all transportation for farm labor from Mango Creek. Significantly, these violations of the union contract came at a time of increasing immigration, when thousands of economic and political refugees vied for jobs in the region. Under new management policies, workers who remained in Mango Creek would be required to get to the farms, some twelve miles away, on their own. "We told them," Winston recalled, "'If you don't like this, there are plenty of aliens who are happy to come into Cowpen, put down their li' hut, and go to work.'" The last union-led strike effort on the area's banana farms occurred in August 1984, when members of a fruit cutting crew at Cowpen demanded a wage increase. By that afternoon, all of the strikers had been fired and replaced by immigrants. The UGWU protested the firings for several weeks, but its appeals fell on deaf ears. By the end of the month union officers consented to an agreement unchanged from the previous year, one that failed to achieve reinstatement of the striking workers.

Although the union contract with the Banana Board had long been openly defied by management, the UGWU continued at least nominally to represent industry workers on the eve of privatization. By then the work force at Cowpen was already comprised largely of recent immigrants who were unaware of the union's once-formidable power in the industry. In a farmwide ballot organized by the board's management, banana workers voted to suspend dues payments to the UGWU in April 1985. When it came, decertification was a more symbolic than substantive gesture, for all existing contracts with the union were in any case nullified when Cowpen farms were sold to private owners later that year. "After the farms were privatized," Winston quipped, "we told the workers, 'You even say the word 'u' . . . and you're fired.'"

### Breaking the Labor Movement in Belize

The emasculation of the UGWU and its expulsion from the banana fields were no isolated incidents at the time. Throughout the 1980s the once-powerful Belizean labor movement found itself increasingly on the defensive and unable to retain the gains made in wages and benefits over the previous decade. By 1993, only thirty-five hundred members of a labor force estimated at sixty-five to ninety thousand belonged to trade unions (Belize Chamber of Commerce 1993, 2), representing a decline of 70 percent in ten years. The head of the national teacher's union attributes falling union participation to "the migration of leaders to North America" (ibid., 3), an oblique reference to the de facto exiling of UGWU activists in the early 1980s. Yet government and employer persecution do not by themselves entirely account for the collapse of the labor movement.

Given the nature of the country's labor laws, the labor movement was faced with formidable obstacles in its drive to organize workplaces through the 1970s. Belize's labor laws were drafted some thirty years earlier to eliminate some of the worst abuses of the "advance-truck" system, a form of debt servitude existing in the timber industry, and to partly pacify rising anticolonial sentiments within the work force. Nonetheless, the UGWU's former vice-president, Felipe Machado, asserted that these laws "still speak in the language of master and servant; they are still colonial in outlook." Machado notes that Belizean labor laws are hobbled by the absence of any binding obligation on the part of employers. Section 30 of the country's labor laws, for example, extends workers the legal right to form and belong to a union (Government of British Honduras 1959). Yet the same statute does not obligate employers to recognize or negotiate with a union, even if it has won a representation election. Collective bargaining is therefore an option entirely at the discretion of the employer. Nor do the country's labor statutes prohibit employer retaliation against workers for trade-union activity.

As long as labor was relatively scarce, as it was in Mango Creek and indeed throughout most of the nation until the 1980s, unions were able to form and press for recognition despite these restrictions. Since the influx of immigrant labor in the early 1980s, however, employers have been free to replace union members with immigrants willing to work for lower wages. The UGWU and the Christian Workers Union have tried since 1982 to unionize the garment industry around Belize City, only to find their organizers and shop stewards repeatedly fired and replaced by immigrants. When the new workers signed union cards, they themselves were replaced with even more recent immigrants. Although representation elections have been won twice in the garment industry, unions have never been able to negotiate a contract with employers because their members were intimidated and fired (Catzim 1992). An additional problem in organizing a non-national work force is that many immigrants are more transitory than Belizean workers. "You need 51 percent of the workers to sign union cards if there is to be a representation poll," Machado notes. "A month or two pass while the Labor Department considers the union's request. In that time, many of the members will have gone back to Honduras or wherever, and when the poll is finally called, we're down to 40 or 45 percent of the work force. Its hard to win a poll under these conditions."

With the collapse of the labor movement, "it is evident," the Belize Chamber of Commerce observes with some satisfaction, "that the majority of workers in Belize do not have and do not want union representation" (Belize Chamber of Commerce 1993, 3). As has been seen here, low rates of unionization in the current work force have resulted from strategies to dismantle unions, rather than from the wishes of those who formerly belonged to them. Such statements have their counterparts in mythical claims that Belizeans left the banana industry because of their aversion to farm work. The transformation of the industry's work force in the 1980s cannot be explained by such alleged cultural preferences. The events that transformed the banana industry may still be inferred, however, from the yellowed pages of archived newspapers and the memories of displaced workers. The abandonment of Belizean labor by the industry followed from the uneven contest of state and employer power against an assertive but ultimately overwhelmed labor movement. Yet the industry's forcible expulsion of unionized workers has already been mythologized out of existence by contemporary workers and management alike, so that the abandonment of Belizean labor is now widely seen as a voluntary act on the part of those displaced. For those who took part in the labor movement in the banana fields, such as Leonard Castillo, this myth making is the most painful legacy of the union's defeat: "Belizean people put that banana industry on its feet. We *started* that industry. We *worked* that industry. We *tended* the fields. We made the first *shipment* from that industry. But they didn't like the kind of money that they were paying, so they found an alternative. Now the immigrants are here, and there's nothing we can do about it. But what I didn't like was when they throw that thing right back at the people. It is one thing when the management put us out of work. Did they then have to turn around and call us lazy too?"

# 5 ❦ Central American Immigration

## THE RESHAPING OF A LABOR MARKET

Juanito was waiting patiently to ask a grower in the Banana Growers' Association office about a job after the farm he had worked on had been
closed. His lined faced and air of resignation belied his forty-four years.
Asked how long he had been in Belize, he volunteered the circumstances that
had forced him to leave his native El Salvador nearly ten years earlier.

Juanito was from Chalatenango, a department fiercely contested by government forces and Farabundo Martí (FMLN) guerrillas throughout the
1980s. He and his teenaged son were at work one morning in their milpa, located some distance from the hamlet where they lived. Hearing vehicles approaching on the road, Juanito and his son crouched, hidden from view, in
their cornfield and strained to get a look at them as they passed. He recognized army markings on the jeeps. Juanito had once or twice encountered the
"muchachos," FMLN combatants who passed through the village seeking
food and water but little else. But since the guerrillas first appeared, Juanito's
family had lived in fear of an army reprisal. He feared that this day was to
bring one, while his wife and three small children remained at home.

He could hear nothing from the hamlet for the next half-hour, and he
thought that the patrol had merely passed through without stopping. Then
he heard a shot, followed by a barrage of gunfire. "I went out of my mind. I
began running, running, like a wild animal. I reached home just as the last
jeep left. Then I saw four young men dead in the street where they were shot."
Juanito would only allude indirectly to what he found when he entered his
home: "For me there was no family to go back to. What they did to them has
no name."

For all the painful detail in which he recounted the day of the army attack,
the following months that brought him to Belize "are like a dream. I don't
even remember when I arrived here." He and his son crossed into Honduras
clandestinely, but feared that to stay there would risk repatriation. The sea

passage from Puerto Cortés to Big Creek cost them the last of their funds. They arrived penniless, but soon found work at Cowpen. Some three months after applying for refugee status from the government, his request for asylum was granted. Now he cannot be returned home involuntarily. "There is peace here, *gracias a Dios*. But this is not my home. We are made to feel that every day. *Los negritos*[1] take advantage of us every way they can. When you have change in your pocket, then they're your friends. But when you need something, they don't even know you."

No one knows how often stories like Juanito's could be repeated among the Central American immigrants who have arrived in Belize since 1980. The magnitude of Hispanic immigration is readily apparent in much of the country, for numerous immigrant enclaves have sprung up in formerly uninhabited rural areas and even on the outskirts of Belmopan. Although immigrant Central Americans are a visible presence everywhere in Belize, consistent data on the size of the immigrant population simply do not exist. In large part, this is because the newcomers often arrive undetected across the country's long and largely unpatrolled border with Guatemala. Once in the country, many fear deportation and avoid contact with representatives of the government's Refugee Office and other agencies ostensibly established to help them. Finally, although some, like Juanito, fled to Belize in genuine fear for their lives, many more have arrived as undocumented "economic migrants," seeking to escape landlessness, unemployment, and economic crisis in Guatemala, Honduras, and El Salvador.

## Influx and Backlash: Belize in the 1980s and 1990s

Throughout the 1980s, estimates of the immigrant population in Belize varied wildly, from ten thousand to as many as sixty thousand individuals. Compounding the difficulties of enumeration, estimates have been subject to manipulation for political purposes. Charging that the PUP government was encouraging Central American immigration in order to "Latinize" the country and register new, pro-government voters among the immigrants, the opposition UDP claimed in 1984 that the actual numbers of immigrants greatly exceeded official estimates. The size of the migrant population and the implications of immigration for Belizean citizens subsequently became major issues in the 1984 national elections (Shoman 1989, 12), as they did again in 1989 and 1993. In 1985, after having won the general elections, the

UDP government headed by Manuel Esquivel claimed that forty-seven thousand immigrants had been allowed to enter Belize during the previous PUP administration. It was claimed that more than half of these were Guatemalan (ibid.). In addition to the prospect of Latinization, such estimates raised the specter for many Belizeans of the long-feared Guatemalan seizure of their country, this time through a silent army of undocumented immigrants.

Refugee-aid officials regard census figures as the most reliable data on Central American immigration to Belize and the least likely to be manipulated for political reasons. In the 1991 census, the total foreign-born population was reported at 25,548, of whom 41.2 percent (10,538) were from Guatemala, 22.1 percent (5,650) from El Salvador, and 9.1 percent (2,329) from Honduras (Government of Belize 1991). As such figures exclude children born to immigrants in Belize, the number of people actually residing in immigrant households remains unknown. According to the government's Refugee Office, some 8,942 individuals had been granted refugee status (that is, political asylum) and remained in the country by 1993, of whom 24 percent are Guatemalan, 69 percent are Salvadoran, 3.5 percent are Nicaraguan, 2.5 percent are Honduran, and 1 percent are of other nationalities. Refugee aid officials concur that the overwhelming majority of refugees intend to settle in the country permanently.

The 1980 and 1991 census figures reveal why immigration has become a major concern of many Belizeans, one that can be readily employed for demagogic purposes by politicians. The terms of ethnic identification used in the two censuses are not entirely comparable, as the Creole and Garifuna populations were combined in 1980 in the category "Negro/Black" but enumerated separately in 1991. Notwithstanding such inconsistencies, the census figures reveal a clear decline in the relative proportion of the Afro-Belizean population over the 1980s, the Creole and Garifuna component falling from 40 percent of the total population to 36.4 percent (Government of Belize 1991). Meanwhile, the Mestizo segment of the population increased from 33.4 percent to 43.6 percent of the total. Similar trends were reported in the Stann Creek District, whose Mestizo population increased from 10.6 percent of the total in 1980 to 23.7 percent in 1991. The census data confirmed what many Belizeans had long suspected to be the result of Central American immigration: Spanish-speaking Mestizos have now become the largest single ethnic group in the country (table 3). At present, the ratio of immigrants to natives in the Belizean population is the highest in the Western Hemisphere, with

Table 3. Belize Population Census, 1980 and 1991

| Ethnic Group | 1980 Population | Percentage of Total | 1991 Population | Percentage of Total |
|---|---|---|---|---|
| Creole | 57,700 | 39.7 | 56,439 | 29.8 |
| Mestizo | 48,100 | 33.1 | 82,575 | 43.6 |
| Garifuna | 11,050 | 7.6 | 12,500 | 6.6 |
| Maya | 13,850 | 9.5 | 21,022 | 11.1 |
| Mennonite | 4,800 | 3.3 | 5,871 | 3.1 |
| East Indian | 3,050 | 2.1 | 6,629 | 3.5 |
| Other[a] | 6,800 | 4.7 | 4,356 | 2.3 |
| TOTAL | 145,350 | 100.0 | 189,392 | 100.0 |

*Sources:* Government of Belize 1983, 1991

[a]The "Other" category includes persons of Syrian, Palestinian, and Chinese descent, as well as North Americans and Europeans.

one out of every six residents of the country having been born in Guatemala, El Salvador, or Honduras (Palacio 1993, 5).

The growth of the Hispanic population has been abetted by out-migration of Afro-Belizeans, many of whom temporarily or permanently seek employment in the United States. Since the 1970s, Belize, like most of the Anglophone Caribbean, has experienced high rates of emigration to the United States (Pastor 1985). Because almost all of this out-migration has occurred among the country's Creole and Garifuna populations, areas of the country occupied by these ethnic groups have experienced constant or declining populations since 1970. The predominately Garifuna town of Dangriga, for example, experienced a population decline of 3.4 percent between 1980 and 1991, while the largely Hispanic towns of Orange Walk and Corozal grew by 34 and 32 percent, respectively (Government of Belize 1991). Approximately seventy thousand Belizeans were estimated to be residing in the United States by 1985, up to one-third of them illegally (Vernon 1990). There is some evidence that this rate of out-migration has increased since 1982, when television first became available in Belize (ibid., 15). Because almost all programming consists of American network transmissions captured on satellite dishes, English-speaking Belizeans have been exposed to a range of consumer goods and living standards not remotely attainable locally.

Belize has had a sizable Hispanic population at least since the 1850s, when thousands of Mestizos and Maya sought refuge in the northern districts of the colony from the bloody Caste Wars of the Yucatán. Notwithstanding the historically diverse nature of the Belizean population, by the late nineteenth century Creoles had effectively attached their cultural and linguistic identities to those of the colony (Bolland and Moberg, 1995). Given their predominance in the all-important mahogany economy and the fact that both their language and religion approximated those of the colonizers, it was perhaps inevitable that Creoles would ascend in the hierarchy of stigma and reward by which the colony's ethnic groups were judged. Long after the formal demise of colonial administration, the ethnic hierarchies that the British erected in Belize continue to cast a long shadow. In part because they were favored for such positions by the British in the waning days of colonialism, Creoles still dominate almost all ranks of the civil service (Bolland 1988, 201), creating the impression that power is wielded by and for Afro-Belizeans.

Although remaining a "polite fiction" in the lives of non-Creole Belizeans (Lewis 1969, 292), the country's officially Anglophone identity is reflected in the use of English in all government activities and correspondence. Regardless of the language spoken in their homes and communities, children throughout Belize are taught exclusively in English from the earliest primary school grades. Even the country's most festive public holiday, celebrated as the Tenth of September, reinforces an Anglophone identity by commemorating the 1798 victory over Spanish naval forces at St. George's Caye. By the mid-nineteenth century, local elites widely interpreted the holiday as a symbolic reconciliation of the colony's class and racial divisions. Until the final days of colonial administration, British officials on the tenth annually extolled the valor of slaves and slave owners who jointly defended the colony against "treacherous" Spanish attack.[2] While promoting closer attachment to empire among the descendants of slaves, this celebration of slave "loyalty" also effaced the coercive nature of the European and African encounter that gave rise to Creole ethnicity. It is by no means uncommon to encounter older Creole residents of Belize City who assert proudly that "we are English," despite the fact that their ancestors were far more likely to be enslaved Africans than English settlers. This affinity for the colonizing culture is all the more poignant given the official racism that thousands of the colony's men endured during World Wars I and II, when they volunteered for military service elsewhere in the empire (see Ashdown 1986).

Throughout their imperial holdings the British encouraged subject peoples to identify their aspirations with those of the colonizers. Given their tenuous hold on Belize against Spanish and Guatemalan claims, however, colonial administrators must have sensed a special imperative in promoting an affinity for England's other Caribbean possessions. For much of its early history, the settlement was officially attached to the West Indies, for its internal affairs were administered from Jamaica prior to its designation as a Crown colony in 1862. The effects of a West Indian educational system and an Anglophile local press persist in the country's resolute cultural orientation toward the Caribbean. To this day, news from the Caribbean remains a regular feature of local newspapers and Radio Belize, with the curious result that Anglophone Belizeans are often much more knowledgeable about the West Indies, more than a thousand miles across the Caribbean, than they are of developments in neighboring Central American countries. Ideologically, English control over the colony also entailed a denigration of the neighboring countries and their institutions. Belizeans pride themselves on a functioning two-party democracy after the Westminster model, an honest civil service, and police and military forces that generally respect human rights, at least those of native Belizeans. In contrast, they often characterize neighboring countries in terms of their high levels of human rights abuse, official corruption, and civil conflict. Yet such features are seen not as the result of inequities and government repression in countries such as El Salvador and Guatemala, but as cultural or even physiological characteristics of their citizens. The comments of a Belizean resident of Cowpen are typical in this regard: "Belizeans are a more milder people than the Spanish. Aliens like to fight and shoot and kill. The Spanish them drink to get drunk. When they block up [get drunk], they bring out their cutlass [machetes] and begin to fight. It seems they are not correct. Their blood supposed to be too thin." Describing the immigrant labor force under his supervision, a Creole captain at Cowpen asserted, "The people who work here are much less civilized than Belizeans. For them, violence is the way they solve all their problems."

Thus, for many Anglophone Belizeans, "Latinization" does not merely imply the increased use of the Spanish language in their country. Rather, it portends a level of violence and political oppression approximating that of neighboring countries, as well as the marginalization that Afro-Caribbean populations have historically experienced elsewhere in Central America. Belize has indeed witnessed a growing number of kidnappings, armed robberies, and assassinations since the early 1980s. Most of these are related to the growth in cocaine transshipment, but because they coincided with a period of high immigration, many Belizeans have directly attributed such acts of violence to the immigrants themselves (Shoman 1989). Such sentiments have been fueled by inflammatory reporting on the part of local newspapers. Even before large numbers of immigrants had entered the country, editorials in Belize's newspapers expressed grave concerns about the policy of granting asylum to refugees from Guatemala and El Salvador: "[The government] is at pains to point out what Belize is getting out of the refugees: refugee aid funds and farming expertise. How about increased incidence of violence, a resurgence of malaria, and a large pool of people with a racist background? We know that the People's United Party is using these people as illegal voters" (*Amandala* 1982a, 7). After the UDP rode such fears to its 1984 victory, the government's official communication medium, Radio Belize, began adopting a similar emphasis in news stories, stressing the "criminality of Central American aliens" (Shoman 1989; translation mine). As recently as late 1993, after the UDP returned to power from a hiatus of four years, a Radio Belize newscast obliquely criticized the previous PUP administration with the charge that "the carrot of refugee aid funds had been used to quietly displace Belizeans and change the country's demography" (Radio Belize 1993).

Given daily recitations in the media of the alleged criminality, violence, and racism of Central American immigrants, it is not surprising that the newcomers have not been well received by many Belizeans. As a report to the United Nation's high commissioner for refugees concluded, "There appears to be an inverse correlation between the size of the Creole population and receptivity to Central American refugees. There are, unfortunately, numerous stories of refugees in Belize City who have been the objects of racial harassment, assaults by Creole youths, or mistreatment at the hands of police" (Montgomery 1991, 15). In public, Belizean youths often relish humiliating jokes at immigrants' expense; in shops Central Americans may be pushed aside and told to wait; on buses they lose their seats to Belizean passengers. Entering a bar frequented by Belizeans, immigrants may be loudly greeted with "Go home, Paisa, we no want no aliens here." "Paisa," short for *paisano*,[3] alternates in private speech with such overtly derogatory references as "yellow-bellied 'Pania" (Spaniard).

For their part, many Central Americans nurture impressions of Afro-Belizeans that are at least as disparaging. Equating light skin color with innate superiority, Hispanic Central Americans often view Afro-Belizeans as inherently indolent, obstreperous, and primitive. One Honduran woman, a resident of Mango Creek, confided that after her arrival in the village she thought that her Creole neighbors were constantly fighting among themselves. Only with the passage of time, she said, did she realize that "that's the way they are. *Los negros no hablan inglés propio* [Blacks don't speak proper English]; they just make noise and scream at each other like monkeys." Similar perceptions are widely represented in popular culture throughout Hispanic Central America, as in novelist Carlos Fallas's depiction of West Indian banana workers in Costa Rica: "They would argue at each other horrifyingly, gesticulating like devils; you would think that they were trying to kill each other" (1975, 134). Although their disdain for Afro-Belizeans is expressed in Spanish, immigrants rarely make an effort to conceal their sentiments from those who might be in earshot, and Afro-Belizeans generally understand enough Spanish to realize when they are the topic of conversation. A few immigrants even engage in deliberately provocative gestures. When asked why he wore a baseball cap emblazoned with the Confederate flag, a Salvadoran worker in Mango Creek grinned mischievously and explained that it offended *los negros,* most of whom knew of the symbol's racist associations in the United States. They didn't know, he continued, that he was equally aware of what the flag represented. Relations between immigrants and Belizeans, then, are fraught with confrontation in part because there are no status criteria shared by both Hispanics and Afro-Belizeans. Whereas Hispanics regard light skin color as the determinant of high status, Creoles and Garifuna consider language and culture more significant. Refusing to acknowledge each other's criteria for discrimination, neither group accedes to the other's disparagement.

If such sentiments do not indicate the full-fledged "ethnic war" that some have predicted in Belize (Topsey 1987), there are nonetheless occasional reports of violence between Afro-Belizeans and Hispanic immigrants. In Mango Creek, attitudes toward Central American immigrants have reportedly softened greatly since the mid-1980s, perhaps due to the fact that hundreds of banana workers spend the greater part of their pay in the village. Until recently, according to a police corporal assigned to Mango Creek, immigrants and Belizeans regularly clashed at local bars on paydays. "Almost every Saturday we had trouble between Belizeans and immigrants. Some Sunday mornings you'd find an alien by the road with his belly sliced open." Since then, such confrontations have nearly disappeared, mainly because immigrant men now avoid places frequented by Belizeans. As the constable noted, "They've learned that if they want to drink, they must do it at home or in their own places." If overtly hostile relations have diminished between the immigrants and Belizeans, then, it is largely because they now move in separate spheres within the same village. The harassment and violence that greeted early immigrants have thus given way to a more stable arrangement, one reminiscent of apartheid.

## The Uses of Immigration and Development Policy

On any weekday morning, the Ministry of Foreign Affairs' Refugee Department in Mango Creek is likely to be filled with ten or more Central Americans, all waiting their turn to provide depositions to the one social worker assigned to the office. It is probable that few are aware of the criteria by which their applications for refugee status will be evaluated. Fewer still will actually be granted asylum. In considering their applications, the government of Belize employs a 1951 United Nations convention, as well as a 1984 Cartagena amendment by the UN high commissioner for refugees.[4] Taken together, these criteria define refugees as persons with a "well-founded fear of being persecuted for reasons of race, religion, nationality, membership in a particular social group or political opinion," as well as those displaced by "external aggression, occupation, foreign domination, or events seriously disturbing public order" (Montgomery 1991, 5). Such criteria may appear straightforward, but because the burden of proof rests with the applicants, in practice most requests for asylum are denied.

Many applicants are declined simply because they were unaware that they had to report to the Refugee Department within fourteen days of entering the country. Applicants who apply within that period of time are provided with a *constancia,* a permit that gives them the right to remain in the country pending the outcome of their asylum application. (By the early 1990s, the backlog of cases had become so great that four to five months usually elapsed from the time of application to an official decision on it.) To be able to work in Belize, however, all resident aliens and asylum applicants must have a work permit issued by the Department of Labor. Permits are obtained by the employer of the immigrant and cost one hundred dollars per year, which the employer invariably deducts from the immigrant's wages. Work permits are retained by the employer during the period of the immigrant's employment:

should the worker quit or be fired from his job, he must obtain a new permit for each subsequent employer, each at a cost of one hundred dollars. Even one of the country's largest banana growers, who benefits from this immobility of labor, privately described the conditions of work permits as "practically slavery. They are chained that way to particular farms."[5]

After providing information for their *constancias,* applicants are granted an interview eliciting their reasons for leaving their home country. Details of the completed interview are then forwarded to the capital, Belmopan, for evaluation by an eligibility committee appointed by the government. The committee consists of nine members: the director of the Refugee Department, its legal protection officer and senior social worker, representatives of the UN high commissioner for refugees, a representative of the chamber of commerce, and a clergyman. The details of the applicant's interview are evaluated relative to the aforementioned criteria, the board accepting or rejecting the application by majority vote. The board's decision is then forwarded to the particular refugee office where the applicant was interviewed. If the committee affirms the application, the asylum seeker is screened for HIV and other infectious diseases. Only if such tests are negative is refugee status granted and a laminated residence permit given to the applicant. Refugees can then remain in Belize indefinitely and are repatriated only voluntarily. Asylum also allows them to work in agriculture without paying for a work permit. This can entail employment in the banana, citrus, or sugar industries, or the cutting of milpa on unoccupied lands in the public domain.

If applicants are turned down by the eligibility committee, they have fourteen days to appeal its decision. The appeal is considered directly by the minister of foreign affairs, whose decision is final. According to the UN high commissioner for refugees, only 5 percent of all asylum applications were granted in the first six months of 1993. The rate of denials has increased substantially since the subsidence of the civil war in El Salvador. In 1989, with the war continuing largely unabated, 53 percent of all Salvadoran applicants were granted refugee status (Stone 1990a, 89). During the first six months of 1992, this number diminished to 35 percent, and fell to 11 percent in the last half of the year (pers. comm. based on interview with UNHCR's refugee protection officer, 2 Sept. 1993).

The composition of asylum seekers has changed in the last several years. Over the 1980s as a whole, 69 percent of all asylum applicants were Salvadoran, 26 percent were Guatemalan, and 5 percent were from elsewhere in

Central America or the Caribbean. By 1992, 39 percent of all asylum applications came from Salvadorans, 41 percent were made by Guatemalans, and 19 percent were made by Hondurans. Representatives of the UN high commissioner for refugees note that the changing composition of prospective refugees is implicated in the increasing rates of rejected applications. As levels of civil conflict in El Salvador declined with the conclusion of peace negotiations between the government and opposition in 1992, fewer immigrants from that nation either sought or were granted asylum. The large majority of Hondurans are also denied asylum as the government regards them as primarily "economic" migrants rather than political refugees.[6] And some United Nations personnel speculate that the Belizean government is less willing to grant asylum to refugees from Guatemala for fear of arousing public opposition over a burgeoning immigrant population from that country.

Those asylum seekers whose application and appeal are rejected are given a month to leave the country. In theory, their *constancias* should be turned in to the refugee office at that point, and they become illegal immigrants unless they apply for resident alien status. This is impossible for many, because they often lack the requisite passports or other evidence of nationality. In actuality, little is heard from most applicants who turn in their *constancias*. Herbert Lewis, the Refugee Department's social worker in Mango Creek, noted with a shrug of resignation, "Once their applications are denied, they don't go back; they stay. Nothing happens. Nothing's done."

The major reason for this, Lewis claimed, was that the government lacked personnel to repatriate illegal immigrants and those whose asylum applications were denied. "Just the other day," Lewis observed, "a Honduranean who was working on a banana farm had some problem with a captain. He was from Honduras also. The worker said he had killed men in Honduras, and he would kill the captain, too. Immigration gave him an expulsion order, to leave the country in forty-eight hours. But I don't know if he gone; he could still be working somewhere in the country." An immigration officer was not assigned to Stann Creek District until December 1992. Formerly, workers' immigration status was checked by the police, but they almost never visited banana farms unless called there by the owners themselves. The Labor Department is charged with ensuring that workplaces are in compliance with immigration policy, but it does not maintain vehicles that would enable personnel to travel to rural areas. When an immigrant is hired, his or her employer is supposed to apply for a work permit, although Lewis stated that no banana growers have ever been penalized for hiring illegal immigrants. As will be seen in chapter 6, all the farms surveyed in the region hire substantial numbers of workers lacking documentation or work permits.

It may seem paradoxical that Belize has instituted elaborate procedures for assigning immigration and refugee status while failing to provide enforcement mechanisms for such procedures. Yet immigration policy has been publicly promulgated and privately disregarded in order to satisfy constituents with mutually exclusive interests. On the one hand, many Belizean citizens fear the cultural and economic changes resulting from uncontrolled immigration, their concerns having been inflamed in many cases for political purposes. To address such concerns, national governments of both parties adopted policies during the 1980s that emphasized border control and high-profile but largely token deportations of illegal immigrants. In 1985, the UDP Ministry of Foreign Affairs invited representatives of the country's media to a deportation of one hundred undocumented immigrants at the Guatemalan border (Shoman 1989, 13). Although it eschewed such inflammatory public relations gestures, the subsequent PUP administration issued a detailed policy statement to the press promising "to control and stem the flow of illegal and economic immigrants" (Government of Belize 1992).

That immigration remains largely uncontrolled despite such symbolic or rhetorical actions suggests that a second, more powerful constituency determines whether or not stated policy is actually enforced. Immigration policy has in the process become captive to the same development priorities that led to the dismantling of the labor movement in the 1980s. In 1984, representatives of the CARICOM nations (the Caribbean Community and Common Market), including Belize, met in the Bahamas to draft a set of common development policies known as the Nassau Understanding (Deere et al. 1990). The Nassau policies endorsed a reversion from import substitution industrialization, whereby the region had promoted the production of manufactured goods for domestic markets, to earlier development priorities emphasizing the region's "comparative advantages" in the production of exportable goods. Among these were climate and land favorable for the production of export crops and, equally important, low prevailing wages. Rather than promoting development through increasing the consumption capacity of its population, Belize has sought to attract investment with the lure of the lowest average wages in CARICOM (Moberg 1992b, 4). Cheap immigrant labor has become critical to this policy, so that any serious effort to control immigration would be opposed by private investors who are now viewed as the very engine of economic growth in Belize.[7]

These development priorities relegate the enforcement of immigration policy to a secondary concern, as the Belizean anthropologist Joseph Palacio notes:

> Government and plantation owners and managers cooperate to ascertain that there remains in the citrus and banana belts . . . a reservoir of labour guaranteed to work for the lowest wages. Every year employers apply for temporary labour permits but the Ministry of Labour does not check whether those with previous permits return to their country at the end of the designated time period. They may remain in the country illegally and compete with a fresh supply coming the following year. (1993, 9–10)

The employment of immigrant labor has generated considerable growth in the banana industry, reflected in the proliferation of consumer goods and luxury four-wheel-drive vehicles among large-scale growers. Yet the benefits of such economic growth have accrued almost exclusively to elites, an inevitable consequence of development policies based on cheap labor. Where banana industry employees are concerned, a resident of Cowpen may have the final word on the type of "development" that results from low-wage strategies: "Look at how the people live here in their little shacks. Here we have no water, no light, no doctor. God Himself has left this place. And every year, we work more and more to earn less and less. *Somos seres humanos o somos esclavos?* [Are we human beings or are we slaves?]"

### Todos Nos Explotan: *Immigrant Labor on Banana Farms*

> Sometimes the dull, prosaic, exhausting life on banana plantations is enlivened by outbreaks of brutality, especially under the stimulus of liquor. Many a laborer, who ordinarily is peaceful and law-abiding, lashed into a frenzy on the aftermath of pay day, settles past and present grudges with machete or gun. Sometimes the murderer is captured by governmental authorities; sometimes he falls before the hand of an avenger; but frequently he escapes to the mountains and the affair is closed. An indication of the prevalence of this law of the jungle is given by the fact that there were sixty-one violent deaths in the Truxillo division of Honduras in 1931. During some previous years the outbreaks of personal violence were much greater. The overwhelming majority of these killings follow gambling, petty squabbles or long-time feuds between laborers.
>
> —Charles Kepner (1936)

Turning onto the unmarked gravel road that leads to Cowpen, there is at first nothing to indicate an approaching human settlement. The road passes a dirt

Fig. 4. Houses and banana fields at Cowpen.

airstrip that, according to area residents, serves at night as a transshipment point for South American cocaine. The banana industry's proximity is presently announced by the sickly sweet smell of rotting fruit, piled in immense mounds alongside the road. This is soon overpowered by an even more penetrating odor, that of the noxious mix of fungicides, oil emulsions, and other chemicals that crop dusters spray on the farms at weekly intervals. Finally, banana fields and the first dwellings come simultaneously into view. Most of the houses in Cowpen occupy narrow spaces between the road and ten-feet-deep drainage ditches that encircle all of the farms. On both sides of the road stand a chaotic profusion of closely crowded shelters, ranging from tar-paper shacks to huts of thatch and palmetto, to a handful of houses constructed with milled lumber and masonry. Spires of antennas on bamboo poles rise from some houses, allowing residents to sporadically receive flickering broadcasts from Honduras on black-and-white sets powered by car batteries.

Confined to the narrow margins of the farms, the houses open directly onto the road. Rear windows and doors, if any, reveal drainage ditches flowing with farm runoff and human waste, and a monotonous backdrop of banana plants. From the road, residents can be readily seen in their houses as they wash, sleep, or take their meals. Small children in rags or naked from the

waist down look up from their play to stare at the pickup truck and its passengers. An occasional chicken or dog rests in the dust of the road, only to stir
itself in midday lethargy to avoid passing trucks and farm equipment. Sur-
rounded on all sides by banana fields, the settlement is denied any breeze that
would otherwise relieve the afternoon heat. Once in Cowpen, it is easy to see
why Belizean residents of Mango Creek refer to the settlement as "little
Melchior," after the wretched border town across the country's western frontier with Guatemala.

A Creole passenger, one of the farm supervisors at Cowpen, has been
quiet until now, but grows increasingly animated as the pickup makes its way
through the village. "These people are willing to accept anything. The big
problem with them is that they do not have the sense of hygiene that Belizeans have. Look at how they eat. They think nothing of eating food after
houseflies have pitched on it. They would look at that puddle and drink
water right from it. That's why so many of them are sick every day."

Why have so many come to work under these conditions? The supervisor,
who has worked at Cowpen since 1975, expresses some ambivalence about
the industry's reliance on immigrant labor:

> Just like everywhere these days, we're looking for the cheapest labor possible.
> That's why we put these people to work. They earn fifteen dollars a day and
> think they're in heaven. But then they turn around and say that Belizeans are too
> lazy to work in bananas. What they forget is that all of this was started by
> Belizeans. Belizeans cleared all of this bush, they planted the bananas and put up
> the cableways. Its not that Belizeans are lazy, but they want a good wage. They
> think that electricity and water are necessities, not luxuries. Well, these people
> are not used to the standards of living that Belizeans consider civilized, so we can
> work them for less. The only reason they are here is because the industry wanted
> the cheapest labor it could get.

At Cowpen the industry has indeed assembled a sizable pool of cheap labor.
Although industry workers acknowledge that pay rates on banana farms in
Belize are up to 60 percent higher than those in Honduras or Guatemala,
where prevailing rates are about five U.S. dollars per day, they are quick to
point out the much greater cost of living in Belize. Further, in both Honduras
and Guatemala, union contracts handsomely supplement prevailing wages
for banana work. Since the 1954 general strike in Honduras, for example,
banana worker unions in that country have won subsidized commissaries,
grievance procedures, pensions, protective clothing, a "thirteenth month"
bonus for every year of employment, and a modicum of medical care. Since

the expulsion of the UGWU from the banana industry in 1985, comparable benefits have been nonexistent on Belizean farms. These factors, combined with frequent complaints of mistreatment and underpayment, suggest that few immigrant workers regard their surroundings or working conditions at Cowpen as anything remotely approaching "heaven."

Severino Diego, a Garifuna man from Honduras, is perhaps more familiar with working conditions in Cowpen than most residents. He worked at Farm 2 for six years before being fired suddenly in 1992. The circumstances of his dismissal indicate the extraordinary discretion farm managers have over their immigrant employees. Diego claims that he was dismissed from his work because his foreman wanted to sleep with his wife, who worked in the farm's packing shed on shipment days. One week after Diego told him to leave his wife alone, he was called into the office by the foreman, who accused him of cutting a cable to sabotage the harvest. Diego knew nothing of the incident, but he was nonetheless fired and blacklisted on the other three farms in Cowpen as a saboteur. "Maybe if I was an español [Mestizo], they would have believed me. But I was the only black working on the cableway, so the management thought I did it. At Farm 2, the management is all español, so they think that any black is no better than a Belizean."

Diego notes that farm managers at Cowpen, other than those at Farm 4, are all immigrants themselves, and most are veterans of the Honduran banana industry. This does not make working conditions for the almost entirely immigrant work force any easier, for managers have recreated the harsh labor relations that existed on Honduran farms prior to unionization, as Diego explains:

> Si, son Hondureños o Guatemaltecos, pero nos tratan como esclavos. Todos nos explotan. [Yes, they're Hondurans or Guatemalans, but they treat us like slaves. They all exploit us.] Here workers are supposed to earn eighteen dollars for a nine-hour day, but you won't find any who brings home more than fourteen to sixteen dollars. I know they are supposed to pay time and a half for work over forty-eight hours, but not one farm here pays that. What can we do? If you complain, they fire you on the spot. I know workers who were poisoned when they were spraying Gramoxone. When they asked to be reassigned to do something else, they were fired instead. The managers have plenty here to take your place.

Interviews with other Cowpen workers suggest that these are not the claims of an isolated malcontent. "Muy oprimido," a captain on Farm 2 described conditions on the farms. "Very oppressive. Fyffes exploits the workers. All the companies have their *orejas* [literally, "ears," or informers]. They pay them to report on people that the companies consider troublemakers. That means no one is going to talk about unions or strikes here, because you don't know whether your best friend is getting a little extra to report what he hears." Geronimo Pop, a Belizean Mopan Maya who resides in the village, speaks in similar terms: "You see, Farms 1, 2, and 3, they are all run by Fyffes. They bring their own bosses from yonder. So they want to work the people like how they work them in Honduras. It's the alien people that get chanced [taken advantage of], not the Belizeans. They jump from there."

If underpayment and summary dismissal are frequent occurrences at Cowpen, neither is it uncommon that workers are not paid at all for prolonged periods. Under Belizean law, farm workers must be paid every two weeks, or *quincena*. The majority of farms observe these provisions, albeit with the conditions mentioned above. Farms 1 and 3 had a history of mismanagement under the ownership of a Danish firm, which subsequently contracted with Fyffes to manage the farms. Yet the Danes continue to have severe cash shortages, with the result that pay periods are often missed entirely. Other than managers, their work force is comprised almost entirely of recent immigrants, as the farms have acquired a bad reputation among more seasoned workers. Some Farm 1 and 3 workers surveyed in Cowpen had gone up to two months without pay. In lieu of wages, both farms occasionally provide groceries to their workers so that they have something to eat. The cost of these provisions, they are told, will be deducted from their pay once it is disbursed to them. Workers themselves express great frustration at their predicament, for many feel that if they leave the Danes to work elsewhere, they will never be able to collect their back pay. As one noted with resignation, "*Qué puedo hacer?* If I leave now, that's two thousand dollars those *cabrones* owe me. Do you think they will pay up if I go somewhere else to work?"

Conditions on these farms are so notorious that other growers and government officials openly express embarrassment at the Danes' participation in the industry. Belizean residents of Mango Creek refer to the Danes derisively as "the cheap planets," for their tendency to defraud their employees as well as a widely held if unconfirmed suspicion that they belong to an otherworldly religious cult.[8] As abusive as the Danish managers are now, growers claim that they were far worse immediately following privatization. "The Ollson crowd was like little gods in those days," one grower recalled of the Danish owner and his managers. "If a worker speak up too much for his rights, they don't just fire him, they want to kill him. One morning, about 5:30, they dump a Salvadorean right in the street across from my house. Well, he was bleeding in the extreme. They had run him over with a vehicle and dump him, just like that." Although the worker survived following emergency surgery in Belize City, he was unwilling to testify against his employers, a fact that some attribute to death threats against him.

This incident, and other alleged human rights abuses, led the Human Rights Commission of Belize, a nongovernmental organization, to investigate working conditions on the Danish farms in 1991. After identifying itself, the initial investigatory team was driven from one of the farms at gunpoint. Several days later, several bilingual commission members reentered the farm under cover, in the guise of farm workers. On that and other Danish-owned farms, commission investigators found child labor extensively employed in the packing shed in violation of the law. Although they were held to the same expectations as adult workers, children were paid just 50 percent of the minimum wage. Farm workers complained that payroll records were poorly kept, with hours worked often being substantially less than the amount of work actually performed. Because most of the workers on the Danish farms are illiterate and virtually none speak English, they are easily tricked on paydays. In the event that workers detect discrepancies in their pay, the presence of heavily armed security guards and a captain wearing a .38 caliber pistol on his belt tends to discourage complaints. A subsequent investigation by the government's Labor Department in 1993 corroborated the Human Rights Commission's findings, leading the government to order the Danes to pay back wages amounting to $250,000. Although the Labor Department claims to be monitoring their compliance with the order, workers on the farms do not report any change in pay procedures.

## Life and Death in the Banana Enclave

If working conditions in Cowpen are often abusive, the conditions under which residents live is acknowledged as dangerous, even by farm owners.[9] Weekly overflights by crop-dusting aircraft douse workers and their families with agricultural chemicals. The only local water supplies consist of wells that residents dig in close proximity to their houses. Drinking water, then, is almost certainly contaminated by pesticides and fertilizers that leach through the topsoil. Because their settlement is established on private land belonging to the banana farms, residents are unable to obtain electricity, water, or other utilities from the government, nor can they apply for formal titles to their house lots. Consequently, they occupy their houses at the discretion of the farm on which they have settled. Managers frequently evict terminated workers from houses they themselves constructed. In one instance, a farm owner attempted to expel a resident after she established a *comedor* (diner) and bar in her home to feed farm workers. The decision to evict her, Dolores Castillo believes, was made because her business was competing successfully with the company-run commissary. Originally from a Mestizo village in Cayo District, Castillo is one of the few residents of Cowpen who is both English-speaking and a Belizean citizen. After she hired a Belize City attorney to represent her in court, a judge ruled that she could not be legally ordered off land she had occupied for eight years, and the eviction was overturned. But few residents of Cowpen have Castillo's citizenship, a comparable length of residence, or the resources and knowledge to defend their claims to lots. Her victory remained partial at best, for Castillo could do nothing to challenge the farm's decision to fire her husband, a dismissal that she attributes to retaliation for her court case.

An estimated 1,777 people reside in Cowpen (Blomberg 1993), all or most of whom are exposed to farm chemicals, contaminated water, endemic malaria, workplace injuries, and the usual maladies occurring in Third World populations. The community has a health post, which is, however, used only for occasional public-health education classes or visiting immunization clinics for children. Cowpen lacks a resident nurse or doctor, or any reliable transportation for reaching the closest medical personnel, who are twelve miles away in Mango Creek. Scheduled buses are useless in emergencies as they enter the village just three times per week. Because only a few residents of the village own motor vehicles, workers turn to their supervisors if they need immediate transportation for medical attention. Managers vary in how they respond to such requests, but according to community residents, most ask for about forty dollars in fuel expenses before providing transportation for an ailing farm worker or his or her family. Montgomery (1991, 17) tells of a resident farm worker losing a baby daughter to infant diarrhea because a manager refused to drive her to Mango Creek without prior payment.

The Belizean government has established a primary school in the community to provide instruction to children residing in the village and nine banana farms to the south. A bus under government contract visits the first of these farms at 6:30 in the morning to bring children to Cowpen, returning them home at 4:30 in the afternoon. According to the school's teachers, a given day's attendance rarely approaches half of the 375 enrollment. Although schooling in Belize is mandatory until standard six (the equivalent of eighth grade in the United States), the school lacks personnel to enforce such laws. Teachers cite several reasons for the low attendance levels. Most of the mothers in the village work in the packing sheds on Mondays and Tuesdays and rely on older children to babysit and prepare meals during their shifts. In addition, adult residents themselves have very low levels of education, with some 32 percent of those surveyed having never attended school. In the words of the school's principal, a prim, elderly Garifuna man, "Until you have an education, you can never know the value of an education. This is a critical problem we face in getting parents to send their children to school."

Although teachers often attribute low attendance to parental attitudes, a more fundamental problem may reside with the medium of instruction. All teaching takes place in English, and only two of eleven teachers speak any Spanish at all, factors that undoubtedly discourage attendance by monolingual Spanish-speaking children. Because only a minority of the children on banana farms attend school regularly, the coordinator of the country's Human Rights Commission fears that a cohort of second-class citizens is being created at Cowpen and surrounding farms in the banana belt. "These children are Belizean, because they were born here," he noted. "But they will grow up without an education, they will be illiterate and unable to speak English. When they are adults, they will be no better off than their parents because they won't be able to demand their rights as Belizean citizens."

If public services are negligible in the community, whatever social amenities exist are improvised in the few evening hours after work. Around 280 school-aged children living in the community attest to a certain proportion of resident families, but the majority of the community's residents are single young men. The demographic structure of the population, combined with the lack of recreational activities, do not make for generally healthy diversions. One exception is the soccer teams that are organized on each farm, which often play each other on Saturday afternoons. Other than this, however, recreation is limited to a billiards hall, the occasional game of dominoes or cards, and the intermittent reception of Honduran television. Given their surroundings, it is no surprise that most young men seek more perilous pleasures to deaden their sense of privation. Communities of largely single young men are notable for attracting a certain measure of prostitution, and Cowpen is no exception. Lack of access to medical personnel, public-health information, and prophylactics place many residents at high risk for sexually transmitted diseases.

More commonly, alcohol provides the desired release from farm workers' surroundings. After each *quincena* the weekend is marked by young men lurching through the streets or brawling over real or imagined slights. Should such fights escalate, as they often do, to the use of knives or machetes, there is little to restrain the participants from seriously hurting one another. Although residents might conceivably call on police in the village to break up such fights, many have learned from experience to avoid contact with local authorities. During a weekend drinking spree in 1993, an intoxicated policeman shot and wounded a Salvadoran without provocation, according to witnesses. He and his partner were not disciplined for the shooting, but were reassigned elsewhere, apparently out of fear of retaliation by the victim's kin or friends. At present, a single policeman is stationed in the village, a Creole who knows just a few words of Spanish. Even he returns home during the weekends, leaving the community without law enforcement at those times when brawls and assaults are most likely to occur. Describing weekends in the village as "dangerous," Victoria Santos, an adult education teacher, said, "Las mujeres tenemos que defendernos" (We women have to defend ourselves). Apparently without irony, she added, "As for me, I stay close to my husband on Saturdays and Sundays."

*always the optimist*

If the foregoing description suggests that the residents of Cowpen experience high levels of what sociologists call anomie and community disorganization, it must be added that some villagers have attempted to foster a degree of cooperation through village self-help projects. Santos, herself a Belizean Mestiza from Corozal District, teaches night classes in English and in hygiene and public health, although she notes that few workers have the energy to attend after a day in the banana fields. Some parents of school children have staged talent shows to raise funds for improvements to the school. And workers on a banana farm south of the village have started a cooperative to help them market the crops they cultivate on their milpas during weekends. Yet such seeds of cooperation have largely fallen on barren ground, for numerous intractable divisions inhibit the entire community's participation. Seeking release from the conditions around them, through means arguably less destructive than rum, hundreds of residents have joined a variety of charismatic evangelical sects that operate in the community. The sectarian squabbling between these groups, and between Protestants and Catholics in gen-

Fig. 5. Immigrant packing-shed worker.

eral, have, however, done little to promote solidarity within the community. Differences of religion overlie deeper and more insoluble differences among immigrants. As Santos explains, "*La gente aquí son de distintas culturas.* [The people here are of different cultures.] They don't get along very well, because since childhood they have been taught that the others are *vagos* [tramps]. Yes, they're almost all Hispanic, but among them you have Hondurans, Salvadorans, Guatemalans. They aren't one nation yet."

If the divisions among village residents inhibit a sense of community, they are all the more pronounced in their effects in the workplace. Divisions of ethnicity, language, and nationality may make the residents of Cowpen and other banana farms an easily malleable work force from the viewpoint of the employer, but such divisions also create unanticipated difficulties in recruiting and retaining that work force. Although ethnicity and nationality diminish the class solidarity that workers need to challenge the conditions under which they labor, they provide new bases of resistance to the authority of employers. Hence, while employers' efforts to dominate the work force remain constant, in the interstices of ethnicity and nationality workers manage to create a breathing space from domination.

# 6 ❧ The Construction of Ethnicity on Banana Farms

The original breakup of Central America after Independence . . . resulted in the creation of five rival nationalisms, carefully fostered by politicos and militarists for their own aggrandizement. Over the years these national-isms have become automatic responses in the unsophisticated popular mind. Not only is a *catracho* [Honduran] supposed to hate a *guanaco* [Salvadoran], and vice versa but this antagonism extends to every rival national group in the area.

—Thomas Anderson (1981)

For a few hours every other Friday evening, the population of Mango Creek is suddenly transformed in ethnicity and nearly doubled in size. Trucks and buses disgorge banana workers by the hundreds in the late afternoon, as workers of five or more area farms are transported to town to collect their pay for the past *quincena*. More than ninety workers from Gregorio Achmed's farm line up outside his store to collect their pay, much of which will immediately be returned to the owner to cancel past debts or purchase new provisions.

By six o'clock, all of the workers have been paid off, and hundreds of Central American immigrants fill the streets, shops, and bars of Mango Creek to partake of town amenities before they are trucked back to the farms later that night. This is one out of two nights during the month that immigrants, in the words of one Creole resident, "take over the town." A local club whose juke-box plays reggae and soca all other nights of the week is for a few hours dominated by loud conversation in Spanish over the strains of *ranchera* music. Profiting immensely from the sale of groceries, clothing, medicine, beer, and rum to the newly paid workers, Belizean residents of Mango Creek are willing to briefly accommodate the immigrants in their short-lived "takeover."

For most of the workers, the novelty of an evening in town is heightened by the fact that, until a few hours earlier, none of them knew they would be here. Most farms in the region pay their workers in cash on the same day, but studiously avoid paying them in the same place every *quincena*. Achmed himself may pay workers at his farm for several pay periods in a row, then alternate with payments in town in ways that defy predictable patterns. These convoluted procedures began after one payday in 1991, when he and his son Tony drove to the farm to disburse a twenty-three-thousand-dollar payroll. A short distance from town, Achmed's son pulled over to pick up a Honduran man hitchhiking along the Southern Highway. Ten minutes later the Honduran fired a .22-caliber handgun through the rear window of their pickup truck, seriously wounding Tony. The truck crashed by the side of the road, throwing the assailant off balance and allowing Gregorio to overpower him. With a bullet still lodged in his lung two years later, Tony recalled the shooting with a combination of disbelief and indignation: "And we knew that man good! He'd worked on our farm for years, and we'd given him credit, a house, any kind of help he needed. It just shows that you can help these people, they can seem to be your friends, but when the chance comes to turn against you, they'll do it." The shooting was by no means an isolated incident. In 1992, a security guard at Farm 2 was shot and killed by a farm worker who escaped with a payroll of twenty-five thousand dollars. Seven months later, a vehicle carrying the payroll for the same farm was ambushed outside of Cowpen by two Salvadorans, one of them a captain on a local farm. The driver and paymaster were both wounded by the assailants' shotgun but nonetheless managed to reach the farm with the payroll intact.

### The Ambivalence of Domination

Periodic attempted robberies of paymasters and owners highlight the ambivalence of labor relations on banana farms. On most farms, paternalism is a regular feature of labor relations, partly to retain experienced workers and partly as a mechanism of domination. On all farms in the region, other than those operated by the Danes, workers reported that they regularly rely on farm owners for loans, advances, and help in emergencies. Surveyed workers report that they are indebted an average of $120, either to farm owners or to the shops owners operate on their farms. For farm owners like Gregorio Achmed, who also operates a store in town, paternalism takes the form of extending credit for items such as bicycles, butane stoves, radios, and other goods that would otherwise be difficult to purchase. Some workers choose to pay in cash at Dangriga stores, where prices are much lower, but the ready credit offered by Achmed attracts a large clientele. The store owner describes his offer of credit to chronically cash-poor banana workers as an act of benevolence, but he derives far more benefit than risk from the arrangement. Because most of Achmed's customers are also his employees, it is seldom difficult to collect debts that can simply be charged against their wages. In effect, indebted workers are paid for much of their labor in the form of goods at high retail markups. If growers are then astonished by their workers' apparent ingratitude, ranging from slander behind their backs to robbery in broad daylight, workers themselves view paternalism in less charitable terms. Although credit and emergency assistance are often acutely necessary and welcomed when they are offered, many workers also recognize a less overt function of such assistance: ensuring control of the work force. When asked about the assistance he had received from his employer, one Honduran worker laughed, "Sí, nos ayudan, como el ganadero engorda al ganado!" (Yes, they help us, like a rancher fattens his cattle!)

Through such ties of dependence, paternalism promotes among workers individual loyalties to growers that fragment their sense of belonging to the same class. A common feature of labor relations on small farms whose employers are intimately acquainted with their workers, paternalism is equally critical to the control of labor on large farms, where most workers are entirely unknown to their employers. With full- and part-time work forces often exceeding two hundred members on each farm, the region's largest growers rely on ties with a few favored workers to maintain control over all others. As the Garifuna manager of one such farm explained,

> We have ways of detecting troublemakers and weeding them out pretty quick. You know, those people who instigate things, who pick fights or get the other workers agitated. We don't put up with any fights on the farm. Some of these people from Honduras come with their ideas of unions and politics and such that they get from the farms that side. It doesn't take long to find out what they're up to and get rid of them. Usually the field captains know what's going on in the village. Even if they don't, some of the workers have been here a long time. They know Ronnie [the farm owner] personally, maybe he's helped them out from time to time. These people usually come right up and tell us if they see or hear something that's not correct.

Fig. 6. Farm payroll truck after an unsuccessful ambush.

If ties of dependence maintain domination over the work force as a whole, they are also important means of retaining experienced workers. Despite the fact that banana workers are typically described as "unskilled" and rarely earn more than the national minimum wage, if that, experienced workers are eagerly sought by all farms. This is because differences in the ability to cut and handle harvested fruit translate into the difference between high quality scores (and correspondingly high profits), and low scores or even entirely rejected harvests. Growers estimate that nearly a year of experience is needed to fully train a worker in most facets of banana farm labor. For growers such as Sancho Nuñez, who owns a farm of just twenty acres, the prevailing high turnover rates of labor represent "a constant loss. Once you get somebody to the point where he can do his job well, he's gone. Either he left for another farm or he gone back to Honduras." The problem of turnover particularly affects small farmers, Nuñez notes, because unlike those who run larger operations, they do not have enough work available to permanently assign workers to specialized tasks. Whereas workers on large farms can be thoroughly trained in just one or two jobs, employees of small farms must be familiar with all or most of the steps involved in banana production. "The only way I can keep people long enough so they know their work is to pay them off," Nuñez declares. "They're always asking me for help, loans and such, and I'm afraid not to give it to them. The problem is, the experienced ones know they can get a job anywhere, so sometimes after I give them a loan, next day, they're gone. That's the last I see of them or my money."

The dangers associated with overt, collective defiance of employer authority do not, paradoxically, diminish worker resistance. Rather, it is channeled into more individualistic and surreptitious forms of noncompliance. Ranging from theft to sabotage and flight, such responses to domination are the "weapons of the weak" Scott (1985) has discerned among the rural poor wherever overt or class-based forms of resistance would be easily detected and quickly repressed. Although the banana fields of Toledo and Stann Creek Districts appear to be quiescent, their work forces divided among themselves by ethnic and national prejudices, the "everyday forms of resistance" exhibited by the Malaysian peasants in Scott's ethnography have their local counterparts in numerous acts of insubordination and destruction.

Slowly eating away at the profitability of banana farms and taxing the efforts of farm managers to ensure labor discipline, the acts of defiant workers are usually described by owners as inherent ingratitude, dishonesty, or indolence. The comments of a grower from the United States are typical in this regard:

> One man I hired was an illegal alien from Honduras. He was caught by the police and put in jail. I got him out and took care of all the paperwork and the work permit. He seemed to work out fine on the farm. Then, a few weeks ago, the foreman discovered that he had been bagging short stems [which should be rejected] and was being paid for it. Of course, I fired him on the spot. One thing I will not tolerate is stealing, above all after I had fixed his problems for him. Now, he must have known that he would be discovered, but he went ahead and stole anyway. These people must be raised with that mentality; it's as if they can't help it, even if it's in their best interests not to steal.

Workers rarely acknowledge such acts, even among themselves, in part because of the feared *orejas* employed on most large farms. Rather, at their most openly defiant, they contrast the harsh living and working conditions they endure on banana farms with the ostentatious wealth and comfort of their employers, who commute from town to farm in late-model, air-conditioned Toyota Landcruisers, the vehicle of choice among the region's elite. The transcript of workers' resistance, then, must be closely read and edited from the comments of farm managers, who contend with numerous, costly, and infuriatingly unattributable acts of defiance.

Asked to describe how the immigrant work force has changed since the industry began importing Central American labor in the early 1980s, growers and managers often assert that workers are less loyal and compliant than in the past. The growing resistance of Central American banana workers to working conditions and labor control on Belizean farms mirrors immigration processes elsewhere. As Griffith notes for North American low-wage industries,

> It has been common for employers to draw upon myths that certain sexes, ethnic groups, or nationalities are somehow predisposed toward working harder or working specific tasks better than others. Certainly this is not entirely myth, since there is ample evidence that new immigrants will perform better, from an employers' perspective, than U.S. workers. They tend to complain less because of language barriers, and they tend to be more grateful for their jobs than native workers, at least in the short run. Yet there is an equal amount of evidence that, over time, these immigrants shed their pliant reputations and behaviors. (1993, 205; see also Massey et al. 1987)

Although many growers acknowledge that they first sought immigrants in the early 1980s to displace militant Belizean workers, they note that with the passage of time these early immigrants have also become skilled at evading their employers' control. An elderly Creole farmer and long-term participant in the industry asserted, "These aliens is getting smart. When they first come to Belize, if you tell them to do something, they'd do it, quick time. Now if you tell them something, you better not turn your back. Some of them has been here ten, fifteen years, but they pretend to not understand English. If you try to talk to them in Spanish, they still pretend to not understand how you speak. It seem they are learning quick how to have their own way." Raisha Sen, an East Indian who manages a farm along the Swasey River, describes similar experiences with the work force under his supervision:

> The Honduraneans and Salvadoraneans give plenty of trouble. These people are too smart. For two hundred acres, forty men should be sufficient, but when I started here there was sixty-five on the payroll. Well, the owner wanted me to control costs, so I called a meeting of the workers. I told the foreman I wanted to see everybody who worked on the farm. Only fifty-five showed up. I made sure I was there on the next payday, and for the first time ten men fail to collect their pay. Then I knew what was happening. The foreman was collecting the pay for those ten, who never worked on the farm. That's how the Spanish people are too smart.

Growers who speak only English often find that language becomes the basis of resistance to their authority. Two U.S. farm owners who hired an entirely immigrant work force noted that they had to personally demonstrate to their foreman the tasks they wanted done. When they eventually fired the foreman because of the slow pace at which he carried out their instructions, all the members of their work force left with him. The growers surmised that the workers and foreman had agreed among themselves to a leisurely pace of work and could rely on the owners' lack of Spanish fluency and unfamiliarity with banana farming to get away with it. On the other three U.S.-owned farms in the banana belt, growers employ bilingual foremen who are either Belizean Mestizos or Maya and who act as intermediaries between the owners and their Spanish-speaking workers. Yet the owners of these farms often mention their frustration at their inability to understand the conversations of their employees, who they suspect may be slandering them in their presence. Despite his inability to speak Spanish, a farm owner from Texas goes to some lengths to ensure that such verbal attacks do not take place, at least in his presence: "Even if I don't understand what they're saying, I can usually tell what they're thinking about me. A lot of times, I'll walk right past them, pretending not to notice. Once I'm about ten feet away, I'll turn around and look at them. I can tell, by their gestures, the look in their eyes, or if their voices drop when they're talking, what they're saying about me. Sometimes that's all it takes to get rid of them."

If theft and foot dragging are widely reported within the industry's work force, a much costlier form of resistance is outright sabotage. After Raisha Sen told the foreman on his farm that he himself would pay workers each *quincena* to prevent padding of the payroll, he noticed a precipitous drop in the quality of fruit entering the packing shed. Nearly 20 percent of the fruit was ruined by rough handling alone. Sen concluded that the foreman had retaliated against his action by encouraging field workers to damage fruit. After warning the foreman that he would be fired if harvest tasks were not done more carefully, the quality of fruit entering the packing shed improved almost immediately. When he subsequently learned from other workers that the foreman had mentioned plans to ambush and kill him, Sen fired him and had him blacklisted at other, nearby farms. A Creole captain at Farm 4 indicated that sabotage is the most common way in which immigrant workers express their grievances to management: "These people you have to supervise all the time. Even the captains will cheat by reporting work that their crews never did. And if you have to lay one off, watch out. The next thing you know, he's out cutting an irrigation line or chopping banana trees. They don't understand that sometimes you have to lay off people, so they're out to sabotage the farm."

A notable feature of these acts of insubordination is that they are not entirely individualistic, but often entail collaboration between immigrant captains and the workers that they supervise. Captains are ordinarily classified as managerial employees and do not engage in heavy physical labor, despite the fact that they earn 40 percent more than average farm workers. Their job classification, type of work, and higher pay enable Belizean field captains to claim some prestige relative to immigrant field workers. Yet a much smaller divide of prestige and experience separates many immigrant captains and workers. Unlike Belizeans, who commute daily from Mango Creek, most immigrant captains endure the same squalid living conditions in Cowpen as field workers. Further, some are related as kin to field or packing-shed workers and consequently have ambiguous or conflicting loyalties to farm owners. When disgruntled, immigrant captains frequently enlist the support of workers in sabotaging production, stealing farm chemicals, or shirking. On Farm 1 at Cowpen, a Salvadoran captain recruited one of his farm workers, also a Salvadoran, in the ambush of a payroll truck in April 1993. Typically, such instances of collaboration occur when captains and farm workers are of the same nationality. Although the large majority of the region's farm and supervisory labor is made up of Central American immigrants, differences of nationality cross-cut this work force. Sancho Nuñez, like most growers, employs Hondurans, Salvadorans, and Guatemalans, but notes that "these different groups don't pull together too good. They have old time frictions among the Central Americans them. They kind of discriminate against each other and keep to themselves."

Such nationalist sentiments can be, and often are, manipulated to extract greater productivity from workers. The American owners of the Southern Pride Farm noted that many of their farm employees asked to work under captains of their own nationality. Initially as an experiment, they divided their nearly sixty field workers into Honduran, Guatemalan, and Salvadoran teams, each of which was supervised by a captain of the same nationality. After each shipment of fruit, the owners then awarded small bonuses to the national team that completed its harvest work with the highest quality scores, which determine the price received for each box of fruit. Such appeals to nationality obviously erode farm workers' perceptions of common interest. Instead of collectively challenging the conditions under which they work, farm workers compete with one another to augment farm profits.

When manipulated in this fashion, national loyalties may become so volatile that they threaten farm production. During one harvest, the Honduran and Guatemalan teams were assigned to adjacent blocks of the Southern Pride Farm. Because the block being worked by Hondurans bore less ripe fruit, they finished their work earlier and were then assigned to help the Guatemalans. Some of the reassigned workers were resentful at having to work overtime and began taunting the Guatemalans as slow, unskilled *indios atrasados* (backward Indians).[1] Members of the two teams began fighting, causing the growers to intervene and separate the groups. Although no one was seriously injured in the brawl, later that evening, the Guatemalan and Honduran captains continued the argument between themselves. The next morning workers found the Guatemalan hacked to death in his bed. The Honduran had fled undetected during the night. The murder of the Guatemalan captain shocked and incensed the Guatemalan workers, many of whom vowed to retaliate. Subsequent acts of violence were averted only by the growers' careful culling of the work force. "The problem was, both captains were the most experienced men we had," one of the growers recounted later. "They had worked in bananas for years before they came to Belize, and we're still paying for the loss of that experience. Plus, we had to get rid of some of the Guatemalans who were talking about revenge. One thing we learned out of all this is not to mess around with national work teams anymore."

Such incidents underscore the potentially explosive balance of worker identity and labor discipline on banana farms. While the U.S. growers anticipated that they could extract more labor from their work force by accentuating such loyalties, national sentiments quickly interfered with the production process itself. Moreover, as has been demonstrated above, nationality often binds workers to captains in ways that encourage sabotage, theft, and other forms of resistance. On Farm 4, managers had long puzzled over the fact that the farm was absorbing an array of costly fertilizers and herbicides in amounts far exceeding recommended application levels. Office managers began to suspect that many of these chemicals were being pilfered by farm workers for use on their own milpas. Their suspicions were confirmed when several immigrant workers and captains were discovered carrying bottles of

Gramoxone home at the end of one workday. Management immediately fired all of the farm's immigrant field captains and replaced them with Afro-Belizeans. Yet if such responses forestall collaborative theft between captains and workers, they also threaten to unify the work force against an exclusively Creole, English-speaking management. As will be seen below, each farm in the region presents a radically different possibility in the deployment of labor. In dialectical fashion, each also creates new possibilities for domination and resistance.

## Labor Recruitment and Labor Control

Data collected on work-force composition on twenty-two of the region's twenty-three active banana farms indicate a wide variety of ways in which the industry's work force is deployed by ethnicity, gender, and nationality. Clearly, the recruitment and deployment of labor take the form of an experiment in progress, for managers are constantly evaluating and reevaluating differing work-force configurations in terms of their effects on production and labor discipline. Each farm has reached differing solutions in attempting to satisfy these imperatives. The only consistent pattern throughout the region is that all farms employ few or no Creoles and Garifuna as farm workers, and many employ none in any capacity.

Afro-Belizeans comprise no more than 12 percent of the field work force of any one farm, and for the industry as a whole, they make up a minuscule 3.4 percent of all farm laborers. On all of the farms, 92.8 percent of field laborers are Central American immigrants, whereas only 7.2 percent are Belizeans. Of the 1,380 full-time field laborers recorded on the twenty-two surveyed farms, 34 percent are Guatemalan, 32.3 percent are Honduran, 25.2 percent are Salvadoran, 4.3 percent are Belizean Maya or Kekchi, 3.2 percent are Creole, .7 percent are Garifuna, and .4 percent are Belizean Mestizos. Given their predominance in the work force as recently as 1982, the absence of Creole and Garifuna workers throughout the banana belt today testifies to the rapidity with which farms can reallocate labor to operate within the constraints imposed by Fyffes and the world market.

As mentioned earlier, growers rationalize the near absence of Afro-Belizeans from banana farms in terms of the purported unwillingness of Creoles and Garifuna to work in agriculture. That similar claims are pervasive in lower Central America attests to the historical exclusion of black labor from the region's banana industries. Having encountered such ideologies even before their arrival in Belize, most immigrant laborers subscribe to them axiomatically, as the comments of a Guatemalan farm worker suggest: "*Los negritos no se encuentran aquí en el banano.* [You won't find blacks here on banana farms.] They don't know anything about agriculture and don't want to work in the countryside. The blacks who are going to work want easy jobs, like office work." On another farm, where Creoles and Garifuna are employed in some numbers as part-time (casual) workers during shipments, a Honduran foreman noted, "Si, los Beliceños trabajan en la empacadora bajo la sombra, pero nunca en la finca bajo en sol" (Sure, Belizeans work in the packing shed under the shade, but never on the farm under the sun). Despite their ubiquity among growers and immigrants alike, prevailing beliefs about cultural predispositions for farm work cannot logically account for work force composition on the region's farms. Growers allege that Creoles and Garifuna lack the agricultural traditions of Hispanics, and are therefore unsuitable as banana workers, but Belizean Mestizos are even less likely to be employed as field labor on banana farms.

Although nearly all growers who have entered the industry since 1985 have declined to extensively recruit Afro-Belizeans as field labor, Brian Seals, a North American grower, relied heavily on Creole workers from Mango Creek when he established his farm in 1991. His experiences are instructive, for they suggest some of the reasons the industry abandoned local labor, regardless of ethnicity, more than a decade ago: "The Creoles can do the work, make no mistake about it, but you can't push or reprimand them. I told one of them that he was making mistakes, and he accused me of embarrassing him. . . . The Belizeans seem to be passive, but I think they have a lot of hostility underneath, particularly if you have a white skin. I heard that some of the guys who used to work for me called me the 'white slaver.' I don't know what the British did here when they were the colonial power, but they sure gave these people an attitude." Seals subsequently replaced his Creole workers with immigrants, primarily because the Belizeans refused to accept his reprimands uncritically. Seals attributed the assertive "attitude" of Creole workers to colonial-era stigmas of class and race, which for many Belizeans are recreated when employed by a white foreigner. Yet as Seals's own ensuing comments suggest, Creole resistance to employers may stem more directly from the widely differing consequences of job loss for Belizeans and immigrants: "For the Belizeans, it's no big deal if they lose a job. They'll just find something else to hustle. But with the Central Americans, they know that if they talk back they might just find themselves back in El Salvador. That makes them just a lot more manageable."

If Creoles and Garifuna are rarely found in the banana fields today, then, it is largely due to growers' efforts to maintain labor discipline on their farms. The precarious returns to banana production create an overriding imperative to lower production costs. As a result, practices such as obligatory overtime (paid at non-overtime rates), underpayment, and harvest shifts of twelve hours or more are commonplace throughout the industry. They also necessitate a work force willing to accept such conditions without overt opposition. As a Creole captain at Cowpen noted, "Belize is too democratic. Our people can work even harder than aliens, but they won't be bossed or treated unfairly. We find that if we work Belizeans alongside the aliens, we don't hear any complaints from them. They either fit in or we replace them. But work lone Belizeans on the farm? Then you'll see what I mean when I say we are too democratic."

Only one segment of the industry employs exclusively Belizean labor: waterfront work at the Big Creek port, where freighters are loaded with bananas at weekly intervals for shipment to Europe. Two work gangs are employed for nine-hour shifts during each of the two shipment days of the week. All forty waterfront workers are Creole men from Mango Creek, and almost all are twenty-five years of age or younger. Unskilled workers on the waterfront warehouse boxes of bananas that have been trucked from the region's farms and load them onto pallets for transfer into the ships' holds. Other unskilled workers are employed in the holds to unload boxes from the pallets. All of this labor is physically demanding, although probably less so than harvest labor on the farms. Unskilled workers are paid $3.00 per hour, or $54.00 per shipment. Two members of each work gang are classed as "semiskilled" laborers, and earn $3.50 per hour to operate forklifts that bring bananas to dockside and the winches that transfer bananas onto the ships. During especially large shipments, men are employed in excess of their nine-hour shifts, for which they are paid time and a half.

Although the waterfront provides only part-time employment, the wages and working conditions there are clearly superior to those of farm work. Waterfront workers are employed by the Banana Growers' Association, as is the foreman who hires them. The foreman, who is himself Creole, was remarkably candid when accounting for the ethnic composition of the waterfront

Fig. 7. Belizean dock workers load bananas on a freighter.

gangs: "I have no opposition to aliens working in the industry, but a lot of people here do. I hire local people for two reasons. First, I can't speak Spanish and these men have to be able to understand and follow my orders. Second, I hire local people so they don't resent what the industry is doing with all the aliens at the farms. If they saw aliens working here too, they might make trouble for the whole industry. That's why you find these people are paid a little more than the aliens at the farms." Such comments indicate that the industry's myths of ethnicity and nation are built on a conscious effacement of historical memory. The consignment of more than a thousand immigrant workers to the banana enclave at Cowpen removes from view any reminder of Belizeans' past exclusion from the industry. Further denial of their displaced status is assured by the token employment of Mango Creek Creoles in waterfront work twice a week.

The confinement of Belizean labor to highly visible, better-paying positions in the industry closely corresponds to class segmentation theories of workplace ethnicity. National differences within the work force are most conspicuous between field laborers and supervisory personnel (table 4). Earning on average 40 percent more than nonsupervisory workers, field captains and other supervisors are more likely to be Belizeans than immigrants. Whereas only 43 (3.4 percent) of the 1,323 immigrants employed on the region's farms on a full-time basis are supervisors, 48 (32.4 percent) of the 148 Belizeans employed full-time are supervisors.[2] The largest number of Belizean supervisors are Creoles (20 of 48), followed by Mopan and Kekchi Maya (13), Mestizos (10), and Garifuna (5). Although the work force is clearly segmented by nationality, Belizean workers and supervisors are not demonstrably segmented by ethnicity. Afro-Belizeans are no more likely to be employed as supervisors than are Mestizos and Maya, as indicated by a chi-square value of .34 (not significant at $p < .05$ and 3 df). In recruiting supervisors, many growers frankly consider Belizean antipathy toward immigrants to be an asset. As one indicated, "If you hire aliens to supervise aliens, before you know it, they get together and start conspiring to give trouble. Belizean captains won't go soft on workers like the aliens will. In fact, most Belizeans enjoy bossing aliens around."

Whereas Afro-Belizeans are confined to a small if comparatively well-paid segment of the industry, Belizeans of other ethnicities are employed as farm labor in larger numbers. Five of the twenty-two farms heavily employ Belizean Mopan and Kekchi Maya as field laborers, albeit in combination with Central American immigrants. Farm owners who hire the Mopan and Kekchi claim that indigenous labor presents certain managerial advantages not present with either Afro-Belizean or immigrant workers. These advantages derive from a patriarchal pattern of social organization that, according to growers, reduces the need for close supervision and numerous administrative personnel. Among both the Mopan and Kekchi, when the eldest males of an extended family seek employment from farm managers, they often bring with them their sons, daughters, and daughters-in-law as well. This pattern of recruitment is highly distinct from the manner in which most immigrants are employed, for Central American immigrants tend to pursue work singly or in small groups of males. On one farm, just three Maya and Kekchi families supply among them twenty of the farm's twenty-eight full- and part-time employees.

Given the voracious demand for labor during shipment periods, growers eagerly seek employees who can bring with them additional family members to work on a part-time basis in the packing sheds. Small- and medium-sized farms face the greatest problems in obtaining adequate supplies of part-time labor for harvest periods. Such farms are invariably newer and located far from established enclaves such as Cowpen and South Stann Creek. Whereas

Table 4. National, Ethnic, and Gender Distribution on Banana Farms

*(N = 22)*

| Nationality/<br>Ethnic Group | Full-Time<br>Field Worker | Office/<br>Supervisory | Casual<br>Labor | Row<br>Total |
|---|---|---|---|---|
| Salvadoran | 284 (25.2%) | M: 7 (8.9%) | M: 34 (6.8%)<br>F: 35 (6.9%) | M: 325<br>F: 35 |
| Honduran | 364 (32.3%) | M: 25 (32.1%)<br>F: 1 (1.3%) | M: 37 (7.3%)<br>F: 87 (17.3%) | M: 426<br>F: 88 |
| Guatemalan | 384 (34.0%) | M: 10 (12.8%) | M: 43 (8.5%)<br>F: 98 (19.4%) | M: 437<br>F: 98 |
| Belizean Maya | 48 (4.3%) | M: 13 (16.7%) | M: 56 (11.1%)<br>F: 40 (7.9%) | M: 117<br>F: 40 |
| Belizean Mestizo | 5 (.4%) | M: 5 (6.4%)<br>F: 1 (1.3%) | M: 2 (.4%)<br>F: 5 (1.0%) | M: 12<br>F: 6 |
| Creole | 36 (3.2%) | M: 10 (12.8%)<br>F: 1 (1.3%) | M: 18 (3.6%)<br>F: 15 (2.9%) | M: 64<br>F: 16 |
| Garifuna | 8 (.7%) | M: 4 (5.1%)<br>F: 1 (1.3%) | M: 14 (2.8%)<br>F: 20 (2.8%) | M: 26<br>F: 21 |
| TOTAL | 1,129 | M: 74<br>F: 4 | M: 204<br>F: 300 | |

*Note:* The total land area under cultivation on twenty-two of the country's twenty-three operational banana farms is 4,412.7 acres, or 96.7 per cent of the total. Surveyed farms employ an average of one field worker per 3.8 acres. Percentages refer to the proportion of the work force in each labor category that is comprised of members of a given ethnic group and gender. On all farms, field workers are males; among casual and office/supervisory workers, *M* denotes male, *F* denotes female.

large, more established farms tend to have many resident families, the work force of newer farms is usually dominated by single young men, placing these farms at a disadvantage in recruiting part-time labor. Large farms at Cowpen and South Stann Creek obtain most of their packing-shed labor by hiring the family members of resident banana workers. Even the many resident households on the farms at South Stann Creek are insufficient for the labor demands of area farms during harvest periods, leading two of the operations to transport Garifuna women as part-time workers from the village of Hopkins, some seventeen miles away.

As indicated in tables 5 and 6, small- and medium-sized farms (those below the industry average of 245 acres) turn more often than large farms to Maya and Kekchi residents for full- and part-time labor.[3] Because much of this additional labor belongs to the same kinship group as that of oldest worker, kin-based and domestic patterns of authority tend to reinforce labor discipline on the farm. One grower from the United States describes his Maya and Kekchi workers as the most productive and least "troublesome" members of his work force, because the patriarch of each family ensures that other family members work reliably and productively: "With the Indians, once the grandfather is at work, what he says, goes. He makes sure that his sons are in the fields and daughters come every week to pack fruit. It's like having a foreman in every family." Because of such kin-based patterns of authority, the grower has just one captain (himself a Mopan Maya) on a 220-acre farm. A farm of comparable size employing nonindigenous labor would usually require four or more captains. On another farm of 180 acres, a single Kekchi captain is employed to supervise all work in the fields and packing shed. "We can do that," the captain indicated, "because all of us are one people here." The twenty-seven Kekchi workers on the farm belong to just five families.

Yet some growers avoid hiring Maya and Kekchi precisely because of their social organization. One Belizean grower claimed, "I would never have more than one or maybe two work for me. They all stick together, so if one stop work, they all stop and the others don't even know why they strike. Then one morning you go to farm and you find they all gone to their milpa. Just like that, with no notice at all." Another grower hired an elderly Mopan man to "deflower" fruit, an undemanding job involving the removal of vestigial buds from fruit prior to packing, largely because he said he could bring his grandson to work in the packing shed. When the older man was laid off because there was no more work for him to do that week, he took his grandson with him, disrupting production during the shipment when the young man was most needed. The tendency of the Maya to view wage labor as supplementary to milpa farming also reduces their permanence in the work force, much to the chagrin of employers who seek a readily available reservoir of labor. Alfred Winston, who employs Kekchi and Mopan Maya as well as immigrants, claims to discern significant differences between the two Amerindian groups in their tendency to abandon wage work with little or no notice. Winston claims that his Mopan workers have become as assertive as Afro-Belizeans, a

Table 5. National, Ethnic, and Gender Distribution on Small- and Medium-
Sized Banana Farms
*(N = 12; <245 ac.)*

| Nationality/ Ethnic Group | Full-Time Field Worker | Office/ Supervisory | Casual Labor | Row Total |
|---|---|---|---|---|
| Salvadoran | 28 (18.3%) | 2 (16.7%) | M: 3 (3.1%) | M: 33 |
| | | | F: 4 (4.2%) | F: 4 |
| Honduran | 17 (11.1%) | 3 (25.0%) | M: 7 (7.3%) | M: 27 |
| | | | F: 13 (13.5%) | F: 13 |
| Guatemalan | 81 (52.9%) | 2 (16.7%) | M: 8 (8.3%) | M: 91 |
| | | | F: 15 (15.6%) | F: 15 |
| Belizean Maya | 22 (14.4%) | 3 (25.0%) | M: 25 (26.0%) | M: 50 |
| | | | F: 18 (18.8%) | F: 18 |
| Belizean Mestizo | 2 (1.3%) | 1 (8.3%) | M: 1 (1.0%) | M: 4 |
| | | | F: 2 (2.1%) | F: 2 |
| Creole | 3 (1.9%) | | | M: 3 |
| Garifuna | | 1 (8.3%) | | M: 1 |
| TOTAL | 153 | 12 | M: 44 | |
| | | | F: 52 | |

*Note:* This table presents data on work-force composition collected on the twelve farms smaller than the industry-wide average of 245 acres. The total land area under cultivation on these farms is 934 acres. Small- and medium-sized farms employ 153 field workers, or an average of one worker per 6.1 acres. Percentages refer to the proportion of the work force in each labor category that is comprised of members of a given ethnic group and gender. All field workers and supervisory staff are males; among casual workers, *M* denotes male, *F* denotes female.

point emphasized by his sarcastic use of Creole when referring to the Mopan: "When we're working shipment, we need every man we can get. But these [Mopan] Maya no de worry. The milpa come first. Now, the Kekchi, they keep their milpas, but they send their wives to work on the milpa or to replace them in the packing shed. But never the Maya. Dem say dey women are just fu cook and make baby."

If such differences between indigenous ethnic groups exist, they may well reflect the differing culture histories of the Mopan and Kekchi. The Kekchi have long been far less integrated with markets and Belizean society as a whole than the more acculturated Mopan (Wilk 1991). Accordingly, the

Mopan are more likely to be fluent in English and literate than the Kekchi, many of whom grew up in remote hamlets in the Toledo District, where formal education is rudimentary or nonexistent. Winston's own comments imply that Mopan workers increasingly see themselves as entitled to the same rights as other Belizeans, with the result that they tend to be more defiant of farm authority: "I don't know what happened to these [Mopan] Maya. They think that because they are Belizean, they have a right to do what they want on the farm. They are getting . . . Creolized. My foreman will tell the Maya Indians, 'Hurry up, you're moving too slow.' And the Maya says back [in Creole],

Table 6. National, Ethnic, and Gender Distribution on Large Banana Farms
(N = 10; >245 ac.)

| Nationality/ Ethnic Group | Full-Time Field Worker | Office/ Supervisory | Casual Labor | Row Total |
|---|---|---|---|---|
| Salvadoran | 256 (26.2%) | M: 5 (7.6%) | M: 31 (7.2%) | M: 292 |
| | | | F: 31 (7.2%) | F: 31 |
| Honduran | 347 (35.5%) | M: 22 (33.3%) | M: 30 (7.0%) | M: 399 |
| | | F: 1 (1.5%) | F: 74 (17.3%) | F: 75 |
| Guatemalan | 303 (31.0%) | M: 8 (12.1%) | M: 35 (8.2%) | M: 346 |
| | | | F: 83 (19.4%) | F: 83 |
| Belizean Maya | 26 (2.6%) | M: 10 (15.2%) | M: 51 (11.9%) | M: 87 |
| | | | F: 22 (5.1%) | F: 22 |
| Belizean Mestizo | 3 (.3%) | M: 4 (6.1%) | M: 1 (.2%) | M: 8 |
| | | F: 1 (1.5%) | F: 3 (.7%) | F: 4 |
| Creole | 33 (3.4%) | M: 10 (15.2%) | M: 18 (4.2%) | M: 61 |
| | | F: 1 (1.5%) | F: 15 (3.5%) | F: 16 |
| Garifuna | 8 (.8%) | M: 3 (4.5%) | M: 14 (3.3%) | M: 25 |
| | | F: 1 (1.5%) | F: 20 (4.7%) | F: 21 |
| TOTAL | 976 | M: 62 | M: 180 | |
| | | F: 4 | F: 248 | |

Note: This table presents data on work-force composition collected on the twelve farms smaller than the industry-wide average of 245 acres. The total land area under cultivation on these farms is 3,478.7 acres. Large farms employ 976 field workers, or an average of one worker per 3.5 acres. Percentages refer to the proportion of the work force in each labor category that is comprised of members of a given ethnic group and gender. All field workers are males; among casual and office workers, M denotes male, F denotes female.

'Me no hurry. Me da Belizean.' If they think they are being mistreated, they run right to the minister [of labor] in Belmopan to complain. When you have people with that way of thinking, its very hard, so little by little I'll be replacing them with aliens. If you have a few aliens working alongside the Maya, they don't give any more trouble." In this sense, much as Thomas (1985) noted for California agriculture, immigrant labor is employed to discipline restive workers holding secure citizenship status.

### Gender in the Work Force

On all large farms, labor is segmented by gender as well as ethnicity and nationality. Nearly all female workers on the region's farms are employed on a part-time basis in the packing sheds. The majority of these are employed in sorting tasks, although a few men may also be assigned to the same work. Sorting work entails evaluating fruit by quality and length and rejecting all fruit that fails to meet company specifications. On the largest two farms at Cowpen, on average 90 percent of the workers who were sorting and rejecting fruit in observations made during harvest periods were women. Unlike harvest labor on the farms, sorting does not require great physical strength, but it is nonetheless exhausting. Packing-shed workers stand in place alongside sorting bins for shifts lasting twelve or more hours. During this time, their hands are immersed in the water-filled bins, but after a few hours of sorting fruit and flinging rejects out of the bins, workers are usually drenched from the neck down. A few improvise "parkas" of plastic bags to help shield them from the water, although such protection is flimsy at best. One Garifuna woman employed on the sorting line described the effects of such work: "It get so with me hands in the water that after eight, nine hours, I can't feel nothing. Me hands stiffen right up. When night fall, you still wearing your wet clothes and by quitting time at 8:00, I shake so hard from the cold I can scarcely stand. Next morning at six the whole thing start right over again."

Throughout the shift, several male supervisors move constantly along the sorting line, occasionally answering workers' questions or measuring fruit with a metal tape curved to the contours of a banana. In general, however, the task of supervisors is to ensure that women remain constantly at work to maintain a rapid throughput from the harvesting of fruit to the point that it is loaded on trucks. Workers talk among themselves over the din of machinery but are quickly reprimanded if they look at one another or their concentration on their tasks wanes. Six times per day a supervisor will strike a long, suspended metal bar with a pipe, the clatter echoing over the sounds of machinery to announce the beginning or end of the work day, lunch breaks, or rest periods. Packing-shed workers receive a half-hour lunch and two ten minute breaks per shift. At the beginning of each break, adult and child vendors converge on the shed to sell sodas or snacks. Workers walk stiffly from their positions, dry their hands and arms, and look for some place to sit down and rest during their brief reprieve from sorting.

The predominance of women in packing-shed employment is not a recent innovation in the banana industry. Photographs of the industry released by the Government Information Service in 1975, the first full year of production under the Banana Board's direction, reveal a line of exclusively female workers sorting bananas floating in water-filled bins (*New Belize* 1979, 13). The scene could pass for any contemporary view of packing operations on a large farm, except that the photos reveal a work force that was entirely Garifuna. Today, fully half (49.9 percent) of packing-shed employees on the region's farms are immigrant women, 12.4 percent are immigrant men, 20.6 percent are Belizean men, and 16.9 percent are Belizean women. On Farm 4 at Cowpen, a few Afro-Belizean women are dispersed through the line, looking uncomfortably excluded from the Spanish conversations taking place around them. Some Creole and Garifuna employees in the Cowpen packing sheds charge that supervisors prefer to hire immigrant women, in large part because they are more easily intimidated by Creole supervisors than are Belizean women. When Farm 4 laid off 35 of its 120 packing-shed workers in April 1993, a disproportionate number of those dismissed were Belizean. One Creole woman who had worked at the shed for five months bitterly commented on her dismissal the previous day, "Them say Belizean First,[4] but it seem the alien first now. All the Belizeans gone home, but the 'Pania keep working. The 'Pania come here but they hate we Belizean. They call we all kind of name. Them say 'negrita'; yesterday one de call me baboon. And now we are second in fu we [our] own country."

Managers offer several rationales for their heavy reliance on female labor in the packing sheds. They note that most men are in need of full-time wages and that the earnings of two days of packing employment per week are insufficient to support their families. Managers also assert that part-time packing shed employment allows women to fulfill their domestic "duties." These rationales overlook the fact that a fair number of Cowpen households are headed by single women, for whom packing shed employment provides needed but far from sufficient income. Nothwithstanding the needs of such households, full-time wage employment for women in rural Belize is in any case nearly nonexistent, except for those few women with accounting or secretarial skills who are employed in the offices of the larger farms. Finally, managers assert that women are inherently better able to evaluate the quality of fruit than men. A supervisor at Farm 4 claimed that "men don't have the patience or skill with their hands that women do." Another, perhaps more telling comment was offered as an afterthought: "After ten hours of doing this, standing here, men sometimes slow down or start to talk back to the supervisors. We can't allow that."

The segmentation of labor by gender complements the supervisor's authority over a work force engaged in the final, critical stages of banana production, when mishandling could easily turn a promising harvest into a near-total loss. Like the Malay factory women described by Ong (1987, 155), labor discipline in packing sheds is buttressed by the differing ethnic and national identities of workers and their supervisors. Much as Belizeans attribute random and explosive acts of violence to Central American immigrants, so Hispanics bear their own myths about Afro-Caribbean men, many relating to their purported sexual appetites and aggressiveness.[5] To the extent that they subscribe to such beliefs about their Creole supervisors, immigrant women in the packing sheds become the captives of their prejudices.

Some immigrant women respond to the conditions of banana industry employment in ways that parallel the experiences of women in societies as diverse as Malaysia (Ong 1987), northern Mexico (Peña 1988), and the United States (Sacks 1988). In all these societies, women of peasant or minority origins occupy secondary labor markets yet often refuse to accept dehumanizing work routines. Rarely engaging in open resistance that would threaten their jobs, women workers in these settings have nonetheless devised ways to critique and resist management in moral terms. Such strategies may prove as costly to employers as strikes led by a unionized work force. In Malaysian factories, for example, female electronics workers experience dramatic bouts of spirit possession that correspond to extended shifts and production speedups (Ong 1987, 164). At such times, production comes to a complete halt until the spirits are exorcised by a healer. If the relegation of immigrant women to part-time work in the banana industry's packing sheds is rationalized by its own myths of gender, these ideologies also contain fatal contradictions that emerge under the intense labor demands of industrial agriculture. Having been assigned to packing-shed employment because it is physically "undemanding," immigrant women are nonetheless expected to endure shifts lasting late into the night during the frenetic harvest periods. Under such conditions, some workers appear to faint or become ill part way through their shifts and must be sent home early. Given their lower expectations of female endurance, it rarely occurs to supervisors to question whether such illness is feigned. When in safe company, however, many packing-shed workers readily acknowledge that it is.

If ethnic, gender, and national divisions within the work force enhance its malleability, such divisions are compounded by an elaborate hierarchy of job classifications and pay rates. These classifications are of relatively recent origin, having been imposed following the privatization of the industry. Prior to 1985, when the union negotiated wage contracts, there were few wage categories in the industry. Among field workers, just three primary classifications existed: harvesters received the highest wages, followed by machete workers, and, finally, general farm workers, who did such relatively undemanding tasks as "deflowering" fruit and bagging stems. In 1984, the last year this wage system remained in place, the highest paid field workers earned approximately 30 percent more than the lowest. Further, by union contract, all jobs were paid with hourly wages, so that workers were paid regardless of the intensity of their work.

In addition to the displacement of militant unionized Belizean workers, management also restructured job assignments and pay rates in ways that closely correspond to the predictions of class segmentation theory. Today, an elaborate and to some extent arbitrary hierarchy of job classifications exists on large farms. Table 7 indicates average pay rates for banana industry labor, as well as the expected daily pay for each category of work. Almost all jobs in the contemporary industry are paid at piece rates, shifting the burden of supervision to the worker. These wage rates also result in widely differing levels of compensation. Harvesters, for example, can earn close to thirty dollars per day, whereas the pay received by field workers is less than half that. Workers' pay now corresponds exactly to the amount of work they complete. Finally, there is some evidence not of ethnic segmentation among immigrant workers (most of whom are Mestizo), but of segmentation by nationality. Of the 148 immigrant banana workers surveyed on six farms, Salvadorans earned just 78 percent of the average earnings of Honduran and Guatemalan workers. (In contrast, the average pay of Belizean field workers is 13 percent higher

Table 7. Average Wage and Piece Rates for Banana Industry Labor

| Type of Labor | Pay Rate ($) | Average Daily Earnings ($) |
|---|---|---|
| Maintenance | | |
| Pruning | 10.00/acre | 14.00 |
| Propping | 1.50/acre | 14.00 |
| Deleafing | 1.50/acre | 13.00 |
| Applying fertilizer | 6.50/acre | 18.00 |
| Applying lime | 10.00/acre | 17.00 |
| Applying nematicide | 5.00/acre | 16.00 |
| Applying herbicide | 4.50/acre | 15.00 |
| Bagging fruit | .06/stem | 11.00 |
| Machete clearing around banana plants | 12.00/acre | 13.00 |
| Deflowering fruit | .06/stem | 11.00 |
| Opening bags | 8.00/1,000 | 13.00 |
| Primary drain cleaning | .03/foot | 13.00 |
| Secondary cleaning | .03/foot | 13.00 |
| Drain digging | 1.70/yard | 19.00 |
| Irrigation | 2.00/hour | 16.00 |
| Replanting | .16/seed | 12.00 |
| Harvest: | | |
| Cutting | 9.20/100 stems | 28.00 |
| Backing (carrying fruit to cable) | 9.20/100 stems | 26.00 |
| Fruit protection | 2.00/hour | 16.00 |
| Hauling (pulling fruit into packing shed) | 12.67/100 stems | 29.00 |

Note: Pay rates and average daily earnings are expressed in Belizean dollars ($2.00 Bze = $1.00 U.S.)

than that of Hondurans and Guatemalans.) The assignment of Salvadorans to the lowest paying jobs on farms was consistently mentioned by workers of all nationalities. As will be seen in chapter 7, Salvadorans are also the least willing of all three nationalities to return to their country voluntarily. As a result, they can be compelled to accept earnings and working conditions that Hondurans, for example, will not.

## Crucible of Conflict: Ethnic Relations on Banana Farms

> One of the [United Fruit] supervisors . . . told me about a murder he had witnessed back when he was a young man.
>
> "Down below me . . . was this here laborer, honing his machete. He was stroking that there knife like it was a woman. Had an edge you could shave by. You know these fellows are proud of their machete and take good care of it."
>
> "Coming down the street is this other man, also a laborer, and the fellow on the stoop looks up real sharp, like he seen a rat. The man just ambles on by, and the fellow with the machete sort of gets up at a crouch, sneaks along behind him, then raises that knife over his head with both hands and comes on down with everything he's got—right here."
>
> [He] pointed to the crown of his own head, then drew a line right down the middle of his face with his index finger.
>
> "Just like a pineapple. Split him down to the shoulders. Two profiles, one half face on either side."
>
> "Jesus," I said. "And what happened then?"
>
> [He] thought it over. "I'll tell you what happened then," he said at last. "I puked, that's what."
>
> —Thomas McCann (1976)

Among the unintended consequences of strategies designed to segment the labor force by nationality, ethnicity, and gender are occasionally lethal conflicts that erupt in the banana fields and adjacent communities. After each payday, a small but predictable stream of farm workers will visit the doctor's clinic in Mango Creek to have their machete cuts dressed, broken bones splinted, or gunshot wounds treated. These are the known casualties of the region's battlefield of identities, whose wounds dramatically attest to a work force in which distrust and animosity run deep. How many personal grievances arising from nationality and ethnicity result in injury will never be known, nor will the number of wounds left untreated or corpses discretely hidden in shallow graves. When workers disappear without a trace it is usually assumed, correctly, that they abruptly left their jobs to seek work elsewhere or return home. Such was the assumption about a Guatemalan farm worker at the Bladen River, who was thought to have quit without notice in early September 1993, after a quarrel with some Honduran co-workers. Four days after his disappearance a captain came upon his decapitated body clumsily concealed under debris in a remote area of the farm.

More than 92 percent of today's banana work force is comprised of Central American immigrants, but these workers are far from homogeneous. Considerable enmity has existed historically among the Central American nations, especially between Honduras and El Salvador, which fought a brief but consequential armed conflict in 1969. The so-called Soccer War between Honduras and El Salvador erupted following a World Cup playoff match between the two countries. For many North American reporters, the prospect of Central Americans warring over the outcome of a soccer match provided irresistible fodder for stereotypes about Latin "volatility." Unmentioned by most of the press, however, was the far more grievous cause of the war—the decision of the Honduran government to forcibly repatriate tens of thousands of Salvadoran settlers in the weeks prior to the football game.[6] Although military and civilian casualties in the hundred-hour skirmish probably did not exceed two thousand, the war itself and the events prior to it displaced up to one hundred thousand Hondurans and Salvadorans (Anderson 1981). Many of these refugees fled to Guatemala, and ultimately to Belize (Schwartz 1987; Stone 1990b). Decades later, the national antagonisms engendered by the Soccer War, which continue to be inflamed by politicians and the press in both countries, occasionally erupt in violence in the banana belt.

A casual conversation with a Honduran worker on Farm 2, a man whose left arm had been amputated below the elbow, leads inevitably to the topic of his injury:

> La mayor parte de la gente aquí se llevan bien. [Most people here get along well.] But some of the Salvadorans still hate us for the war all those years ago. They are still looking for revenge. One of them on Farm 2 had been threatening me for months, but I ignored him. Well, after the way he acted, I carried my machete wherever I went. A man has a right to defend himself, no? I was playing checkers with a friend one Saturday and he came up drunk and started in on us. 'Hey, you sons of bitches, you cabrones, why don't you fight, you cowards?' We tried to push him away, but he swung at my arm before I could get my machete. When I saw the wound . . . son of a bitch! He cut right through the bone.

Touching the scarred site where his forearm had been amputated, the worker continued, "By the time we got to Mango [Creek], the doctor said he would have to finish the job. The hand couldn't be saved."

While many immigrants insist they left their national conflicts behind them when they came to Belize, incidents such as these suggest that such animosities are not quickly forgotten by all members of the work force. Interviews with farm workers and managers alike indicate that violent confrontations almost invariably occur after drinking on paydays, when inhibitions are at their lowest. Yet once an initial dispute occurs under intoxication, it is often prosecuted to its conclusion long after the effects of alcohol have subsided. At a farm on the Swasey River, a Honduran and Salvadoran began quarreling one Friday night after each had been drinking. The argument abated without violence, only to arise with renewed force the next morning when the men began drinking again. The men drew their machetes but were quickly separated by other workers. Late that evening, as the Salvadoran was emerging from a bath in the river, his antagonist fired a shotgun at his chest at point-blank range. The man's body was found suspended from a cableway used to haul bananas, the Honduran having escaped before the murder was detected.

Although most violent conflicts are reported to occur between Hondurans and Salvadorans, divisions periodically flare up between other segments of the work force as well. Within the immigrant work force, Mestizos and Indians retain many of the mutual animosities prevailing between them in countries such as Guatemala. A Honduran worker described the Guatemalan Maya he worked with as *anuentes,* passive to the point of lacking any initiative. Some jobs, such as digging drains, he said, were simply beyond their reasoning power: "*Los inditos no tienen la inteligencia para eso.* [Indians don't have the intelligence for that.] The Spanish are more aware of a task. They don't have to have it explained to them. But the Indians have to be told to do it, over and over again. They should be more like the Spanish. We know there is work to be done if money is to be made." For their part, Belizean as well as Guatemalan Maya state that they avoid socializing with immigrant co-workers. The Belizean Kekchi manager of a farm commissary seethed as she mentioned the Mestizo workers employed on the farm: "The Spanish don't like the Indians and the Indians don't like the Spanish. They're always talking about us, thinking we don't understand what they say. They like to call us *indios brutos.* But they are the ones that act like animals. Just the other week, a Guatemaltecan chop a Honduranean on the farm and killed him, just like that. Then he run back to his country before the police catch him." The woman stopped short in her discussion when an immigrant worker entered the store to buy a Coke, but she served him with unconcealed disdain.

In addition to ethnicity, religion must be added to the sources of conflict within the work force, albeit one that does not result in violence. Among the most dramatic cultural changes to have taken place in Central America in the last twenty years has been the diffusion of evangelical Christianity throughout the region, often as the result of missionary activities sponsored by North American fundamentalist churches. Propagated in the context of profound economic crisis and state and paramilitary persecution of an increasingly activist Catholic church, "the apocalyptic religion offered by the protestants—a gospel of tears, shouting and speaking in tongues—was sustaining and seemingly appropriate for the times" (Annis 1987, 79). Such creeds have found fertile ground among Central America's poor. Many Central American immigrants in Belize are heavily involved in charismatic Protestant sects. Three separate and often squabbling evangelical churches vie for the loyalties of Protestants in Cowpen, whereas the organized Catholic presence is limited to twice monthly visits by a North American priest based in Dangriga. Pentacostalist groups have been the most prominent and vocal of these sects among banana workers and, according to farm managers, the most divisive as well. One grower noted:

> I find the [workers] that give problems are the religious ones. They instigate the others a lot. The good workers like their beer and rum on Saturdays. I don't mind if they get drunk on their own, as long as you're at work Monday to Friday and sober. The religious ones start to give them hell, and then they take it into the fields, and the supervisor has to get involved. On one farm I was managing they had one group, and then another evangelist come in and form a second group, and the two groups started to quarrel. Oh man, big problems. So first thing I ask a new worker, "Do you drink?" If he tells me no and starts talking his religion to me, I might not hire him.

With their ranks divided by ethnicity, language, phenotype, nationality, gender, and faith, the region's banana workers can collectively summon little systematic resistance to the conditions of their employment. What resistance they offer is of a surreptitious and individualized variety, albeit costly in the long run for many employers. In the ten years after the breaking of the UGWU in the banana industry in 1985, only one attempted strike has involved the participation of an entire farm work force. Significantly, this strike occurred on Farm 2 at Cowpen, which employs a greater number of Hondurans than any other banana farm in the country. Employers have often preferred to hire Hondurans over other workers since the first immigrant labor was imported from that country in 1982. This is largely because of the extensive experience many Hondurans have in banana work. Yet many employers also recognize that this recruitment strategy is a risky one from the vantage point of labor control. Banana workers in Honduras, unlike their contemporary counterparts in Belize, are unionized and have a long history of militant confrontations with United Fruit and the other banana companies operating in that country (MacCameron 1983; Argueta 1992). Workers bring such experiences with them to Belize, but there their militancy is diffused by the multinational and multiethnic composition of the work force. Indeed, many growers acknowledge that they would not allow any single nationality, above all Hondurans, to comprise a majority of their workers. On Farm 2 at the time of the 1992 strike, some 63 percent of the field laborers were Honduran immigrants, compared to just over 26 percent on the region's farms as a whole.

In December of every year, recently arrived Honduran workers invariably approach their employers to request Christmas bonuses. Following years of agitation, banana workers in Honduras won such benefits not through the strike weapon but by mandate from the Honduran national assembly. By law, Honduran banana farms are required to provide a "thirteenth month" payment in December equivalent to a full month's earnings. Many Honduran workers assume that similar practices are followed in the Belizean banana industry, and are understandably upset to learn that neither law nor custom requires the payment of bonuses in Belize.[7] In December 1992 the new owner of Farm 4 in Cowpen was besieged by requests for bonuses by a group of recently hired Honduran employees. Warned by a captain that a good deal of sabotage might result if he completely ignored the requests, the owner told the farm's management to provide cash advances at Christmas. Alfred Winston laughed as he recalled the events leading up to the strike: "It just so happen that Farm 4 they played a trick on the workers. They give the workers ninety dollars each just before Christmas. Now that ninety dollars is an advance on their vacation, but they never know that right away. See, they only find out it's an advance one at a time when they come up for vacation, and that's long after Christmas. Before Christmas, they all thought they got a bonus. When word reach Farm 2 with all those Honduraneans, they said, we want a bonus, too. That's how the strike happen."

The strike on Farm 2, when it came, was of less than one day's duration. Yet it was unprecedented in the seven years since the industry's privatization, as it involved the participation of all of the farm's 154 field laborers, regardless of their nationality and ethnicity. Alarmed by the news of the work stoppage, the farm's owner (a monolingual Jamaican) asked the chairman of the Banana Grower's Association to speak to the workers and encourage them to return to the fields. The farm owner announced his willingness to match the offer of Farm 4, omitting, of course, that this offer entailed an advance rather than a bonus, as the workers had thought. By the time a vehicle arrived with the added payroll late on the afternoon of the strike, the BGA chairman had reassured the strikers of management's willingness to match payments with Farm 4. Hearing what appeared to be the owner's capitulation, most of the workers were already on their way back to the fields. Not until March of the following year, when workers began planning to return home for Easter, did it become general knowledge among workers on Farms 4 and 2 that they had been paid advances on their two-week annual vacations rather than Christmas bonuses. Renewed calls for a strike might have been expected as a result, but the time that had elapsed since the subterfuge enabled the management of both farms to call upon their networks of informers. Workers who had led the demand for bonuses were quietly identified, and then terminated long before knowledge of the deception had spread throughout the work force. In addition to removing a potential leadership of future strikes, the terminations served notice to other workers of the consequences of overt resistance.

The ease with which management defeated the Farm 2 strike suggests that the antecedent experiences of workers offer little match against the industry's determination to remain free of unions. That the strikers were defeated through deception, and the consequences of the deception contained through persecution of strike leaders, suggests that collective resistance will elicit whatever management response is needed to crush it. Given the state's preference for low-wage development strategies based on export agriculture, as well as the overwhelmingly immigrant composition of the industry's work force, outside intervention to secure workers' rights within the industry is a remote prospect at best. Indeed, as will be seen in the epilogue to this book, which deals with a union organizing drive in summer 1995, state power is far more likely to be exercised on behalf of management than labor. Short of a regionwide general strike, a practical impossibility given the distance and lack of communication between farms, banana workers stand little chance of collectively improving the conditions of their employment. Divided among themselves and lacking allies in other industries or within the state, banana workers are forced to sublimate their resistance. The tragedy of this psychic repression is not the occasional anonymous destruction of farm equipment or crops, but the violence turned toward oneself and outwardly toward other workers. Internalizing the despair under which they live and work, many immigrant workers become brutalized agents of their own destruction.

# 7 ❧ Transnational Identities
and Trajectories in the Banana Belt

Contemporary Belizean discourse on ethnicity leads inevitably to the effects of immigration on national culture. Given the magnitude of the Hispanic influx since 1980, and Afro-Belizeans' historically grounded fears of minority status, it is only fair to note that Belizeans are probably less xenophobic than most nationalities. For many natives of Belize, however, immigration provides a ready explanation for any untoward social change, ranging from a rising incidence of malaria to spiraling real estate prices. Foreigners regardless of ethnicity and provenance are subsumed under the unsavory connotations of the term *alien*. This label encompasses investors from Hong Kong who speculate in desirable residential lots around Belize City, North American tourists who dabble in marijuana smuggling, and, above all, Hispanic Central Americans who are alleged to be at the root of the country's escalating drug trade and violence. When finer distinctions among foreigners are merited (at least in polite company), the latter are referred to simply as Central American aliens.

In order to define the faceless migrants who figure so prominently in policy and scholarly debates on immigration and ethnicity, I analyzed survey data collected from a systematic random sample of households at Cowpen and two smaller farms to the south, as well as work-force surveys completed on twenty-two of the country's twenty-three commercial banana farms (see the appendix). The survey entailed structured interviews with the heads of 157 households, encompassing a total of 576 rural residents. Among those heads of household interviewed, 56 (35.7 percent) were of Guatemalan origin, 51 (32.5 percent) were originally from Honduras, and 41 (26.1 percent) were from El Salvador. Only 9 households (5.7 percent) were headed by native Belizeans, attesting to the overwhelmingly immigrant character of banana worker settlements.

Survey data reveal an immigrant population so varied by nationality, ethnicity, experience, and ideology as to defy most facile claims regarding the background or propensity of "aliens." All immigrants in one way or another have been displaced to Belize by the economic and political crises of their homelands. Yet data from the banana belt indicate that the region's work force is in many ways distinct from the residents of the few immigrant communities elsewhere in the country that have been extensively studied previously, such as refugee settlements on the rural fringes of Belmopan (Stone 1990a, 1990b). Notwithstanding their differences, immigrant communities in Belize highlight the distinctive character of contemporary immigration and the dilemmas of identity that it poses for emerging nation-states.

## Transnationalism and Immigration Policy

Reflecting the unprecedented magnitude, character, and consequences of contemporary immigration, the concept of transnationalism now dominates scholarly discourse on international population movements. Transnationalism refers to "the processes by which immigrants forge and sustain multistranded social relations that link together their societies of origin and settlement" (Basch, Glick-Schiller, and Blanc-Szanton 1994, 7). Whereas previous studies suggested that immigrants permanently broke with their natal societies or returned home after short-term migratory labor abroad, recent research suggests that many immigrants instead have "their feet in two societies" (Chaney 1979, 209). These "transmigrants" are "a new kind of migrating population . . . whose networks, activities and patterns of life encompass both their host and home societies" (Glick-Schiller, Basch, and Blanc-Szanton 1992, 1). Many of those who permanently settle abroad, for example, retain close economic, cultural, and political ties to their communities of origin. Transmigrants usually support family members and community organizations in their homeland through remittances, and may return there for periods ranging from brief vacations to more protracted periods of work or eventual retirement.

Political economists attribute the transnational character of contemporary population movements to the accelerating globalization of capital and labor in the late twentieth century (Lash and Urry 1987; Harvey 1989). Rural Central America has been incorporated into world commodity markets for centuries, but patterns of land use throughout the region have been radically transformed in recent decades by capital-intensive varieties of export agriculture. As traditional export crops have been supplanted by large-scale cotton and beef production, the demand for agricultural labor in all countries of the region has sharply declined. Rendered suddenly redundant by mechanization and the conversion of farmland to pasture, much of the region's rural population has witnessed plummeting living standards since the 1970s (see, for example, Brockett 1990, 67ff.). Nor have urban working classes been spared the effects of globalization, for national industries have been devastated by neoliberal economic policies that prescribe the dismantling of tariff barriers and other "impediments" to the mobility of foreign capital (Nash 1994, 12). In El Salvador, Nicaragua, Guatemala, and Honduras, the internationalization of agriculture has amplified already inequitable land tenures, fueling in turn the insurrections and repression that drove much of the region's population into exile in succeeding decades (Williams 1986).

Displaced from their homelands by often horrific events, Central American refugees have become "deterritorialized groups" for whom "the homeland is partly invented" (Appadurai 1991, 193). In reconstituting elements of their natal communities in their countries of settlement, both refugees and economic migrants subvert traditional conceptions of nationality that equated bounded territories with national identities. By maintaining distinct sets of allegiances across borders, they are involved in the nation-building processes of more than one state—often unwillingly, as their presence becomes a rallying point for nativists who assert older equations of nation with race and language. Such are the transnational processes that underlie the growing Latinization of Belize, and all the attendant debates on its contested racial, linguistic, and national identity as a Commonwealth country in Central America.

Much recent scholarship on immigration documents transnational processes in remittance flows and circular migration across borders (Rubenstein 1983; Gonzalez 1988; Gmelch 1992); less often examined are the determinants of migration strategies among individual workers. Some transnational migrants eventually return to live in their homelands, but many more will permanently settle in their adopted countries. The determinants of migrant trajectories are of acute interest to immigration theory and policy, above all with respect to displaced Central Americans. Immigration policy makers in the United States, for example, have assumed that the flow of migrants from the region will lessen in the years to come. The government of El Salvador and the opposition FMLN reached a reconciliation accord in 1992 that, despite some violations, has since reduced violence in that nation. In the wake of this agreement and the gradual subsidence of civil war in Guatemala, some have predicted a large-scale return of displaced persons to the region (Chavez 1994, 57). Belizean policy makers also expect that the troubling question of national identity will simply revert to the *status quo ante* with a voluntary exodus of thousands of Central American immigrants to their countries of origin.

Contrary to such expectations, research among Central Americans living in the United States suggests that peace has come too late to alter the decisions of many migrants, even those with undocumented status (Chavez 1994). However much political conditions may have forced them to leave their homelands, many immigrants have no intention of returning, regardless of diminished civil conflict. Similar sentiments may be discerned among Central Americans residing in Belize. By the end of 1993, only 260 refugees out of more than 9,000 registered nationally had chosen to return home, indicating that most wish to remain in the country permanently. Even if many of those who return no longer need fear for their physical safety, prospects for employment or land remain bleak at best in much of Guatemala and El Salvador. Indeed, nearly 35 percent of the banana workers from the latter country first arrived in Belize *after* the cessation of guerrilla war and counterinsurgency in 1992. This implies, as do theories of the globalization of capital and labor, that political refugees and economic migrants were displaced by differing manifestations of the same process. It also suggests, much as many Afro-Belizeans fear, that the racial and cultural transformation of their country is probably irreversible.

## Origins and Immigration Status of Banana Workers

Drawn to Cowpen and other farms by the industry's voracious appetite for labor, immigrant workers create enclaves that bear few of the marks of natural communities. The peculiar character of such settlements is at once apparent from their skewed demography, distinguished from other communities (including those of immigrants elsewhere in the country) by a disproportionate number of single young men. The contrast between surveyed banana workers and those immigrants that Stone (1990a, 1990b) surveyed in the vicinity of Belmopan aptly illustrates the diversity of immigrant experiences. The average age of household heads in the banana worker survey (36.9 years) is not substantially lower than that of other immigrant settlements, where the reported average is 39 years (Stone 1990b, 3). Yet the much lower average number of children in banana worker households (1.9 compared to 4.1 at the Valley of Peace[1] in Cayo District) indicates a relatively small proportion of nuclear family households among farm workers. Among all immigrants surveyed, the number of adult males aged 18 and above considerably exceeds the number of adult women residing on banana farms (fig. 8). For the household survey as a whole, the adult male to female ratio ranges from 2.3 among Hondurans to 2.5 among Guatemalans and 2.9 for Salvadorans.

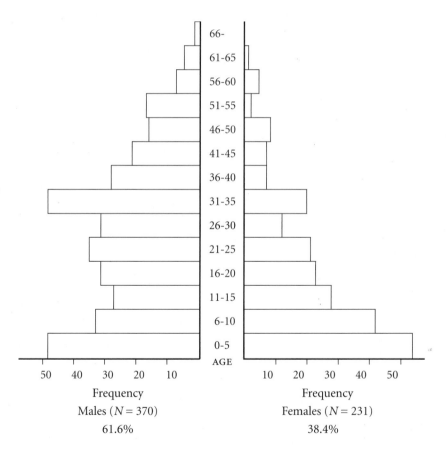

Fig. 8. Sex and age distribution for members of immigrant households in banana enclaves.

In Cowpen, the substantial number of households headed by co-resident men and women (74 out of 127 total households) as well as 11 female-headed households attest to somewhat lower (albeit still substantial) sex ratio imbalances. Elsewhere, however, single men predominate, especially on more remote and smaller farms, where few or no amenities exist. Only a handful of women and children reside on the two farms located at an isolated, highly malarious site on the Bladen River, twenty-five miles south of Mango Creek. On one of these farms adult men outnumber resident women by nearly six to one. In such places, where workers' recreational outlets are literally limited to drinking and the occasional brawl following payday, frustration and violence reach endemic levels, exceeding even those reported in Cowpen. This lack of demographic balance on banana farms, as well as the transience of many of their workers, also robs such settlements of much of the cohesion recorded in some immigrant communities. More than 53 percent of the residents at the Valley of Peace were involved in some community development organization relating to agriculture, health, or women's issues (Stone 1990b, 5). Comparable groups, as noted in chapter 5, are nearly nonexistent among the residents of Cowpen and other banana farms.

Immigrants arrive in Belize under a wide array of circumstances, ranging from harrowing flights from army patrols to the pursuit of hard currency en route to the United States. From these antecedent motives, policy makers distill a simple distinction between political refugees and economic migrants. Many refugee-aid officials reject the validity of this division, noting that the effects of civil war in neighboring countries include not only political persecution but also landlessness, recession, and unemployment. As a Canadian UN official noted in frustration, "Economic migrants are denied rights and can be sent back, while refugees are free to stay. But what difference is there between starving to death and being killed by a death squad?" However arbitrary in origin, the distinction between refugees and economic migrants is important in practice. Economic migrants enjoy little of the residential security of refugees or naturalized citizens, and in turn must tolerate working conditions that more secure immigrants might not.

Both formal refugee resettlement projects, such as the Valley of Peace, and the spontaneous settlements that have formed around Belmopan, are comprised almost exclusively of Salvadoran and Guatemalan immigrants who have applied for or received formal refugee status. Of 211 immigrant heads of household surveyed at the Valley of Peace in 1990, 87.7 percent identified civil conflict or political oppression as their primary reason for emigrating to Belize, and only 7.1 percent listed economic reasons for migration (Stone 1990b). The large number of Hondurans in the banana work force, virtually none of whom satisfy official criteria for refugee status, is one indication of the distinctive character of the immigrant communities in the banana belt. So are the reasons mentioned by banana workers for emigration from their home-lands. Residents of Cowpen and other farms often indicate that the decision to emigrate was a complex one, entailing both a hope for improved economic opportunities and social peace. Yet when asked their primary reason for com-ing to Belize, most Central American immigrants other than Salvadorans specify economic conditions. Among all three nationalities these economic motivations include a lack of employment, inadequate prevailing wages, or a lack of available land at home (table 8). Farm residents also mentioned as a reason for migration their effort to seek "a better life," which seemed to en-compass a desire for both better economic conditions and social peace.

If a minority of immigrant banana workers fled to Belize because of overt political persecution, even fewer have been granted refugee status. Only ten (6.8 percent) of the immigrants surveyed were officially classified as refugees, and the majority (52 percent) were instead residing in Belize on temporary work permits. Notwithstanding Labor Department requirements that immi-grant workers hold annual work permits, another 34.5 percent of those sur-veyed acknowledged that they had obtained no such documentation or held expired permits. Hence, a substantial minority of banana workers are in effect illegal immigrants. As expected, Salvadorans predominate among docu-mented refugees (seven out of forty-one, or 17.1 percent of all surveyed Salva-

Table 8. Banana Workers' Primary Reason for Emigration to Belize, by Nationality
(N = 148)

| Reason | Hondurans | Guatemalans | Salvadorans | Total |
|---|---|---|---|---|
| Economic conditions | 48 (94.1%) | 42 (75.0%) | 20 (48.8%) | 110 (74.3%) |
| Political conditions | 3 (5.9%) | 14 (25.0%) | 21 (51.2%) | 38 (25.7%) |
| TOTAL | 51 (100.0%) | 56 (100.0%) | 41 (100.0%) | |

Note: Chi-square = 24.5, significant at p <. 0002 with 2 df.

dorans are so classified). Yet even among Salvadorans, a much greater number (sixteen, or 39 percent) are working illegally in the country. Reflecting their longer residence in the country, Hondurans are more likely to both hold work permits and be naturalized Belizean citizens (table 9).

Although the places of origin of immigrant banana workers (table 10) often differ from those recorded among immigrants elsewhere in Belize, they closely reflect ongoing processes of agro-export development and population displacement from the neighboring countries. Very few Hondurans reside around Belmopan, for example, yet Honduran immigrants comprise nearly a third of the banana work force. Since 1982, there has been a continuing flow of labor from the Honduran banana industry to its Belizean counterpart. More than 59 percent of Honduran immigrants come from the departments of Atlantida, Yoro, and Cortés, which make up the primary banana-producing regions of that country. Some 22 percent of Hondurans reported employment as banana workers prior to entering Belize, and another 60 percent mentioned "agriculture" as their previous employment. A similar circulation of labor has also developed between Guatemalan plantations and those in Belize. Unlike the Guatemalans residing around Belmopan, an overwhelming number of whom originated in El Petén, less than 4 percent of the surveyed Guatemalan banana workers came from that department. The difference in migrant origins may account for the large numbers of Guatemalan refugees around Belmopan, for El Petén was a site of intense armed conflict during much of the 1980s (Stone 1990a, 100). In the banana belt, 52 percent of all

Table 9. Banana Workers' Immigration Status, by Nationality
(N = 143)

| Status | Hondurans | Guatemalans | Salvadorans | Total |
|---|---|---|---|---|
| Refugee | 0 | 3 (5.6%) | 7 (17.1%) | 10 (6.9%) |
| Work permit | 31 (64.5%) | 28 (51.9%) | 18 (43.9%) | 77 (53.8%) |
| Illegal | 14 (29.1%) | 21 (38.9%) | 16 (39.0%) | 51 (35.6%) |
| Naturalized citizen | 3 (6.3%) | 2 (3.7%) | 0 | 5 (3.5%) |
| TOTAL | 48 (99.9%) | 54 (100.1%) | 41 (100.0%) | |

Note: Number missing or no response = 5. Due to rounding, some columns do not add up to 100%.

Guatemalan workers originated in five departments (Zacapa, Jutiapa, Escuintla, Chiquimula, and El Progreso). Since the 1960s, all of these regions have witnessed rapid growth in agro-export production, primarily of cattle, with an attendant displacement of subsistence farmers (Williams 1986, 134ff.). The largest single source of Guatemalan banana workers is the adjacent department of Izabal, center of Guatemala's banana industry. Not surprisingly, some 17 percent of the Guatemalan immigrants reported employment on banana farms prior to entering Belize.

The expulsion of labor from banana-producing regions of Guatemala and Honduras reflects an ongoing reorganization of the banana industries throughout the Americas. This, in turn, follows from the decisions of multinational banana exporters to rid themselves of some immovable assets, such as land and packing facilities, and adopt more flexible operations. Chiquita and its former subsidiary, Fyffes, increasingly purchase their fruit from private suppliers who assume all risks of production (Davies 1990, 234). Although exports from Guatemala and Honduras have remained stable in recent decades, the sale of some corporate holdings to private growers and technological changes have reduced the banana work force in both countries (Ruhl 1983, 126). This accounts for much of the emigration of banana workers to Belize, where in contrast to surrounding countries, farms are still in a state of expansion and are increasing their use of labor.

Where Salvadorans' motivations for migration are concerned, it bears mention that radio broadcasts in El Salvador have long promoted Belize as a country of peace and plentiful land. Although such broadcasts are unattributed, Stone (1990a, 98) speculates that they may originate with a Salvadoran government agency. Much as they regarded Honduras prior to the Soccer War, Salvadoran military and political leaders have long considered Belize to be a potential agricultural frontier and "safety valve" for peasants displaced by its authoritarian model of development. In 1971, the Salvadoran and Guatemalan militaries reportedly planned a joint invasion of Belize for the following year, to be followed by the resettlement of one hundred thousand Salvadoran peasant families in Belize. Detected by British and U.S. intelligence and apparently deterred by the dispatch of three thousand British troops to Belize, invasion plans were rescinded (at least by the Salvadoran army). But broadcasts encouraging emigration to Belize may be having a effect not unlike that of the planned invasion (ibid.).

The origins of Salvadoran workers in the banana industry more closely

Table 10. Immigrant Banana Workers' Places of Origin
(N = 148)

| Department | Frequency | Percentage of Total |
|---|---|---|
| | Hondurans | |
| Yoro | 16 | 31.4 |
| Atlantida | 11 | 21.6 |
| Cortés | 7 | 13.8 |
| Valle | 4 | 7.8 |
| La Libertad | 3 | 5.9 |
| Copán | 2 | 3.9 |
| Lima | 2 | 3.9 |
| Santa Barbara | 2 | 3.9 |
| Lempira | 1 | 1.9 |
| Guatemala | 2 | 3.9 |
| El Salvador | 1 | 1.9 |
| TOTAL | 51 | 99.9 |
| | Guatemalans | |
| Izabal | 22 | 39.3 |
| Zacapa | 10 | 17.9 |
| Jutiapa | 8 | 14.2 |
| Escuintla | 6 | 10.8 |
| Chiquimula | 3 | 5.4 |
| El Progreso | 2 | 3.6 |
| Alta Verapaz | 2 | 3.6 |
| El Petén | 2 | 3.6 |
| Baja Verapaz | 1 | 1.7 |
| TOTAL | 56 | 100.1 |
| | Salvadorans | |
| La Libertad | 10 | 24.4 |
| Chalatenango | 8 | 19.5 |
| Sonsonate | 6 | 14.6 |
| Cabañas | 5 | 12.3 |
| San Salvador | 3 | 7.3 |
| Santa Ana | 3 | 7.3 |
| La Union | 3 | 7.3 |
| Metapan | 1 | 2.4 |
| San Miguel | 1 | 2.4 |
| Usulután | 1 | 2.4 |
| TOTAL | 41 | 99.9 |

Note: Due to rounding, totals do not add up to 100%.

resemble those of Salvadoran immigrants elsewhere in the country. Some 74 percent of Salvadoran household heads on the Belmopan periphery originated in five war-ravaged departments of that country (Cabañas, Chalatenango, La Libertad, San Salvador, and Santa Ana) (ibid., 131), and the same departments were places of origin for 71 percent of Salvadoran banana workers. Yet Salvadorans' stated motives for coming to Belize are also rapidly changing. The reasons for migration offered by recent arrivals indicate that economic hardship, an aftermath of the country's civil war, has supplanted persecution as a motive for emigration. Nearly 35 percent of the Salvadoran banana workers surveyed had arrived in Belize since 1992, by which time rural violence had lessened substantially. As the peace accords did not alter El Salvador's notoriously inequitable land distribution, however, large numbers of displaced peasants continue to leave the country in search of livelihoods elsewhere. More than 69 percent of Salvadoran banana workers arriving in Belize prior to 1992 specified political conditions as their primary motive for emigration, a reason given by just 31 percent of the arrivals since then.[2]

Because most immigrant banana workers originate in the largely Mestizo lowlands, they exhibit less ethnic diversity than their nations as a whole. Some 97.6 percent of Salvadorans and all of the surveyed Hondurans reported their home language as Spanish. The large majority of these Salvadoran and Honduran workers identified themselves ethnically as Mestizo or by equivalent terms (*ladino* or *español*). Three individuals among the forty-one Salvadoran workers identified themselves as Maya, and just one Maya and one Garifuna were identified among the fifty-one Hondurans. Guatemalan workers exhibit somewhat more ethnic diversity, although the Mestizo component of this immigrant group (78.6 percent) remains considerably greater than the proportion of Mestizos in Guatemala's national population, which is estimated at 56 percent (Goodwin 1992, 31). Nine Guatemalan workers reported their ethnic group membership as Maya and three as Kekchi. Their evident fluency in Spanish, and the fact that all but three of these workers reported Spanish as their home language, indicate a high degree of acculturation among indigenous Guatemalans in the banana work force. Although the large majority of Guatemalan workers are either Mestizo or conform to Mestizo linguistic norms, members of other immigrant nationalities emphasize and exaggerate Indian ethnicity in their descriptions of Guatemalans. Hondurans and Salvadorans occasionally refer disparagingly to all Guatemalans as *indios* or claim that as a nationality they are *atrasado* (backwards), ostensibly due to their Mayan and Hispanic admixture. That such attitudes are directed even toward *ladino* Guatemalans, who at home often view the Maya as an inferior race (Brintnall 1979), must be galling to them, however poetically just.

If the immigrant work force is fairly homogeneous by ethnicity and language, there are nonetheless intense ideological divisions that cross-cut those of nationality. Most apparent are religious differences, for substantial numbers of immigrants report affiliations with evangelical Protestant sects. Of all immigrant workers surveyed, 84.5 percent reported some religious affiliation, and of these 57.3 percent identified themselves as Catholic. Three evangelical churches active in the region (Assembly of God [Pentecostalists], Nazarenes, and Baptists) claimed the loyalty of the remaining 42.7 percent of immigrants stating a religious affiliation. Among Salvadorans, workers with evangelical affiliations even exceeded Catholics (45.7 percent versus 40 percent). Such figures are substantially higher than the 17.3 percent Protestant population recorded among immigrants at the Valley of Peace (Stone 1990b, 5). To an extent, these data reflect a strengthening missionization effort throughout Central America (including southern Belize) by North American evangelical churches, but they also indicate the comparative absence of an institutionalized Catholic presence in immigrant enclaves. Evangelical churches are deeply entrenched at Cowpen and Mango Creek, where local residents act as preachers during services. In contrast, a Catholic Mass is celebrated in the village only at twice monthly intervals by an American priest based in Dangriga. Many residents of the village, then, may have gravitated to evangelical sects simply by default. A more likely reason for the participation of many workers in such groups, however, is that intensely charismatic faiths have historically appealed to the impoverished and oppressed, as has been noted in other Central American contexts (Annis 1987). Undoubtedly, their appeal extends as well to immigrants living in the banana belt. By the same token, the absence of nonreligious community organizations in Cowpen may further the polarizing effects of intense religious loyalties.

Other ideological divisions among immigrants contribute to an occasionally palpable undercurrent of distrust in banana worker enclaves. Among those Salvadorans and Guatemalans surveyed in the banana belt who left their countries for political reasons, a large majority (84.4 percent) indicated they had done so to flee governmental or paramilitary violence. A smaller but not insignificant number, however, (15.6 percent) reported intimidation at the hands of antigovernment guerrillas, or Communists, as some labeled them. One of these respondents is the pastor of a local evangelical church, highlighting the politically conservative orientation of such sects. To an extent, then, the political divisions of rural Guatemala and El Salvador have been reproduced in banana worker communities in Belize. Of more immediate concern to many refugees is the fact that former members of the Guatemalan and Salvadoran security forces have infiltrated some refugee communities in Belize, apparently to monitor the movements of asylum seekers (Stone 1990a, 88). The fact that some refugees have been denounced as "subversives" to Belizean authorities, and that unexplained deaths and disappearances persist in immigrant communities, suggests that immigrants find at best a partial haven from political violence in Belize. Needless to say, such political divisions contribute to the further corrosion of class consciousness among banana workers.

## Transnationalism and Permanence in the Banana Belt

Debates about Central American immigration in Belize, as in the United States, entertain the possibility that immigrants will return home following the reduction of civil conflict in their native lands. Such claims overlook the fact that civil war is just one manifestation—albeit the most dramatic—of long-term political and economic transformations that have displaced much of the region's population. The cessation of hostilities has not altered these processes, as the continuing Central American influx into Belize attests. Regardless of nationality, the majority of immigrants wish to permanently settle in Belize. Yet as theories of transnational migration suggest, many of these "permanent" migrants have repeatedly visited home and continue to maintain economic and social networks that extend across national borders. Conversely, a still sizable number of immigrant banana workers (43 or 32 percent of the total) plan to resettle in their homelands some day. Salvadorans, who are most likely to have fled their country for political reasons, also most often plan to return home. As seen in tables 11 and 12, nationality and immigration status are associated with planned permanent resettlement. Whereas only about 26 percent of the banana workers holding work permits intend to resettle in their homelands, almost half of all undocumented workers plan to do so. This may account for the fact that on average banana workers with legal status have resided in Belize for a substantially longer period of time (mean = 6.3 years) than undocumented workers (mean = 3.5 years).

Immigration status and nationality are strongly associated with prior vis-

Table 11. Immigrants' Plans to Return Home, by Nationality
*(N = 136)*

| Plan | Hondurans | Guatemalans | Salvadorans | Total |
|------|-----------|-------------|-------------|-------|
| Will return home permanently | 10 (20.8%) | 17 (32.7%) | 17 (47.2%) | 44 (32.4%) |
| Will settle in Belize | 38 (79.2%) | 35 (67.3%) | 19 (52.8%) | 92 (67.6%) |
| TOTAL | 48 (100.0%) | 52 (100.0%) | 36 (100.0%) | |

*Note:* Number missing or no response = 12. Chi-square = 6.55, significant at p < .038 with 2 df.

Table 12. Immigrants' Plans to Return Home, by Immigration Status
*(N = 129)*

| Plan | Refugee | Work Permit | Undocumented | Total |
|------|---------|-------------|--------------|-------|
| Will return home permanently | 1 (16.7%) | 20 (26.3%) | 23 (48.9%) | 44 (34.1%) |
| Will settle in Belize | 5 (83.3%) | 56 (73.7%) | 24 (51.1%) | 85 (65.9%) |
| TOTAL | 6 (100.0%) | 76 (100.0%) | 47 (100.0%) | |

*Note:* Number missing or no response = 19. Chi-square = 9.94, significant at p < .01 with 2 df.

its home (tables 13 and 14). About 51 percent of surveyed banana workers had visited their country of origin at least once since coming to Belize. Although many Guatemalan and Salvadoran banana workers fled political violence in their homelands, about 64 percent and 37 percent of the workers from these countries, respectively, have returned home at some point. Some 63 percent of documented workers visited their countries of origin at least once since arriving in Belize, but only 38 percent of undocumented workers had done so. Given the difficulties they would face in attempting to reenter Belize after a visit home, it is not surprising that many undocumented workers refrain from leaving the country.

Immigrants who have returned to their homelands at least once since their arrival are also the most likely to want to settle in Belize permanently (table 15). These data suggest that workers who settle in Belize nonetheless retain a transnational orientation through repeat visits to their homelands. These migrants also evidence greater stability in their domestic circumstances and residential status in Belize. As seen in table 16, banana workers accompanied by wives or common-law partners are much more likely to plan to remain in Belize than the many single men who comprise much of the industry's work force. Workers who plan to remain in Belize average 39 years of age, whereas those who plan to return home permanently are younger (mean = 33.3 years; $|t|$ = 2.7, significant at $p < .0079$ with 102 df) and have fewer, if any, co-resident children ($|t|$ = 2.63, significant at $p < .01$ with 71.9 df). Indeed, immigrants who wish to remain in Belize often explain their decision in terms of their

Table 13. Immigrants' Visits Home since Coming to Belize, by Immigration Status
*(N = 140)*

| Number of Visits | Refugee | Work Permit | Undocumented | Total |
|---|---|---|---|---|
| One or more | 2 (20.0%) | 50 (62.5%) | 19 (38.0%) | 71 (50.7%) |
| None | 8 (80.0%) | 30 (37.5%) | 31 (62.0%) | 69 (49.3%) |
| TOTAL | 10 (100.0%) | 80 (100.0%) | 50 (100.0%) | |

*Note:* Number missing = 8. Chi-square = 31.16, significant at $p < .001$ with 2 df.

Table 14. Immigrants' Visits Home since Coming to Belize, by Nationality
*(N = 146)*

| Number of Visits | Hondurans | Guatemalans | Salvadorans | Total |
|---|---|---|---|---|
| One or more | 24 (48.0%) | 35 (63.6%) | 15 (36.6%) | 74 (50.7%) |
| None | 26 (52.0%) | 20 (36.4%) | 26 (63.4%) | 72 (49.3%) |
| TOTAL | 50 (100.0%) | 55 (100.0%) | 41 (100.0%) | |

*Note:* Number missing = 2. Chi-square = 7.09, significant at $p < .029$ with 2 df.

children's Belizean citizenship and the putative opportunities it offers them. Finally, the average length of residence in Belize is also significantly greater for those workers who plan to remain in the country permanently (mean = 6.9 years) than for those who plan to return home (mean = 2.5 years; |t| = 5.1, significant at p < .0001 with 134 df). Despite the radically different conditions encountered by immigrants in southern Belize and those in the United States, these findings are remarkably consistent with the predictors of permanent residence among Central Americans in the United States, as recently reported by Chavez (1994).

Banana workers who plan to return home typically come to Belize on a temporary basis to save money, and often plan to remain in the country for no more than a year or two. In contrast to Guatemalan immigrants on the Belmopan periphery, 39 percent of whom had arrived in Belize prior to 1980 (Stone 1990a, 99), only 9 percent of surveyed Guatemalans in the banana belt had resided in Belize that long. On average, immigrant workers of all three nationalities have resided in Belize slightly more than five years, and have worked at their present farm for twenty-five months. Averages tend to be misleading, however, for employment and residence data are highly unevenly distributed, as indicated in the histogram of arrival dates by nationality (fig. 9). One-half of the workers surveyed have been employed at their present farm seven months or less and fully one-quarter for one month or less.

Employment on banana farms is not seasonal, but these work histories suggest that most workers are nonetheless highly transitory, shifting from farm to farm or even returning to their countries of origin as the occasion and resources permit. It is not surprising, then, that banana workers exhibit so little of the sense of community identity and attachment to Belize that has been documented in the more stable and demographically balanced refugee communities around Belmopan (Stone 1990a, 1990b). Such data suggest that, official reassurances to the contrary, there is little prospect that immigrant workers in the banana industry will become more fully integrated into Belizean society in the future. Some 32 percent of immigrant banana workers never attended school, and fully half have two years or less of completed education. Because the vast majority of workers speak only Spanish, few are able to defend their rights in the workplace or even to learn what those rights are. A more troubling possibility is suggested by the low levels of attendance at the Cowpen school (see chapter 5). Having been born in Belize, children in immigrant households are nominally Belizean citizens, but in the absence of lit-

Table 15. Cross-Tabulation of Immigrants' Past Visits Home and Plans to Return Home
(N = 135)

| | Visits Home | | |
|---|---|---|---|
| Plan | One or More | None | Total |
| Will return home permanently | 16 (22.9%) | 27 (41.5%) | 43 (31.8%) |
| Will settle in Belize | 54 (77.1%) | 38 (58.5%) | 92 (68.1%) |
| TOTAL | 70 (100.0%) | 65 (100.0%) | |

*Note:* Number missing = 13. Chi-square = 5.4, significant at p < .02 and 1 df. Phi coefficient = -.20.

Table 16. Cross-Tabulation of Male Workers' Marital Status and Plans to Return Home
(N = 126)

| | Marital Status | | |
|---|---|---|---|
| Plan | Single or Non-Resident Spouse | Coresident Spouse | Total |
| Will return home permanently | 25 (47.2%) | 18 (24.7%) | 43 (34.1%) |
| Will settle in Belize | 28 (52.8%) | 55 (75.3%) | 83 (65.9%) |
| TOTAL | 53 (100.0%) | 73 (100.0%) | |

*Note:* Number missing = 22. Chi-square = 6.9, significant at p < .009 and 1 df.

eracy and English fluency, many will be ill equipped to claim the rights that accompany citizenship. Nor will such rights be automatically extended to those of Belizean birth, for, according to the Belizean solicitor general, "the law will not come to the aid" of children born in Belize whose parents are there illegally (Stone 1990a, 115).

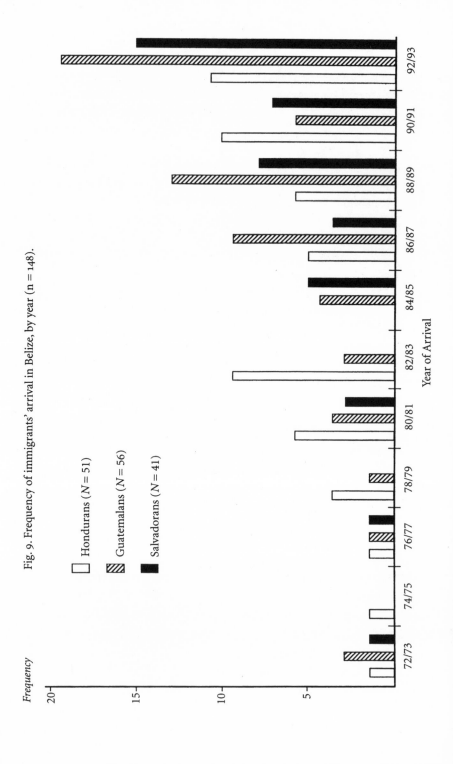

Fig. 9. Frequency of immigrants' arrival in Belize, by year (n = 148).

## Immigrant Networks

For many immigrants, the mere fact of arrival in an English-speaking and occasionally hostile land is a daunting prospect. All the more formidable is the task of regularizing one's immigration status (or alternately eluding authorities), avoiding potentially predatory employers or fellow immigrants, and obtaining work. Like immigrants everywhere, those who have recently arrived in Belize usually turn to their more established counterparts for information and advice. Employers as well as prospective workers are aware of such ties, and farm managers regularly ask their workers to help them recruit new arrivals as farm workers. Along immigrant networks is passed information about employers' reputations and the location of farms, so that many immigrants have in mind fairly precise destinations in the banana belt even before arriving in Belize. Yet significant differences also exist in the extent to which immigrants of different nationalities call upon established networks of fellow nationals to help them adapt to life in Belize.

Although a majority (60.3 percent) of all surveyed banana workers report that they found out about their jobs through their own efforts, substantial differences exist between nationalities in their ability to obtain assistance in finding work. Whereas 45.1 percent of Guatemalan farm workers and 48.1 percent of Honduran immigrants obtained help from others in locating a job, only 21.9 percent of Salvadorans did so. Further, the source of such information differs significantly between Guatemalans and Hondurans on the one hand and Salvadorans on the other. Salvadorans who learn of work from others more often do so from employers themselves rather than from compatriots or family members, as is the case for other Central Americans (table 17). The implication of these findings is that information networks among Salvadoran immigrants are comparatively truncated, placing Salvadorans at a disadvantage in access to knowledge about jobs and working conditions on the region's farms. It may be for this reason that the Danish-owned Tropical Produce operation at Monkey River, which is widely regarded as the country's most abusive farm with respect to working conditions and pay, employs a disproportionate number of immigrants from El Salvador.[3] Some 67.8 percent of that farm's labor force is from El Salvador, compared to a total industry work force that is only 20.6 percent Salvadoran.

These characteristics of Salvadoran workers can be accounted for by their origins and time of arrival in Belize. Salvadoran workers in general are much more recent migrants than are Honduran or Guatemalan banana workers.

Table 17. Immigrants' Sources of Information about Their Banana Industry Jobs
*(N = 146)*

| Source | Hondurans | Guatemalans | Salvadorans |
|---|---|---|---|
| Friend | 14 (27.4%) | 12 (22.2%) | 3 (7.3%) |
| Relative | 0 | 4 (7.4%) | 0 |
| Captain or employer | 9 (17.6%) | 10 (18.5%) | 6 (14.6%) |
| Own efforts | 28 (54.9%) | 28 (51.8%) | 32 (78.1%) |
| TOTAL | 51 (99.9%) | 54 (99.9%) | 41 (100.0%) |

*Note:* Number missing = 2. Due to rounding, some columns do not add up to 100%.

The average period of time that surveyed Salvadorans have been in the country is slightly more than four years, compared to nearly six years for the other nationalities. As mentioned earlier, more than a third of all Salvadorans had resided in Belize a year or less at the time of the survey. Accordingly, Salvadorans are in many instances less informed about working conditions on the region's farms than are members of other nationalities. Compounding this lack of knowledge is a lack of contact between Salvadoran immigrants in Belize and prospective emigrants in El Salvador. Although, as mentioned earlier, some Salvadorans return home on temporary visits after arriving in Belize, those who do so are significantly fewer in number than the other nationalities (see table 14). Hence, it is probable that comparatively little information about working and living conditions in Belize is disseminated from Salvadoran immigrants in the banana belt to prospective emigrants in El Salvador itself. Probably because many are unaware of alternatives following their arrival in Belize, Salvadorans are often treated more harshly by employers than are other immigrants, or are slower to leave especially abusive workplaces.

Survey data on employees' earnings offer some evidence for discriminatory treatment of workers by nationality. On average, nonsupervisory Salvadoran banana workers included in the survey report earnings of $152 per *quincena,* compared to $170 for Guatemalans, $167 for Hondurans, and $187 for Belizeans.[4] Such disparities are not attributable to job classifications, prior experience, or the length of time spent at work each *quincena.* Workers belonging to all nationalities report average work weeks that vary only slightly (between 4.8 and 5.1 days), and Salvadorans and Hondurans report work weeks of nearly identical length. Although substantial differences exist between immigrants in their length of employment in the banana industry, except for the subsample of Guatemalan workers there is no measurable association between length of employment and reported earnings. Further, this association disappears when supervisory personnel are deleted from the sample. Finally, the magnitude of workers' earnings is not related to their prior employment experience, for, other than supervisors, immigrants formerly employed on banana farms in Honduras and Guatemala report no higher incomes than workers from nonagricultural backgrounds. For nonsupervisory personnel, then, income disparities appear to result from the disparate treatment of workers of different nationalities. As indicated in chapter 6, workers of all nationalities, as well as many growers, report that Salvadorans are less often represented among supervisors than Belizeans, Guatemalans, or Hondurans, and are typically assigned to less desirable and lower paying jobs. Lacking the cohesive ties with earlier immigrants reported by Honduran and Guatemalans, many Salvadorans lack as well the means to resist or escape the more abusive aspects of labor control in the banana belt. Further, they may be obliged by their greater desire to remain in Belize to accept working conditions and wages that others will not.

## Ancillary Economic Strategies

Working an average of 4.9 nine-hour shifts per week, banana workers have little time left over for other income-generating or subsistence activities. Farming for household use, which serves as a supplement to wages for low-paid workers throughout the Third World, is heavily constrained in the banana belt by both the lack of spare time and land available to farm workers. The symbiosis noted elsewhere between household and estate agriculture, in which domestic production is encouraged by commercial farms to subsidize low wages and maintain work forces during the off season (de Janvry 1981; Painter 1985), is here largely nonexistent. Demanding a full-time work force available throughout each week of the year, the managers of banana farms view their employees' part-time economic activities as rivals to the compulsions of wage labor. Their concerns are well founded, for the amount of land workers cultivate in their spare time correlates inversely with the number of days they work per week ($r = -.28$, $p = .006$). Lacking either the subsidy of household agriculture or the consumption capacity of higher wages, most workers on the region's banana farms are reluctant but necessarily full-time proletarians.

Banana workers' full-time commitment to wage labor is enforced by a variety of mechanisms at the disposal of employers, in addition to those of low earnings and routine underpayment. Although milpas in Belize are cut on otherwise unoccupied public or private lands, all four of the farms in Cowpen prohibit milpa farming on nearby unused lands under their control. Farm workers charge that the banana farms at Cowpen acquired such lands simply to deny them to would-be *milperos*, although the managers of the plantations claim that the lands are sites of intended farm expansion. Whatever its motive, the banana industry's monopolization of rich alluvial lands in the vicinity of Cowpen leaves little nearby arable land available to residents. As each of the four farms at Cowpen expands its area under cultivation, milpa farming on the periphery of the settlement is pushed farther into less accessible areas. Just 13.6 percent of the surveyed residents of Cowpen maintain milpas, their size averaging 3.5 acres. While most *milperos* cultivate staple crops (generally maize and beans) exclusively for household use, a few also report local sales of crops. Farther to the south, where the two farms at the Bladen River are situated in a vast unoccupied and largely unclaimed hinterland of primary forest, farm workers report somewhat more involvement in part-time agriculture. There, some 37 percent of all workers' households maintain milpas, which average 4.8 acres in area. Bladen Branch workers who keep milpas earn an average of $398 annually from the sale of crops, compared to $416 among Cowpen *milperos*. The slightly higher earnings from crop sales among the latter, despite the lower average area of their farms, probably relate to the lower incidence of milpa farming among Cowpen residents overall. Both the demand and price for produce are greater in Cowpen.

The availability of credit at local shops, which in most cases are operated by the farms themselves, creates as well a significant disincentive to the production of food for home use. A majority of banana workers purchase food with cash, a few traveling as far as Dangriga to patronize the more competitive shops in that town. Because Hispanic immigrants are frequently harassed or cheated by Garifuna and Creole residents in Dangriga (Kroshus Medina 1992b), however, it is little surprise that most immigrants opt for the higher prices but lessened intimidation of farm shops and stores in Mango Creek. A substantial number (38.1 percent) of surveyed workers report that they are indebted to farm commissaries or rural merchants. Further, these indebted workers tend to be in the lowest paid segments of the farm work force. Levels of indebtedness inversely correlate ($r = -.49$, $p = .002$) with reported earnings per *quincena*. Credit allows such workers to survive on the scanty returns of banana employment, but the high retail markups of farm-run shops leave workers with little purchasing power after their debts are cleared. Given the high level of illiteracy (and presumably innumeracy) among farm workers, merchants can easily augment their profits by subtly cheating their customers. Although workers often complain that merchants require them to pay more than they actually owe in debt, they usually have no way of proving their suspicions.

Banana workers are unique among the labor forces of export agriculture for their near total reliance on wages and store-bought food for survival. Of all workers employed full time in the banana industry, 71.2 percent engage in no other source of livelihood. On average, workers earn only about $241 per year from sources other than banana farm employment. By far the most common of these ancillary activities is maintaining a milpa, but this is reported by only 20.3 percent of all surveyed workers. Ten female heads of household (13.8 percent of surveyed banana workers) are employed in packing sheds on a part-time basis but supplement their wages by sewing, operating a *comedor*, baking bread for sale, washing clothes, or operating a shop. Only two male banana workers engage in cash-earning or subsistence activities other than milpa farming, one (a Belizean citizen) as a justice of the peace and the other as an evangelical minister. The lack of an off season in banana production creates few opportunities to engage in other work or subsistence activities that could supplement household nutritional needs. Indeed, what is striking about farm workers' diets is their monotony and expense even when compared with those of Belizeans at large, who have devised from a long history of reliance on imported canned and processed British foods one the most unvaried diets of any Central American nation.[5]

Solitary male workers often contract with local *comedores* for their meals at a cost of sixty to seventy dollars per *quincena*. Consuming a third or more of their earnings, these arrangements are out of the question for workers who support families. Such workers instead rely on the narrow range of staples and expensive, invariably imported canned foods, or cured pork parts (tails and snouts), available in local shops. Some surveyed workers (eighteen, or 11.4 percent of the total) report that they maintain chickens, and three (1.9

percent) keep pigs to supplement their diets and incomes. The fact that the remainder choose to purchase expensive fresh or cured meat at local shops may appear paradoxical, given the seemingly low costs of maintaining fowl. Yet many workers note that free-ranging fowl and even pigs may be surreptitiously stolen by other farm residents, and the costs of penning and feeding animals are prohibitive. Further, by 1994 managers of Cowpen Farm 2 began claiming that chickens and other livestock were destroying young banana plants, and they ordered farm security guards to shoot such animals on sight. Consequently, the keeping of livestock may appear to be a low-cost source of food but is simply seen as too risky by many farm residents.

Given the high cost of living in the banana belt, and on the region's farms in particular, many households must draw on the wages of several of their members in order to survive. Of all households containing more than one family member of employable age, 42.1 percent (48 out of 114 surveyed) have more than one member employed in the banana industry. In 25 of these households, adult women are employed on a part-time basis in packing-shed labor. Another 17 households contain male relatives (generally sons of the head of household) who are employed full time in farm labor. Finally, six households contain both part-time female workers and full-time male farm laborers. In many cases, such workers contribute substantially to household budgets. On average, those households containing multiple wage workers supplement their total incomes per *quincena* by $135, according to survey data on family members' earnings.

### Banana Enclaves and "Natural" Communities

To a large extent, the survey data presented in this chapter corroborate in quantitative terms the portrayals of banana worker enclaves offered in previous chapters. They also suggest why such settlements differ so strikingly from the more demographically balanced and stable immigrant communities elsewhere in the country. The rootlessness and anomie that pervade the lives of many immigrant workers become understandable when the demography and origins of such workers are examined. Having been expelled from other nations by agrarian transformations that robbed them of employment or the prospect of land ownership, thousands of single young men predominate in the banana work force. Their transitoriness, in part the result of abusive living and working conditions, and in part a response to insecure immigration status, does little to remedy the frustration and violence characterizing the banana worker enclaves at Cowpen or Bladen Branch.

Unlike most of their counterparts in other agricultural sectors, banana workers are fully proletarianized. Most work full time for wages throughout the year. Because the majority of banana workers lack the opportunities or access to land required for other subsistence activities, wages must fulfill all or most of their subsistence requirements. Yet the high costs of processed and imported foods purchased at local shops often exceed the buying power of their wages. As a result, they enjoy neither the relative security of full-time urban work forces (who usually have access to price-controlled staples [Moberg 1991b]) nor the fall-back activities that seasonal agricultural workers rely upon. Notwithstanding their full-time employment status, banana workers comprise, in the archaic if still relevant nineteenth-century usage, a lumpenproletariat whose survival is by no means assured by their full-time wages. In order to support themselves banana workers often rely on debt, illicit activities, and, finally, flight to other farms, regions, or countries. The elites who organize cocaine transshipment through southern Belize encounter any number of immigrant workers willing to endure the perils of loading the aircraft that periodically land near Cowpen.[6] It is widely believed, by both immigrants and Belizeans, that some Cowpen residents have completely forsaken banana industry employment for perilous but comparatively lucrative work in the drug trade. In addition to the dangerous work of loading aircraft, some immigrants are thought to cultivate marijuana on concealed plots in the foothills several miles east of the village. Although such rumors remain beyond confirmation, it is notable that the lightly armed police stationed in Mango Creek not only vigorously affirm the existence of such farms but adamantly refuse to enter the foothill region without more heavily armed military escorts.

Much as the rapid turnover and migration to other farms allow workers to escape, if temporarily, the abuses of employers and immigration authorities, so they permit workers to elude the consequences of their actions. As a result, the "mutuality" (Scott 1985, 261) of workers' experiences—the recognition of a common interest in resisting employers' domination—is undermined by the absence of enduring community among immigrant banana workers. Whether reflected in the theft of a chicken from another worker's household or the channeling of rage into an impromptu brawl, rootlessness fragments class consciousness as effectively as the most divisive ideologies of ethnic or national chauvinism. More than once did interviewed banana workers voice the singularly incredulous outrage that comes from a gesture of kindness or solidarity betrayed by another immigrant's predation and calculated self-interest. A Cowpen resident tells of inviting two recent and apparently penniless migrants from his own department in Honduras to stay at his house, only to later be robbed by the same men at knife point. The anger expressed in retelling the incident far transcends the danger and material loss entailed in the robbery; indeed, it speaks of a class and national identity betrayed.

So, too, do the data presented here illustrate the cynical manipulation of ethnicity and nationality for employers' own ends, a manipulation that is often disguised from workers themselves. The deep disparities of earnings by nationality are explicable in no terms other than nationality itself and provide clear evidence that employment practices in the banana belt are far from neutral where nationality and immigration status are concerned. The causes and consequences of these practices shall be examined in chapter 8, as will an alternative vision of national development that could unite rather than divide Belizeans and the newcomers to their nation.

# 8 ❧ *Toward Paths That Unite*

## STRATEGIES OF NATIONHOOD

## AND DEVELOPMENT

> The chief result of the banana strikes has been the rise of an organized labor movement among banana workers. In spite of the varieties of political and economic convictions of leaders and workers, and in spite of divided counsels in regard to strike policies, the workers have discovered they can offset the strength of a mighty corporation and wealthy planters by collective action. In Caribbean countries, which are predominantly agricultural rather than industrial, organized banana workers are likely to constitute the spearhead of the labor movement of the future.
>
> —Charles Kepner (1936)

Kepner's predictions, based on his reports of several brutally repressed strikes on United Fruit plantations in the early 1930s, have been echoed in much subsequent research on Central American banana enclaves. Observing that labor-management relations on banana farms remained "explosive" more than fifty years later, Bourgois noted that Latin American banana workers have always been "exceptionally combative," their ranks claiming "the forefront of the labor union movement in Central America" (1989, 9).

Yet if the combativeness of banana workers is beyond dispute, there is little evidence that as an organized labor movement they have attained lasting concessions directly from their employers. Every challenge to working conditions and pay rates imposed by banana corporations has been met—usually successfully—by a counterstrategy designed to diffuse, divide, and defeat striking workers. Even rare instances of prolonged labor solidarity over large regions, such as the general strike that paralyzed all Honduran banana production for sixty-six days in 1954, achieved only token concessions from employers and left working conditions largely intact (Becerra 1985, 101). Able to compensate for work stoppages in one area by resorting to production from other regions and nations, the banana multinationals have little difficulty in waiting out and defeating strikes through sheer exhaustion. More expeditiously, of course, strikes have been ended through company recruitment of strikebreakers and the persecution of labor leaders by local authorities.

## Dilemmas of Class and Citizenship

Ethnicity and nationality have played major but by no means exclusive roles in employers' strategies of labor control throughout the banana belt. This pattern can be generalized as well to all Central American banana industries. After more than a century of coexistence in the banana-producing lowlands, Afro-Caribbean and Mestizo workers still profoundly distrust one another, in large part because of the conscious manipulation of ethnicity as a means of defeating banana strikes (Purcell 1993, 32). While banana workers as a class remain paralyzed by such crude tactics as hiring racially and nationally distinct replacement workers, the multinationals are able to devise ever more innovative strategies of control. Concluding, at least for public relations purposes, that a continued refusal to recognize banana workers' unions would prove self-defeating in the long term, United Fruit revised its tactics in the 1950s by promoting docile promanagement unions on its tropical divisions. The banana worker unions recognized by management were typically affiliated with international anticommunist labor organizations and have often received assistance and training from the American Institute for Free Labor Development, which in turn has been partly funded by the CIA (Agee 1975). Company efforts to steer workers into such unions even take the form of staged events for which co-opted leaders have been coached to appear combative when dealing with company managers. Although seemingly novel, such innovations are in reality variations on a long-established theme. Emblematic of the grim efficiency of corporate labor control tactics are the notorious and ever-expanding company blacklists of "troublemakers." Since the 1940s, each United Fruit division has maintained and updated blacklists of union activists and strike leaders. Forty years later the blacklists were technologically modernized in the form of a computerized database of more than four thousand names shared by all the banana companies in Costa Rica (Bourgois 1989, 12).

Workers and their employers are necessarily in conflict over working and living conditions on banana farms, but labor struggles do not occur in isolation. The state always forms a prominent backdrop to labor-management relations, although its presence may be overtly apparent only in those instances in which coercive authority is employed against labor activists. Central American states have historically acted in close approximation of instrumentalist state models favored by some political economists (e.g., Milliband 1983), in which the state is viewed as a blunt instrument acting in favor of elite interests. At least until the Second World War, states in the region did indeed operate as compliant agents of foreign capital, making resources available to United Fruit and its competitors on a massive scale and employing their military and juridical powers against banana workers to facilitate corporate labor control and profit making. As seen in chapter 2, such was the case as well for the ostensibly "impartial" colonial administrators governing Belize during United Fruit's ascendancy. In more recent decades, however, the region's states have gained greater nominal autonomy from direct corporate control. This is not because of greater integrity among the region's leaders, nor any newfound resistance to commerce with the banana multinationals. Rather, to preserve both personal power and "political stability" (that is, prevailing modes of capital accumulation), governments began to articulate policies that at least rhetorically recognized a set of national interests independent of the claims of the banana multinationals. Hence, organized banana workers, having attained very little by means of strikes and direct confrontation with employers, were not wholly unsuccessful in pressuring governments of the region to implement substantive reforms over corporate operations. If banana workers of the region today enjoy some degree of health care, bonuses, paid vacations, and other benefits, it is less because of their organized threat to corporate well-being than because of their predominance as constituents of the state. Only by sheer force of numbers do banana workers make themselves heard by state officials over the prevailing interests of the banana multinationals.

Those who employ banana workers in Belize lack the singlemindedness of multinational corporate strategies of labor control. Unlike banana growing regions of Honduras, Guatemala, and Costa Rica, where most production occurs on corporate estates, in Belize the banana industry is entirely based on independent farms of widely varying sizes. In addition, the labor force available to banana growers is characterized by continuing flux, determined by changing levels of repression and economic crisis elsewhere in Central

America, and correspondingly high rates of attrition and circular migration. As a result, no unitary form of labor control characterizes the Belizean banana industry, unlike the monolithic corporate control exercised on the massive United Fruit division documented by Bourgois (1989). As seen in chapter 6, small and large farms are not distinguished, like their counterparts in U.S. industry, by "simple" forms of labor control (i.e., coercion and paternalism) and "technical" forms based on multiple job and wage classifications (Thomas 1985, 18). Paternalism and coercion remain critical instruments of control on even the largest farms, where carefully cultivated relationships between management and a few favored workers translate into surveillance of the many who remain personally unknown to growers. In Belize, banana growers continually experiment with new forms of labor control and recruitment to obtain workers and reliably extract their labor at the lowest possible cost. For their part, banana workers devise strategies of resistance to these practices, by far the least common of which is overt and class-based. In these confrontations of capital and labor, each side has weapons in its arsenal; however unequal the terms of engagement, even the most wretched immigrant is not entirely powerless in contending with his employer.

The greatest liability for most banana workers in Belize, and the greatest asset for their employers, is their immigrant status. For employers, the benefits provided by an overwhelmingly immigrant work force are not, as might be initially thought, a result of its insecure residence. Except for those apprehended for a crime or unlucky enough to be deported as a gesture of political symbolism, immigrants are very rarely forced to leave the country. The threat of deportation, which is widely employed elsewhere as a mechanism of labor control, is in Belize rarely used to enforce compliance with workplace authority. Rather, immigrant workers are more easily controlled than Belizeans because they are not constituents of the state. They are not only unaware of their rights in the workplace, but as immigrants have no recourse to secure those rights. Political candidates, government ministers, and departmental civil servants have much to lose and nothing to gain from the enforcement of labor laws that would improve working conditions in the banana industry. Very few immigrant workers are eligible to vote or otherwise reward government intervention on their behalf. Indeed, to the extent that officials rectify conditions that violate immigrant workers' rights, they alienate farm owners, whose ranks include their most powerful constituents in the southern third of the country.

In Belize, as in the rest of Central America, the state looms large in the background as a partner in confrontations between labor and capital. With the dramatic exception detailed in the epilogue to this book, the state's role on Belizean banana farms is one of determined laissez-faire, allowing an uninterrupted extraction of surplus value (and creation of desired export earnings) while neglecting the enforcement of laws that would adversely affect the state's most vocal and valued constituents. State policies in Belize, as elsewhere, are motivated in large part by the interests of officials who enact them, foremost of which is the retention of power (see Moberg 1994). The minimal rights extended to Honduran banana workers in that country (including social security, collective bargaining, and paid vacations) were rights granted by the state rather than employers, and came about as the holders of state power slowly recognized the importance and volatility of this sector of citizenry (Becerra 1985, 101). As noncitizens, most banana workers in Belize fail to comprise any sort of constituency in their own right and are accordingly denied even the slightest protection of the state. As seen in chapter 4, the employment of noncitizens in the industry has also been used to steadily diminish the position of Belizean workers relative to their employers by eroding the rights to strike, join unions, and collectively bargain that workers formerly enjoyed. This dilution of effective citizenship among native workers is in most respects similar to the effects of undocumented immigrant labor in low-wage sectors of the United States (Thomas 1985, 210).

However repressive the forms of labor control prevailing throughout the Stann Creek and Toledo Districts, the structure of the Belizean industry also accords banana workers a degree of self-defense (mostly through anonymity) that would be unthinkable in Honduras. In Belize, banana workers easily escape the sort of ubiquitous control wielded by a few corporations over entire national work forces in the neighboring countries. Although owners of adjacent farms often share information about troublemakers or otherwise undesirable workers, there are no formal blacklists operating throughout the entirety of the Belizean banana industry. Workers can and do move from one farm to another with no questions asked, very often after incurring major debts and other obligations to former employers. The absence of corporate control over production thus facilitates the varieties of "subterranean" everyday resistance documented in previous chapters. In part because of the small size of most farms, efforts to organize collective resistance are easily detected and punished. Given the ease with which farm workers leave one farm for employment at another, however, relatively few effective sanctions exist against sabotage, shirking, and theft.

One arrangement intended to inhibit movement between farms is the temporary work permit system, which ostensibly ties farm workers to particular employers through the duration of a permit. Theoretically, to leave one farm for another entails application for a new permit and a deduction of one hundred dollars from the farm worker's wages to pay for it. As has been seen, however, more than a third of the banana workers surveyed either had no documentation or held lapsed work permits, suggesting that in practice the permit system serves as neither a means of immigration nor labor control. A few efforts have been undertaken by banana growers as a class to recreate something of the monolithic forms of labor control existing in the neighboring countries. Hence, the Banana Growers' Association has attempted to establish a common set of wage guidelines for field and packing-shed labor in order to diminish the attractiveness of some farms over others for workers seeking higher wages. Yet there is no evidence that individual growers adhere to these guidelines, and many admit to raising wages for certain critical tasks in order to attract skilled workers from other farms. While growers share common interests in maintaining an abundant supply of compliant labor, their mode of production forces them to vie with one another for experienced workers and in this respect diminishes their cohesiveness as a class. This competition within the ranks of employers becomes in turn a major asset in the arsenal of banana workers, allowing them to avert some of the more ubiquitous aspects of labor control found on Honduran and Guatemalan banana plantations.

### Comparative Advantage and Immigration Policy

With the demise of centrally planned economies in eastern Europe and worsening economic crises in much of the Third World, worldwide movements of displaced workers and dispossessed peasantries have reached unprecedented levels since the end of the 1980s. Belize is far from unique in exhibiting a backlash against impoverished immigrants willing to undercut the wages of native workers. The rise of neo-Nazi violence in Europe and passage of xenophobic ballot initiatives in the United States refute any claim to greater tolerance for ethnically distinct immigrants in the developed world. Public officials in such nations placate a fearful and economically insecure citizenry by advocating deportation of undocumented immigrants, revocation of citizenship to the children of immigrants, and virtual border closures against newcomers. Such anti-immigrant discourse has its counterpart in Belize, where government publications flatly assert that Central American immigrants "have had an explosive impact on our way of life, [creating] negative repercussions on land use, labour, health, and public services" (*Belize Today* 1987, 2).

Policy statements issued by public officials in most areas of high immigration invariably pledge to "crack down" or "get tough" with illegal immigrants. Increased expenditures for immigration enforcement and highly visible deportations usually follow, albeit with little net effect other than garnering voter support for the elected authors of such policies. If public consumption is one of the intended goals of immigration policy, of much less visibility is the primary objective, that of securing a steady flow of workers to economic sectors requiring large quantities of cheap, often seasonal labor.

Immigration policy in the United States achieves such goals by coupling harsh public rhetoric with lax or sporadic enforcement. Through approaches such as lightly staffed border watches (rather than employment checks in farms and factories) and the suspension of raids during harvest periods, the U.S. Border Patrol conspicuously avoids antagonizing prominent employers dependent on illegal immigrant labor (Portes and Walton 1981, 58). Of several studies of immigration policy and the labor needs of U.S. agribusiness, "the consensus is that the role of the Border Patrol has been to 'regulate' the illegal flow of labor rather than to prevent it" (ibid.). In like fashion, only after ten years of intense public controversy on Central American immigration did the Belizean government assign an immigration official to the southern districts of Stann Creek and Toledo, where thousands of Central Americans are employed in the banana and citrus industries. Other than a token deportation of one hundred Guatemalans in 1985 and the occasional apprehension of immigrant criminals, no effort was made to return illegal immigrants to their countries of origin prior to the events described in the epilogue to this book. To an even greater extent than in the United States, then, immigration policy in Belize has the primary effect of maintaining porous borders to enable low-wage employers to recruit large numbers of poorly paid and disposable workers. Should those workers become an organized threat to prevailing patterns of capital accumulation and labor relations, of course, the mechanisms remain in place to deport such workers and defuse their challenge to a development strategy based on low-wage labor. Hence, in Belize as well as the

United States, immigration policy prevents foreign labor from becoming "stabilized," that is, residentially secure to the extent that immigrant workers can exert upward pressure on wages (Thomas 1985).

Yet it remains the thesis of this book that immigration policies originate not in the cynicism or corruption of public officials but in the strategies of development that nations adopt. Since the debt crisis that engulfed much of the Third World in the early 1980s, Belize has embarked on a structural adjustment program to ameliorate deteriorating terms of trade for its traditional exports. As mandated by multilateral lending institutions such as the International Monetary Fund and the World Bank, structural adjustment has entailed sharp reductions in public expenditures and deflationary policies intended to reduce budget and trade deficits. In addition, such programs promote nontraditional agricultural and manufacturing industries as mechanisms of export-led growth. These strategies represent a break with development models of import substitution that prevailed through the 1970s, in which the countries of the region attempted to promote growth through tariff protection and public subsidies to domestic industries. In their place, today's neoliberal strategies emphasize the region's "comparative advantage" in producing commodities for the world economy, foremost of which is an abundant supply of low-wage labor.

In Belize, structural adjustment and the promotion of export-led growth have had several immediate effects on labor in the banana industry. The decision to sell public holdings in the banana industry to private investors was a direct consequence of a mandate from the IMF that the Belizean government reduce subsidies to or rid itself entirely of unprofitable state enterprises. As has been seen, privatization ended formal union representation of industry workers, concluding the state's decade-long battle with a unionized work force. Of greater long-term consequence was the state's endorsement of a strategy of development based on low-wage labor, one that was to be achieved through largely uncontrolled immigration. Although management efforts to import banana workers from Honduras had earlier played a critical role in neutralizing unions and excluding militant Belizean labor from the industry, the creation of a low-wage work force was consummated by the subsequent influx of political and economic refugees.

By the late 1980s immigration into the region had nearly doubled the population of rural Stann Creek District, bringing newcomers into competition with earlier immigrants for jobs. The effect of such competition was to place additional downward pressure on wages in commercial agriculture, usually well below the levels Belizeans considered necessary to survive. As Belizean workers were marginalized, they turned increasingly to a precarious livelihood pieced together from seasonal and part-time labor. For many youths faced with few or no legitimate employment prospects, the pursuit of income has led inexorably to the desperate, downward spiral of drug dealing and prostitution. Accordingly, epidemics of HIV infection and crack cocaine addiction threaten an entire generation of Belizeans. Sensing few possibilities for stable employment locally, other displaced workers have fled to the equally dubious opportunities offered in Belizean immigrant enclaves in inner cities of the United States. On the strife-torn streets of Brooklyn, the South Side of Chicago, and south-central Los Angeles are to be found more than a few of the banana industry's castoff workers and their families.

As suggested above, immigrant workers are cheap not merely because they are abundant or in many instances afraid to return home, but above all because they are noncitizens and therefore powerless vis-à-vis the state (Castells 1975). It is in this regard that immigration policy most closely complements a development policy based on the comparative advantages of low-wage labor: "The function of migrant labor has not been—as conventional economics suggests—to increase the supply of labor, but rather to increase the supply of *cheap* labor" (Portes and Walton 1981, 49). This imperative has been so great in the banana industry that immigration was encouraged even when an adequate number of local workers could be found in the villages adjacent to the region's banana farms. As studies of labor immigration into other areas would suggest (Portes and Bach 1985; Radcliffe 1990), labor migration into the Belizean banana industry was a consciously engineered process, one that closely complemented the state's own development priorities.

### Nationhood, Development, and the Costs of Peace

From the neoliberal perspective of currently dominant development models, Third World economic growth is predicated on low wages and "labor peace," defined as an absence of disruptive strikes or overt challenges to managerial authority. Those who subscribe to these models would probably find much that is laudatory in the recent performance of the Belizean economy. By the early 1990s, Belize's annual economic growth rate reached an astonishing 10 percent, far surpassing the rest of Central America (Central Bank of Belize

1991, 1992). As the country's growth rates soared to unprecedented heights, union membership fell to its lowest point since unions were legalized in the 1940s, and strikes became virtually nonexistent. Although tourism led as the country's fastest growing industry, it was followed closely by expansion in the export-oriented citrus, banana, and garment manufacturing industries. With the exception of the tourism sector, most of whose physical infrastructure remains in the hands of expatriate investors, all of these sectors of the economy are dominated by low-wage immigrant labor. Indeed, it may be argued that Afro-Belizean workers retain a foothold in tourism only by virtue of their English fluency and the fact that the large majority of tourists visiting the country are North Americans.

Less often acknowledged in the recounting of Belize's purported "economic miracle" are the potentially explosive social dislocations that underlie the country's recent growth. Expansion in these leading sectors has done little to alleviate unemployment in town and urban areas, where much of the country's Creole and Garifuna population languishes out of work. It is not lost on many of the unemployed that the country's economic growth entailed their displacement from the labor market by lower-paid, ethnically and linguistically distinct immigrants. Based as it is on the suppression of labor costs, the country's newfound path of development has generated considerable revenue for government and wealth for entrepreneurial elites but left the consumption capacity of the general population virtually unchanged. Further, in polarizing the country ethnically by dividing its work force, it threatens to destabilize what have historically been ambivalent but at least peaceful relations across ethnic boundaries.

This book has examined how labor control in the banana industry has been engineered by the manipulation of workers' attitudes regarding ethnicity, nationality, and gender—powerful, but far from primordial, sentiments. Antagonisms based on ethnicity or nationality result instead from the contradictory pressures of centuries of empire and nation building, as well as the contemporary machinations of employers. Indeed, the history of ethnic confrontation and exclusion along the Caribbean littoral underlies many of the current fears expressed by Afro-Belizeans at their prospect of minority status in an increasingly Hispanic country. It is evident by now that, however much employers strive to attain a quiescent work force by manipulating the ethnic and national composition of their employees, labor peace in some absolute sense will remain forever out of their reach. Strikers and union organizers may be fired, and workers may be cajoled, deceived, or coerced into compliance, but the costs of control will be paid elsewhere—usually in production losses from shirking, theft, or destruction. These are losses that most employers appear willing to bear in exchange for a work force unrepresented by unions and largely unconscious of its rights. Yet this level of relative labor peace carries social costs as well that are never recorded in aggregate economic statistics or other indices of "development." These costs are apparent to even the most casual observer of contemporary ethnic relations in Belize.

To the extent that a malleable work force has been crafted in commercial agriculture, ethnic tensions have been augmented by the displacement of native workers, whose unions had earlier accrued significant victories in pay and working conditions. As detailed in chapter 4, the assault on a unionized work force entailed the creation of ethnic myths that denigrated Belizean workers and extolled the willingness of immigrants to labor for long hours and low wages in commercial agriculture. Immigrants in most instances subscribe to these myths uncritically, even while they themselves become steadily less compliant in the eyes of their employers. For their part, Belizeans in the banana belt are keenly aware of their loss of employment and income (as well as status) with the arrival of the immigrants. The result of these changes in the work force are readily apparent in communities such as Mango Creek, where ethnic relations are fraught with tension, mutual animosity, and stereotyping. Belize may not stand on the verge of the "ethnic war" that some (Topsey 1987) have predicted, but it is clear that the major casualty of labor peace in the banana industry (and the work force as a whole) has been the effort of Belizeans of all ethnic groups to forge a nationwide pan-ethnic truce in the wake of colonialism. Perhaps the most tragic legacy of the growing ethnic conflict within the work force will be the resurrection of ethnic ideologies rooted in the colonial era, which consciously pit members of different ethnic groups against one another. Efforts to cultivate a multicultural Belizean identity in the years leading to independence have been all but abandoned in the current climate of fear and resentment.

Anti–Central American sentiments have flourished in southern Belize not merely because Belizean workers have been displaced by immigrants, however much this has caused economic hardship for Creoles and Garifuna in places like Mango Creek. Rather, the displacement of Belizean workers from the banana industry has been accompanied by the creation of rationales that symbolically invert their conceptions of self-worth and national identity.

From once being considered the "real producers" (Williams 1991, 28) of their society and the embodiment of its national identity, working-class Belizeans of African descent find themselves becoming not only demographically and economically overtaken but symbolically marginalized as well. Now that Central American Mestizos, who were once distrusted and disparaged in national ideology, have come to dominate the industry's work force, Afro-Belizeans find themselves ridiculed by their former employers as indolent, inept in agriculture, and combative. When Creoles lament that they are "losing" their country to immigrants, their comments should be understood as well in this symbolic sense. Whereas the institutions of a Westminster parliamentary system and functioning judiciary left by the departing British are sure to remain, the ideologies they imparted to secure Creoles a favorable position in a postcolonial society are rapidly waning.

However much these cultural struggles are waged symbolically, they will ultimately be resolved at the material level, by the strategy of development that Belizeans adopt. It is not too late to envision a path of development that unites rather than divides the many ethnic components of Belizean society. Such strategies would also break from the neoliberal path of economic growth that rests on the suppression of wages and living standards for those employed in export industries. A corollary of the class segmentation theories that inform this work is that discrimination within the work force, although appearing to benefit workers belonging to a dominant ethnic group, in actuality diminishes the well-being of all working people. This is because ethnic divisions, as amply illustrated in the banana industry, impair the ability of all workers to collectively attain improved wages and working conditions. Where class consciousness is concerned, then, one of the more corrosive effects of labor market segmentation is that workers of dominant ethnic groups and genders who occupy primary labor markets fail to perceive their common interests with ethnically distinct workers in secondary markets. Historically, only those labor movements that have attempted to transcend color, ethnicity, and language have attained lasting benefits for workers in all labor markets. In 1938, trade union federations such as the Congress of Industrial Organizations (antecedent of the AFL-CIO) first denounced racial discrimination as a means of "depriv[ing] [workers] of their full economic strength, by arousing prejudices based on race, creed, color, or nationality" (Reich 1981, 257). It was no coincidence that the labor movement's evocation of this principle, however imperfect in its observance, occurred on the eve of a historic expansion of union membership in the United States.

It follows that practices intended to reinforce class segmentation, such as wage differentials and job classifications based on ethnicity, or more formal de jure segregation advocated by some Belizean adversaries of immigrant rights, will ultimately harm most Belizean working people as well. An alternate strategy would be to equally ensure the rights of Belizeans and immigrants within the workplace, and to facilitate their representation by trade unions. Such measures would obviously be opposed by those who benefit from prevailing patterns of accumulation in the banana industry, which are based on low wages and widespread underpayment, and the gender and ethnic segmentation that make them possible. Like all development strategies, these measures are inherently political, for they determine the distribution of the benefits of economic growth.

Employers' unwillingness to improve the welfare of their workers could only be overcome, and workers' rights better protected, if the state were to modernize its labor laws and enforce those that currently exist. Such measures have been promised by political leaders of both national parties to garner the votes of working people, although once in power these same officials have refused to implement their earlier pledges. Given the formal and popular democratic traditions of Belize, traditions rare if not unique in the region, it is not inconceivable that working people could make their voices heard in state policy. Such changes present formidable challenges to the unity and organization of Belizean workers, already fragmented by the demagogic use of ethnic ideologies by politicians and employers. Failing them, however, it is highly possible that their country's future, at least in terms of the widespread social peace that distinguishes it from other countries of the region, will converge with the tragic recent history of their Central American neighbors. For Belizeans and immigrants alike, this alternative is almost too painful to contemplate.

# Epilogue

## THE CRUSHING OF BANDERAS UNIDAS

One of the things that disturbed a lot of citizens in Belize City was when they saw the news coverage and saw the Belizean army dressed as if they were in Salvador or Guatemala and carrying big guns. It was difficult to appreciate that we were looking at a section of Belizean society and that this was going on.

—television reporter on the arrest of striking banana workers in Cowpen, June 1995.

Why don't we just kill all these Spanish and dig a big hole and put them in there?

—policeman during the Cowpen strike

To the residents of Belize City, a news broadcast on 14 June 1995 offered an astonishing revelation of their country's political convergence with Central America. Rarely do televised events in the "districts" intrude upon the insularity of city dwellers, unless they are bland publicity stories orchestrated by government. That evening, however, many Belize City residents viewed conditions in Cowpen for the first time in a news report on the suppression of a banana workers' strike. If the settlement's conspicuous poverty and improvised housing evoked the "Spanish republics" for some viewers, the impression was complemented by the sight of dozens of soldiers dressed in battle camouflage and armed with automatic weapons. What disturbed many Belizeans, as well as the reporters on the scene, was the fact that these troops were not Guatemalan or Salvadoran, but members of the Belize Defence Force (BDF) called out at the behest of growers to deport nearly two hundred Cowpen residents. In the overt intimidation of banana workers by heavily armed soldiers, the mythology of human rights by which Belizeans distinguish their polity from the "republics" was visibly refuted. To those familiar with security guards and guns as features of daily life in the banana belt, the use of force against immigrant workers was less surprising than the manifest support enjoyed by a strike involving all of the nationalities of Cowpen. Acknowledging this decisively changed outlook themselves, workers christened their movement Banderas Unidas, or the United Banners Union.

The union originated in the conditions described throughout this book, and in the efforts of a Belizean woman to seek redress for them. Marciana Funez, a Mestiza resident of Mango Creek, had gained some familiarity with the working and living conditions of Cowpen residents between 1976 and 1986, when she occasionally visited the settlement to sell groceries, produce, and merchandise. After an eight-year absence, she resumed itinerant trading in 1994 and found that, notwithstanding the ever-expanding scale of banana cultivation, the abuses suffered by workers had only worsened after privatization. Her concern with working conditions at Cowpen was initially piqued by the difficulties she experienced as a merchant in the settlement. Many of her customers, despite their full-time employment, lacked ready cash to purchase necessities. She extended them credit, but on returning to the village on payday she found that many were still unable to pay for their earlier purchases. Funez was initially skeptical of workers' claims to be without cash, but when several showed their pay stubs she learned that they had been left with little or no net pay after the deduction of their debts at farm-run stores. Such deductions often exceed Belizean law, which permits a maximum of one-quarter of any given paycheck to be withheld for employee debts. Other workers found that in practice contract rates for their work did not enable them to earn the minimum hourly wage, and many were further docked by supervisors, allegedly for the quality of their work. Other irregularities followed from these initial discoveries. All workers have social security contributions deducted from their pay, for example, but when Funez checked with the Social Security Department she learned that many workers' names did not appear on department registers. She concluded that some employers were retaining workers' social security "contributions" for their own use.

By February 1995, Funez was meeting regularly with Cowpen workers to coordinate a list of demands and decide on a strategy to achieve them. It emerged that most workers' grievances concerned Farms 1, 2, and 3 of Cowpen, all of which are partly owned or managed by Fyffes. In addition to their complaints about excessive deductions, low contract rates, and the abusive behavior of captains, workers objected to harassment by security guards employed on all three farms. Claiming that livestock was destroying immature banana plants, security guards had begun shooting the chickens and pigs with which many workers supplemented their earnings. Much of the harassment by guards appeared to be of a more arbitrary nature, however, as in the accusations of several workers who said they were beaten for taking drinking water from an irrigation line at Farm 2.

A final grievance concerned Fyffes's plan to relocate workers away from the farms, where many are exposed to chemicals applied through aerial spraying. The company proposed to resettle workers to a zone at the northern entrance to Cowpen. Eligibility for company-built housing at the site would be limited to naturalized or native Belizeans, who, as seen in chapter 7, constituted less than 8 percent of Cowpen's residents. At a meeting in Cowpen to discuss the relocation plan, the village alcalde (who is also manager of the Farm 2 store) said that the cost of houses would be seven thousand dollars, payable in monthly installments of one hundred dollars. She neglected to mention that interest charges would bring their final cost to ten thousand dollars. Given their difficulty surviving on average monthly earnings of less than four hundred dollars, most workers doubted that they could afford the monthly installments. They were concerned as well that the plan seemed to strengthen the company's control over them. Fyffes would be responsible for all amenities at the site and could evict workers should they lose their jobs, fall behind in payments, or seek work outside of Cowpen. Workers proposed as an alternative that each household be loaned five hundred dollars' worth of materials that they could then use to construct their own houses. Under this proposal, the loans could be repaid with deductions from farm workers' wages and they would be permitted to choose where they constructed their houses. Bella Vista, an alternative site near Cowpen's southern entrance, was more attractive to workers because it was not under Fyffes's control and would permit them greater freedom to change employers in the future if they want. When it became evident that this alternative was supported by most of the workers in attendance, the village alcalde and Fyffes representatives quickly brought the meeting to a close without resolution.

By April 1995, a union had emerged from the meetings in Cowpen earlier organized by Funez. The decision to seek collective bargaining transcended the national differences that had occasionally divided workers in the past, for, as Funez expressed it, "everyone here has finally learned that we have to unite if we are to survive; this is the meaning of Banderas Unidas." Elections for the union's executive were held in April and were limited to nonfarm workers in order to prevent retaliation by employers. As soon as shop stewards were named on individual farms, they began to experience harassment and arbitrary dismissal. Representing the union, a delegation of workers met with the owner of Farm 2, who promised to restrain the behavior of his security guards. After the meeting, however, he took Funez aside and pointedly warned her, "It's useless to have a union here because the BDF will only come to deport them."

After Banderas Unidas was registered with the government's Labor Department on 17 May, it attempted to open negotiations with the Banana Growers' Association on working conditions and pay. The BGA refused each of its five written requests for negotiation, claiming that the union had not demonstrated that it represented the banana work force. When the union asked growers to schedule a representational poll of their workers, however, this request too was ignored.[1] By the end of May, the union claimed to have collected 490 signatures on its membership list. For its part, the Banana Growers' Association responded that many of the union's supporters were not employees of the banana industry, and that these "outsiders" had intimidated workers into signing the list against their will. While disputing the union's claims to represent the Cowpen work force, the BGA still refused to schedule a representation election. On 29 May, the union informed the district's labor officer that an "industrial action" would take place in Cowpen on 12 June unless the BGA agreed to a meeting to discuss union grievances. Two days later, the Cowpen alcalde and representatives of Fyffes, the BGA, and Labor Department met to coordinate a response to the union's threatened strike. No members of the work force or union representatives were invited to the 31 May meeting.

On Sunday, 11 June 1995, more than six hundred people attended a rally in Cowpen organized by Banderas Unidas. By a show of hands, those attending the meeting voted overwhelmingly to strike against Farms 1, 2, and 3 over the union's grievances concerning pay and working conditions. The following day, the beginning of the week's harvest, the packing sheds on the three farms were shut down, representing a huge potential loss to the operations. The strike soon spread as a sympathy action to Farms 4 and 15, which, although not mentioned in the union's grievances, drew most of their work force from Cowpen. By late Monday, a detachment of BDF soldiers and police had arrived in the village, ostensibly to protect company property. At this point, the former PUP area representative from the National Assembly intervened to seek a negotiated end to the strike. By Tuesday, he had obtained pledges from the union to encourage its members to return to work, and from growers to permit a representational poll. A joint meeting between growers, union leaders, and the country's acting labor commissioner was scheduled for ten o'clock Wednesday morning.

Union leaders were encouraged by the agreement, for they believed that Banderas Unidas would win an election if it were conducted fairly. Their faith in the settlement proved to be misplaced, however. Around nine o'clock Wednesday morning, BDF soldiers and police began rousing union members from their homes and loading them onto four buses that had been earlier parked outside the Farm 2 office. Reportedly, the owner of Farm 2, a Fyffes representative, and farm security guards all pointed out union members and strike participants for arrest, even as the government's labor commissioner stood by and watched. A total of 190 men and 3 women were rounded up and then transported to Benque Viejo, four hours away on the Guatemalan border. There, Belizean immigration officials attempted to deport all the detainees, but some 159 who were reportedly Honduran or Salvadoran were barred from entry by Guatemalan authorities. They were then taken to a Belizean army camp and interned overnight.

By the following day, the consuls of Guatemala, Honduras, and El Salvador had lodged protests with the Belizean government over the treatment and attempted expulsion of their nationals. Heightening the embarrassment of the government, the former Guatemalan president Efrain Rios Montt, then running in that country's presidential elections, vowed publicly to support the cause of the Guatemalan deportees. With the deportation looming as a potential diplomatic crisis between Belize and Guatemala, the Belizean government was forced to accept the return of the Guatemalans. All 193 former workers were then loaded onto buses for transportation back to Stann Creek District. After the unsuccessful deportation attempt, most workers were released in Mango Creek, but about a dozen shop stewards and other leaders were detained at the police station. There, according to Funez, they were beaten by the police and immigration officials, and all were given twenty-one-day departure notices.

In the weeks following the attempted strike, about one-third of the former workers left the country, and another third remained out of work in the banana belt. Having anticipated the strike, Farm 2 had already recruited replacements from Honduras before the attempted deportation. The strikebreakers were at work on the farm by the following week's harvest. Because the other farms were unable to recruit a full contingent of replacements, however, about one-third of the former union members were eventually rehired by their previous employers. On Farms 1 and 3, replacements were reportedly warned not to interact with rehired workers and were threatened with dismissal and deportation if they were seen to mix with them. Retaliation by the growers extended as well to Belizean supporters of Banderas Unidas. Once she emerged as the union's most visible Belizean proponent in the nation's broadcast and print media, Funez found herself increasingly harassed by the police and Fyffes security guards. On the second day of the strike, she was arrested and charged with drug possession at her home in Mango Creek. She recalled that on the morning of her arrest she had noticed a powdered milk can in her yard but merely assumed that a child had left it there after playing with it. Later a policeman arrived with a search warrant, turned over the can, and found about forty grams of marijuana inside it. When she was later released on her own recognizance, she found that the engine of the pickup truck with which she made her living had been destroyed by sabotage.

The response to the strike by the Belizean labor movement, or its remnants, was generally belated. To some extent, the country's existing unions were reluctant to provide immediate support simply because they were unfamiliar with working conditions in the banana industry or even the existence of a union there. Banderas Unidas had failed to confer with other unions on issues of strategy and organizing, so that the strike came as a complete surprise to the labor movement. The Public Service Union, representing government workers, issued a statement of solidarity with the strikers when the attempted deportation occurred. Other unions, including the remnants of the once-militant UGWU, were more cautious. More than a month after the suppression of the strike, the National Trade Union Council sent a delegation to the banana belt to investigate working conditions there. It reported that banana workers had experienced a "gross violation of freedom of association" and appealed for support from all segments of the labor movement for immigrant workers, noting that "this situation reflects directly on the welfare of all Belizean workers" (Radio Belize 1995).

There is evidence that these convictions were not widely shared by Belizeans elsewhere in the country, however. In the weeks following the strike and the adverse publicity it generated for Fyffes and its local partners, the banana growers went on a media offensive. The owner of Farm 2 and manager of the BGA appeared on several television interview programs in which they reiterated their claim that most union members were not banana workers. On one program, the industry spokesmen fielded calls from viewers, the large majority of whom resided in Belize City. Far from being reproached by callers, they were complemented for having "done something" to "clean up that mess down there," in the words of one. Most callers were indignant not at the bad faith of the employers in refusing to hold a representational poll, but at the "aliens" who had organized the strike in the first place. Failing to see any relationship between conditions experienced by immigrant workers and their own wages and working conditions, most Afro-Belizean callers sided with the growers. In a direct and unmediated way, then, the issues of ethnicity and immigration that have dominated Belizean political discourse since 1980 have been enlisted by agro-export elites in suppressing unionization.

Although the union was chastened by its initial battle with Cowpen employers, it acquired formidable allies in the ensuing months. The country's Catholic Church, which inspired an earlier generation of independence and labor leaders but had retreated from social activism in recent years, spoke out anew on the rights of workers. Not long after the deportation attempt, the Bishop of Belize City publicly denounced the banana industry's "blatant disregard for human rights." The country's Jesuit Superior visited Cowpen to celebrate a Mass of solidarity with banana workers, and Sisters of Charity aided workers who had been fired after the strike attempt. With assistance from the nongovernmental Society for the Promotion of Education and Research (SPEAR), the union also brought its message to consumers and potential supporters in the developing countries. In May 1996, Marciana Funez led a delegation to Ireland both to meet with Fyffes executives and to organize a possible consumer boycott of the company should it fail to ameliorate conditions for workers in Belize. Notwithstanding these efforts and allies, however, the union reported on the first anniversary of the Cowpen strike that employers remained as intransigent as ever in their refusal to countenance a unionized work force (Shoman, pers. comm. 1996).

The attempt to crush Banderas Unidas remains an unfinished story at this juncture, for the union continues to demand recognition from the Cowpen growers. Yet if the final pages of the narrative are not yet written, its direction should be familiar enough from a century of confrontation in Central America's banana fields. "Men make their own history," Marx observed, "but they do not make it just as they please; they do not make it under circumstances chosen by themselves, but under circumstances directly encountered, given, and transmitted from the past" (1977b, 300). The effort to collectively win a measure of dignity and well-being has signaled a break from the myths of ethnicity and nation that have long divided banana workers; in this sense, some of the living have indeed freed themselves from the "tradition of all the dead generations" (ibid.). Yet the present abounds as well with historical ironies, suggesting that the past also repeats itself, if in altered fashion. On a news report from Cowpen, a union member from Honduras passionately protested his dismissal for union activity after thirteen years of employment. Among the immigrants recently expelled from the banana belt, then, are some whose presence in Belize was probably owed to the earlier assault on banana workers in 1982. To judge from the deepening deprivations that fueled the cause of Banderas Unidas, as well as the emergent international identity of its members, it is unlikely that the current generation of strikebreakers will be any less resistant than the workers they replaced. If so, the banana fields will not wait another thirteen years to experience their next convulsion.

# Appendix

## METHODS

The field research on which this book is based entailed eight months of residence in Mango Creek, Stann Creek District, Belize, between January and September 1993. More than two years of prior research experience in the region in the mid- and late 1980s, as well as reconnaissance visits in 1991 and 1992, significantly augmented the 1993 field research. In the course of this project, I visited all twenty-three of the region's commercial banana farms at least once, and those in the Cowpen area were the site of almost daily ethnographic research. In addition, I conducted archival research at the Public Records Office of Great Britain (Kew) in September 1994 and at the National Archives of Belize (Belmopan) in July 1995. Ethnographic research undertaken during my 1995 residence in Belize entailed interviews with members of the Banderas Unidas movement and resulted in the epilogue to this book.

During the 1993 fieldwork, I conducted fifty-seven formal interviews with growers, farm general managers, and other administrative personnel in the industry. These interviews followed numerous unstructured interviews with growers and farm managers, which contributed to the later formulation of interview protocols. In addition, I conducted sixty unstructured interviews with banana workers at Mango Creek, Cowpen, and seven farms outside of the Cowpen area. These yielded questions for later inclusion on a structured survey administered to a systematic random sample of residents of the region's farms, the vast majority of whom were workers. The survey instrument elicited information on immigrants' place of origin, length of residence in Belize, motives for migration, residence status, survival strategies and income, and household composition.

As suggested in the preface to this book, ethnographic research in the banana industry posed some complex methodological and ethical dilemmas. Although I was ethically committed at first to informing all participants of the purpose of the study, once several of the region's most powerful growers learned of my interest in the industry's labor and ethnic relations, they evidenced distrust of my motives. I soon recognized that the need to protect relatively powerless informants from retaliation at the hands of their employers or the state would have to take precedence over the full disclosure of my research interests and preliminary findings. The ensuing compromise may not be an optimal solution to the conflicting ethical demands made upon me as a field worker. I am confident at least that if any harm accrues from this project, it will be to my ability to conduct further research in the industry rather than to any of its participants.

Employers, of course, were not alone in regarding my presence with skepticism. The banana industry's extreme class and ethnic stratification, and the vulnerability of many workers to deportation, also inhibited my initial interactions and interviews with many immigrants. After repeated visits, most of this apprehension waned and I eventually developed close working and personal relationships with workers and managers on several farms. The attitude of some, but by no means all, growers proved more intractable. In general, the region's largest growers remained anxious about the goals of my research and tended to greet my questions with extreme reticence. Their suspicion was attributable, I think, to the violations of labor laws and fundamental human rights that remain so evident throughout the industry. Unlike Philippe Bourgois, who reported that United Fruit managers freely volunteered information because they assumed that he shared their class and ethnic prejudices (1989, xiii), I was barred by several growers from observing meetings of the Banana Growers Association and three growers I contacted would not participate in interviews of any kind. A number of expatriate North American growers, small- or medium-scale Belizean farmers, and one member of the elite "Achmed" family provided most of the material attributed to growers in this book, including several secondhand descriptions of BGA meetings.

When traveling to farms to interview resident managers, I almost always encountered far greater cooperation, notwithstanding the usually unanticipated nature of my visits. I was able to interview managers and/or owners on twenty-two of the region's twenty-three commercial banana farms. These individuals also provided information on the ethnic, gender, and national identity of each of their employees, as well as their job classification. The collection of these data usually provoked a good deal of free-flowing discussion concerning their perceptions and "management" of ethnicity, nationality, and gender as worker attributes.

For several reasons, I chose to hire and train Central American (Belizean and immigrant) research assistants to administer the household survey to residents of Cowpen. Although I was eventually well recognized by many workers in the settlement, residents of its periphery were much less familiar with my activities. Initially, I believed that the administration of the questionnaire by Hispanic assistants would improve the validity of survey data, particularly among workers who were not well acquainted with my research goals. In retrospect, my concerns about validity may have been unwarranted, as undocumented immigrants were just as likely to report their residence status to me as to my assistants.

Nonetheless, for reasons entirely unrelated to informants' perceptions of my activities, it would probably have been difficult if not impossible to survey the Cowpen work force by myself. I became aware of these potential barriers to administering the survey when several growers pointedly advised me against interviewing residents of the village. Although some of these warnings were phrased as concern for my welfare (one grower even predicted that I would be viewed as a drug enforcement agent and ambushed), owners of two of the Cowpen farms implied that they would not tolerate my efforts to interview workers on farm property. Because almost all workers' residences at Cowpen are located on private land belonging to the farm owners, I by no means enjoyed guaranteed access to the settlement. A certain amount of stealth, then, was involved in my reliance on Hispanic research assistants, for their inconspicuousness allowed them to conduct the survey without interference. To minimize the dangers to assistants working in Cowpen, I hired only Belizeans or naturalized immigrants who were not employed in the industry itself. Further, I asked them to emphasize the confidential and anonymous nature of the survey to prospective informants and to respect individuals' decisions to decline interviews. Fortunately, none of the assistants reported interference from managers or owners in the process of administering surveys. Nor did workers apparently find the process intimidating, as only four household heads in Cowpen refused to be interviewed.

I personally administered the surveys on two smaller farms at Bladen Branch whose owners consented to my presence for the purpose. At Bladen Branch, I interviewed the heads of 50 percent of all households (n = 29) by visiting alternate residences from the entrance to each farm. Where houses were unoccupied, I sampled the neighboring house to the left or right on the basis of a coin toss. My assistants followed similar procedures at Cowpen, but, given the much larger sampling frame, instead selected every fourth residence for a subsample of 128 households. The individuals interviewed in the combined sample of 157 households closely approximate the composition of the work force as a whole, as reflected in the aggregate data on worker ethnicity and nationality collected from twenty-two of the region's farms. The compositions of the sample and the overall work force differ slightly in that the former underrepresents Belizean Maya workers, few of whom reside at Cowpen or Bladen Branch.

Although the majority of the ethnographic data in this book was derived from interviews, there were also many opportunities for participant observation at Mango Creek and Cowpen. My frequent but admittedly nonsystematic observations of daily life at Cowpen and other farms figure prominently in several of the preceding chapters. Most apparent from these observations was the paucity of community-wide organizations or recreational diversions on banana farms, with fairly widespread alcohol abuse and violence following paydays. Lest these descriptions appear merely to reiterate the stereotypes that many Belizeans hold about immigrants in general, I would note that many aspects of my account are corroborated by other ethnographic analyses of banana enclaves in Central America (for example, Kepner 1967 and Bourgois 1989).

# Notes

## Preface

1. McCann reports that United Fruit's chairman of the late 1960s, Eli Black, returned from his first visit to the company's Central American divisions appalled at the condition of workers' housing: "What disturbed him . . . was that the workers in the tropics were living wretchedly because they had absolutely no sense of pride in themselves or their homes, and that they were letting *our* housing fall into ruin. He suggested . . . that a film be made showing these people how to take care of the company's property" (McCann 1976, 146).

2. The complete Rolston letter is quoted in Peckenham and Street 1985, 44. Some have challenged its authenticity, although most historians of Honduras consider it an accurate statement of banana company operating strategies (see Peckenham and Street 1985 and Lapper and Painter 1985).

3. In actuality, all such "off-grade" fruit supplied to Fyffes by growers in Belize is in turn sold to English retailers or institutional buyers, although growers are not paid for it.

## Introduction: Caste and Class in Southern Belize

1. Use of crack cocaine has expanded dramatically in Belize since the country became a major transshipment point for South American cocaine in the late 1980s. Many low-level drug workers are paid not in cash but with crack, which is then sold on the local market.

2. "Social relations are closely bound up with productive forces. In acquiring new productive forces men change their mode of production; and in changing their mode of production, in changing the way of earning their living, they change all their social relations. The hand-mill gives you society with the feudal lord; the steam-mill, society with the industrial capitalist" (Marx 1977a, 202).

3. In the crab-processing industry of coastal Alabama, employers were initially reluctant to make use of readily available nonwhite labor, despite a rapidly diminishing pool of white workers by the 1970s. The subsequent employment of Vietnamese, Cambodian, and Laotian immigrants in seafood plants engendered much public opposition as Asians were assigned to what were traditionally considered "white" jobs (Moberg and Thomas 1993).

4. None of which are in fact large. The two biggest settlements of the South, Dangriga and Punta Gorda, have a combined population of fewer than twelve thousand residents.

5. Older debates between "primordialist" and "instrumentalist" analyses of ethnicity primarily concern the basis of shared perceptions of ethnic-group membership (Bentley 1987). Instrumentalists (Barth 1969) regard ethnicity as a conscious manipulation of identity for common political or economic interests, whereas primordial models (Geertz 1963; Keyes 1976) ground ethnic identity in symbols of powerful communal affect. However important the symbolic content of ethnicity, it is in the hierarchical relations between ethnic groups that primordial sentiments acquire their greatest significance and meaning (Bourgois 1988, 329).

## Chapter 1. Culture and History in the Forgotten District

1. Although Belize did not achieve formal independence from Great Britain until 1981, mainly because of unresolved Guatemalan claims to the territory, it was granted internal self-rule in 1963. Under this arrangement, Britain retained control only of the country's defense and some aspects of its foreign policy.

2. Rudimentary as it is, completion of the Southern Highway in 1966 encouraged a new generation of commercial elites to acquire large blocks of land for citrus and banana cultivation. By the mid-1980s, there was no longer any unclaimed arable land adjacent to the highway between Dangriga and Mango Creek.

3. "We belong here; everybody else came here."

4. For slave owners and colonial officials, the legendary battle actually served dual ideological purposes. While emphasizing the Creoles' loyalty to empire, it also exonerated settlers of moral responsibility for their treatment of slaves. As the Baymen themselves addressed a visiting English nobleman within a year of the battle, "We have rendered the galling yoke of Slavery so light and easy as to animate our Negroes to a gallant defence of their Masters, by whose sides they fought with the most determined bravery and fidelity" (Burdon 1931, 272).

5. Stone (1994, 269) interprets pay rates on two late-nineteenth-century sugar plantations in Toledo District as evidence of differential job assignment and payment by ethnicity in colonial agriculture. Although the handful of Chinese laborers employed on the farms were indeed paid significantly less than other ethnic groups, Stone's quantitative data actually suggest that Creoles, Garifuna, and "Spaniards" employed on the farms were compensated in nearly identical ways. It remains possible, of course, that employers still treated ethnically distinct workers in qualitatively different ways, as some supervisors themselves implied (ibid., 227).

6. This text was withdrawn from use in schools by the subsequent United Democratic Party government.

## Chapter 2. Boom, Bust, and Monopoly Control

1. The perception that colonial governments were impartial mediators among local elites, foreign capital, and the working classes is prevalent among some Caribbean historians (see, for example, Green 1984). Perhaps for this reason, colonial governors are often depicted in historians' accounts as less venal and corrupt than Central American leaders. As Bolland (1984) and Ashdown (1982) demonstrate, characterizations of most colonial governors as disinterested administrators do not withstand close scrutiny for the Belizean case.

2. By the late 1920s, the Vaccaro Brothers company was to become incorporated into Standard Fruit (now part of Dole), one of the three major banana multinationals in the region today.

3. The company successfully repeated the same tactic two years later, when the Southern Steamship line of Mobile began calling at fruit-producing areas of the coast (*Colonial Guardian*, 26 Mar. 1904, 1).

4. Generally, colonial newspapers of the time were allied with British capital and the timber industry and consequently viewed the government's promotion of commercial agriculture with some hostility.

5. The outcry over land prices in the Stann Creek Valley did not, however, lower land prices for smallholders throughout the colony. In a 1912 dispatch, Governor Swayne encouraged West Indian smallholders to settle in the chronically labor-scarce colony with "grants of land on liberal terms" (PRO CO 123 273). These terms required smallholders to lease lands at fifty cents in gold per acre until half or more of the land was under cultivation. Only at that point could land be purchased, and then for two dollars in gold per acre. Hence, while West Indian smallholders would be cumulatively charged far more than twice the land price granted United Fruit, they were also held to stricter cultivation standards for purchase. Failing compliance with these conditions, smallholders would lose the land they had applied for and forfeit all previously paid rent.

6. Among the names mentioned in the governor's dispatch was W. A. Bowman, who later founded the Stann Creek Valley's citrus industry and became the district's largest landowner by the late 1920s.

7. As might be inferred from these events, climatic conditions in Belize are among the most unsettled and variable of any zone on the Caribbean littoral of Central America. Tropical disturbances and wildly fluctuating levels of precipitation have been identified as major risks facing the country's agriculturalists (Hall 1983).

8. In 1982, each box of Belizean bananas cost Fyffes $15.24. According to a comparative analysis of banana companies operating in the UK market in that year, Fyffes generated a profit of $9.06 on every box of bananas from Belize, compared to $4.58 from its dollar-area sources, and $3.90 earned by independent importers from dollar areas (Shoman 1988, 46). These data suggest that "the Banana Control Board

was subsidizing the operations of U.B. [United Brands] under the existing agreements" with the company (ibid.; translation mine).

9. The actual sale of state assets in the banana industry was conducted in 1985 by the newly elected UDP government, but privatization plans were drafted in the previous year while the PUP remained in power.

## Chapter 3. Local and International Contexts of Production

1. Union contracts in force until 1985 mandated protective clothing and face masks for those handling farm chemicals. Since the union's exclusion from the industry in that year, such provisions have been suspended on every one of the banana farms in Belize.

2. Holt (1992) and Black (1984) recount one instance of such competition, when United Fruit sought to cripple the Jamaica Banana Producers' Association, a growers' cooperative active in the colony in the 1930s. Equipped with a shipping fleet of its own and offering a higher price to its members than United Fruit, the cooperative was diminishing the multinational's supplies of fruit from Jamaica and forcing it to pay higher producer prices than it otherwise would. "Sam Zemurray, President of the U.F.C., regarded this as an intolerable situation, especially as a successful cooperative in Jamaica might well lead growers in other banana-producing countries to follow this example" (Black 1984, 77). The corporation's response was to raise its producer prices in Jamaica far beyond market value, which it could afford to do "for as long as necessary because . . . what they lost of Jamaican bananas could be made up on bananas from other sources" (ibid.). The cooperative soon lost many of its independent suppliers, eventually allowing United Fruit to dictate the terms of surrender in the price war. The cooperative was forced to agree to become a shareholding company, to leave the U.S. market, to limit exports to Britain to 25 percent of that country's market, and to pay its suppliers no more than the prevailing price paid by United Fruit.

Kepner and Soothill (1935) describe similar strategies employed by United Fruit to drive its competitors out of business in Central America.

3. The U.S.-based multinationals that controlled banana exports from dollar areas strenuously protested the EU quotas, claiming that they limited their access to the European market. Acting on their behalf, the U.S. government in 1995 threatened to bring action against the EU under the recently approved GATT (General Agreement on Tariffs and Trade) unless it suspended its preferences for ACP fruit.

4. Fyffes representatives deny that scores reflect anything other than fruit quality. Yet some precedent exists for growers' concerns about the consistency and objectives of fruit scoring. Kepner recorded more than a generation ago that United Fruit, which graded bananas before they left port in Central America, arbitrarily lowered scoring criteria to accommodate influential growers or raised them to rid itself of excess cargo:

When the company is clamoring for more fruit, or when a planter influential in politics is concerned, the inspector tends to be more lenient than usual in inspecting the fruit. Sometimes, however, there is more available fruit than the steamer at the dock can carry, or market prices are dropping and a sizzling radio message arrives from Boston, saying, "Reduce your cargoes," or "Ship only good fruit." Then the tropical division manager and his superintendent of export, who do not want to be blamed for payments for large quantities of fruit that the company prefers *not to accept and market,* check up the inspectors, who often work 18 to 24 hours at a stretch, ordering them to be especially careful not to receive any but "the best fruit." (Kepner 1935, 267)

## Chapter 4. Out of Work in the Fields of Gold

1. Despite growers' complaints about the costs of transporting workers in the past, they were a relatively minor component of production costs. According to the Banana Board's 1984 annual report, management spent over three times as much to transport packed bananas from Cowpen to the wharf as it did to transport workers from Mango Creek, Georgetown, and Seine Bight to the packing sheds at Cowpen (Banana Control Board 1984).

2. The fact that Greene and Atkins's entire work force resided at the farm rather than at Mango Creek is invariably overlooked by those asserting the unwillingness of Belizeans to forego village life.

3. Mawema's emphasis on a nationwide, multiethnic workers' movement recalls the rhetoric of Antonio Soberanis, a leader of the early movement for independence and workers' rights in the 1930s. Like Mawema in the 1980s, Soberanis was detested by the country's elites, who found his views "offensive and inflammatory" (Bolland 1988, 174).

4. In Creole, "taking for puppetshow" means being played with, deceived, or not taken seriously.

5. The union was affiliated, however, with the World Federation of Trade Unions, which claimed many affiliates in Eastern Bloc countries. This fact was often cited by the UGWU's opponents in the labor movement as evidence for the union's communist character. One of the more bizarre accusations against the union was made in 1979 by the deputy party leader of the UDP, who claimed that a jeep filled with "firearms for communists and labour leaders in Dangriga" (*Belize Times* 1979, 12) had been intercepted by the police several miles outside of town. Although Mawema immediately discredited the accusation and the police denied any knowledge of the alleged incident, the party leader's claims were repeated verbatim by the opposition press (ibid.).

6. The act prescribed penalties for "any person . . . employed in any Essential Service to absent himself from his place of work without lawful excuse, the burden of proof of which shall lie upon him" (Government of Belize 1981).

7. The AIFLD is affiliated with the AFL-CIO but has received CIA funding in the past. During the Reagan administration, the AIFLD was seen as a primary means of promoting conservative trade unions in Central America that would preempt more left-wing alternatives.

8. The population of Corozal, a predominately Spanish-speaking district in northern Belize, is of largely Mestizo and Maya origin. Since Corozal was the constituency represented by Florencio Marin, then the minister of agriculture, it is likely that the decision to replace banana workers with Corozal residents originated with Marin himself.

## Chapter 5. Central American Immigration

1. The use of the diminutive form (i.e., *negrito* instead of *negro*) when referring to Creoles and Garifuna conveys a disparaging racial reference, a fact that even monolingual Afro-Belizeans recognize and resent. More politely, Hispanic Central Americans refer to persons of Afro-Caribbean origin as *morenos,* but this term is rarely encountered among immigrants in Belize.

2. It is characteristic of colonial ideology that the slaves' efforts at self-preservation during the battle were later represented as "the devotion and zeal of the Negroes in the Defence of their Masters' lives and properties" (an 1824 account, quoted in Bolland 1988, 20). As Bolland demonstrates, many of the slaves who ostensibly fought in defense of their owners subsequently sought to escape from them (ibid., 40).

3. *Paisano* means "compatriot" in Spanish and is a friendly term of reference when used in Guatemala. Most immigrants interviewed recognize and resent its mocking connotations when used by Belizeans.

4. Throughout the late 1980s, the UDP government refused to recognize the 1951 protocol because to do so, it claimed, would preclude the exclusion of thousands of Guatemalans from national territory (Shoman 1989, 14). A subsequent PUP government quietly acceded to the convention in 1991, two years after having returned to power.

5. The potential for abuse of employees under the work permit system is obvious, given its restriction of labor mobility. It is worth noting that in the United States low-wage employers make use of a similarly restrictive H2 "nonimmigrant" class visa to bind foreign workers to their firms (Griffith 1993, 11). Despite protests by immigrants' rights groups and organized labor, the use of workers recruited under H2 visas is now commonplace in agriculture and poultry and seafood processing in the United States.

6. Such assumptions overlook the emerging evidence of widespread human rights abuses in Honduras throughout the 1980s, when the country served as a staging ground for *contras* fighting the Sandinista government in Nicaragua. The Commission for the Defense of Human Rights in Honduras has documented more

than 120 "disappearances" of Honduran political activists between 1981 and 1991, most of which have been attributed to the country's armed forces and *contra* rebels. The commission has also documented the existence of twelve clandestine cemeteries where the bodies of dissidents were concealed. Throughout this period, the Honduran military received most of it training by advisors from the United States and Argentina, a country whose military systematically relied on kidnapping and torture in its "dirty war" against political opponents.

7. Immigration is but one of several factors lowering the cost of labor in the national economy. Food price controls also suppress wage levels, albeit at the expense of the agricultural sector (Moberg 1991b). In addition, remittances sent by migrants in the United States, which in 1986 were estimated at around $42 million, tend to lower the labor costs of Belizeans who remain at home (Vernon 1990, 15): "Not only is union membership low and less stable because of emigration, not only do unions lose important leaders to emigration, but remittances . . . serve as supplements to wages that decrease upward pressures on wages. And in our present situation of the large supply of cheap migrant labour from the region, a Belizean labour force that is smaller because of emigration makes it easier for employers to keep unions out and wages down" (ibid., 18).

8. Several Belizean government officials claimed in separate interviews that the owners had organized themselves as a church in order to qualify for tax-free status in Denmark.

9. With the support of Fyffes, a co-owner of one of the farms at Cowpen, the government announced in 1992 that it would encourage Cowpen residents to move to a site on the Southern Highway several miles away from the existing settlement. The stated reason for the relocation was to remove workers and their families from the farms and their associated health hazards. In addition, residents of the new village, to be known as San Juan Blas, would be eligible for public utilities and secure house lots. Although streets for the new settlement and house lots were surveyed in early 1993, by September, only four households had chosen to relocate. This was mainly because residents were to receive no compensation for the houses and businesses they left behind or other assistance in the relocation. Owners of the other three farms at Cowpen were also reported to be opposed to the relocation, as they would then have to transport their workers to and from the farms on a daily basis.

## Chapter 6. The Construction of Ethnicity on Banana Farms

1. As will be seen in chapter 7, the large majority of Guatemalan workers are actually Mestizo. Interestingly, Guatemalan nationality tends to be conflated with Mayan ethnicity in the minds of other Central American workers.

2. A chi-square analysis of the field and supervisory work force by nationality yields a value of 195.46 (significant at $p < .05$ with 3 df), indicating that Belizeans are

significantly more likely than immigrants to be employed in supervisory positions on farms.

3. Smaller farms employ less labor per acre than large farms. On average the twelve farms smaller than 245 acres employ one full worker for every 6.1 acres under cultivation, whereas the ten large farms employ one worker for every 3.6 acres cultivated. The smaller relative work forces on small farms may be attributable to two factors. Small-scale growers more often have cash-flow problems and respond by maintaining small payrolls, although labor shortages in the long run of course compound production problems. Second, many growers with farms in remote areas note some difficulty in recruiting and retaining workers willing to live where amenities and transportation are minimal.

4. "Belizeans First" was the campaign slogan of the PUP in the 1989 general elections, when it recaptured the national government. Although the PUP has been less overt than the UDP in its use of the immigration issue during electoral campaigns, the 1989 party slogan played effectively on many Belizeans' fears about immigration.

5. Purcell (1993, 38), Bourgois (1989, 87), and Rout (1976, 276) detail some of the beliefs widely held in Costa Rica and Panama about West Indians' sexual appetites.

6. Most Salvadoran immigrants in Honduras had been displaced from their homeland by the expansion of export agriculture in the 1950s and 1960s, which occurred at the expense of peasant landholdings (see Durham 1979; Brockett 1990).

7. Paid vacation benefits for industry workers were originally negotiated in 1975 by the DIU. By 1981, when the UGWU negotiated its first contract, workers received four weeks of paid vacation and two weeks of paid sick leave per year. At present, workers receive on average two weeks of paid vacation and no sick leave.

## Chapter 7. Transnational Identities and Trajectories in the Banana Belt

1. The Valley of Peace settlement was established in 1982 by the government of Belize with support from the United Nations high commissioner of refugees. The project initially entailed the placement of equal numbers of Salvadoran refugees and Belizean farming families in a settlement designed to more fully integrate refugees into Belizean rural society. The Valley of Peace subsequently received village status from the national government and now functions like other rural settlements in its local governance. Since its inception, however, the village has been marked by a major outflow of its Belizean residents (Stone 1990b, 1).

2. Granting the complexity of immigrants' decisions to leave their country of origin, the primary stated reasons for migration can generally be divided into "economic" or "political" motives. Comparison of reported reasons for migration among Salvadorans since 1992 with migrants arriving in 1991 or earlier yields a chi-square value of 5.57, significant at $p < .05$ with 1 df. This indicates that recent

migrants are significantly more likely to report economic hardship than fear of political persecution as the most important reason for their emigration.

3. Alternately, it may be argued that Salvadorans' fear of deportation to their homeland allows employers such as Tropical Produce to take advantage of them. Until the events of 1995 discussed in the epilogue, however, the region's employers had never relied on deportations to rid themselves of recalcitrant workers. The efforts to deport strikers in that year demonstrate that repatriation serves as a means of labor control when other, informal methods fail.

4. These national differences are not statistically significant, except when Belizeans are compared with other Central Americans as a whole.

5. Lewis notes that the nineteenth-century suppression of agriculture and reliance on imported goods engendered a persisting "dietetic snobbery despising local produce of all kinds, so that . . . the Creole [British] Honduran came to believe that fresh milk was a tasteless liquid as compared with sweetened condensed milk" (1969, 294).

6. Such work is considered dangerous not because of potential detection by authorities but because drug traffickers are reluctant to leave witnesses to their activities. In northern Belize it has been reported that immigrants employed in loading aircraft have been executed en masse after completing their work.

## Epilogue

1. In separate meetings with the government's labor officer stationed in Stann Creek District and an investigative mission from the nongovernmental organization SPEAR (Society for the Promotion of Education and Research), the chairman and secretary of the Banana Growers' Association vowed that they would never negotiate with a union in the banana industry.

# References

## Archival Sources

ARCHIVES OF BELIZE, BELMOPAN

AB 318-33a. Minute paper, 22 Mar. 1933. Colonial Secretary H. G. Pilling to Secretary of State for External Affairs, Ottawa, Canada.

AB 318-33b. 1933. Extract from memorandum by the Agricultural Development Committee.

AB M.C. 1056. Minute paper, 16 Dec. 1922. Confidential memorandum, Chairman of the Riversdale Inspection Committee to Colonial Secretary, detailing an outbreak of Panama disease.

*Clarion.* 22 July 1909 and 26 Mar. 1911.

*Colonial Guardian.* 1 Jan. 1887, 22 Dec. 1900, 1 Jan. 1902, 8 Mar. 1902, 26 July 1902, 26 Mar. 1904, and 11 Dec. 1910.

PUBLIC RECORDS OFFICE, KEW, GREAT BRITAIN

PRO CO 123 165. Dispatch, Gov. Barlee to Secretary of State for the Colonies, 29 Mar. 1880.

PRO CO 123 233. Dispatch, Gov. Wilson to Secretary of State for the Colonies, 3 Aug. 1899, marked confidential.

PRO CO 123 240. Dispatch, Gov. Wilson to Secretary of State for the Colonies, 13 Feb. 1902.

PRO CO 123 240. Henry Keith to Gov. Wilson, 8 Feb. 1902, contained in Gov. Wilson's dispatch.

PRO CO 123 240. Fairweather, Cuthbert, and Woods, unofficial members of the Legislative Council, to Secretary of State for the Colonies, 6 Mar. 1902, contained in Gov. Wilson's dispatch.

PRO CO 123 240. Colonial Office minute paper commenting on letter from Fairweather, Cuthbert, and Woods, n.d.

PRO CO 123 255. Dispatch, Governor Swayne to Secretary of State for the Colonies, 18 Apr. 1907, concerning sale of land in Stann Creek Valley, marked confidential.

PRO CO 123 261. Dispatch, Gov. Swayne to Secretary of State for the Colonies, 11 Feb. 1909, accompanying draft agreement with United Fruit Company for Colonial Office approval.

PRO CO 123 267. Report of the Committee on Landing Rights for Submarine Cables on the Application by United Fruit Company for Permission to Establish a Wireless Telegraph Station in British Honduras, 10 Dec. 1909, marked confidential.

PRO CO 123 268. Dispatch, Gov. Swayne to Secretary of State for the Colonies, 29 May 1911, detailing United Fruit's suspension of passenger service, marked confidential.

PRO CO 123 268. C. H. Ellis of United Fruit to Governor Swayne, 18 Feb. 1911, contained in Gov. Swayne's dispatch.

PRO CO 123 271. Correspondence between Colonial Office and House of Commons, 11 July 1911, concerning cost overruns on Stann Creek Railway.

PRO CO 123 273. Gov. Swayne to Secretary of State for the Colonies, 3 Apr. 1912, Panama, concerning the proposed settlement of Barbardian smallholders in British Honduras.

PRO CO 123 284. Annual Report for 1915 on the Stann Creek Railway, Apr. 1916, submitted by the railway superintendent.

PRO CO 123 291. Dispatch, Acting Gov. Walter to Secretary of State for the Colonies, 1 Apr. 1918, discussing flooding damage in the Stann Creek Valley.

PRO CO 123 292. Dispatch, Gov. Bennett to Secretary of State for the Colonies, 8 Aug. 1918, detailing financial woes of the Stann Creek Railway.

PRO CO 123 295a. Dispatch, Gov. Hutson to Secretary of State for the Colonies, 24 May 1919, detailing impending collapse of banana industry.

PRO CO 123 295b. Dispatch, Gov. Hutson to Secretary of State for the Colonies, 3 July 1919, detailing negotiations with G. M. Shaw, division manager for United Fruit Company in Guatemala.

PRO CO 123 300. Dispatch, Gov. Hutson to Secretary of State for the Colonies, 5 Apr. 1920.

PRO CO 123 300. Railway Superintendent to Gov. Hutson, asking that higher freight rates be levied on United Fruit, transmitted in Gov. Hutson's dispatch.

PRO CO 123 300. Colonial Secretary in Belize to the President of United Fruit in Boston, 11 Feb. 1920, requesting higher producer prices for the colony's bananas and transmitted in Gov. Hutson's dispatch.

PRO CO 123 300. Agricultural report for Riversdale by W. R. Dunlop, transmitted with Gov. Hutson's dispatch.

PRO CO 123 302. Dispatch, Gov. Hutson to Secretary of State for Colonies, 18 Aug. 1921, discussing governor's reluctance to seek legal action against United Fruit.

PRO CO 123 316. Telegram, Gov. Hutson to Secretary of State for Colonies, 16 Nov. 1923, announcing United Fruit's plans to sell the Middlesex Estate for fifteen thousand dollars.

PRO CO 123 329/2. Agricultural Reconnaissance of the Stann Creek Valley, by C. L. Stocker, Agricultural Officer, 1928.

## *Printed and Secondary Sources*

Agee, Phillip
    1975     *Inside the Company: CIA Diary.* New York: Bantam Books.
Alonso, Oscar
    1987     "Workers' Organization in the Banana Industry of Belize." Handwritten
             MS in the collection of SPEAR (Society for the Promotion of Education
             and Research), Belize City.
*Amandala* (Belize City)
    1978     "From Near and Far." 14 Apr., p. 9.
    1982a    "Of Refugees, Rogers, and Radio." 5 Mar., p. 7.
    1982b    "Foreigners Have More Rights than Belizeans in the Banana Industry."
             Letter to the Editor. 12 Mar., p. 2.
    1982c    "Banana Republic in Southern Belize." Letter to the Editor. 9 July, p. 2.
    1991a    "A Message to the Garinagu." 15 Nov., p. 2.
    1991b    "Between the Lines." 22 Nov., p. 5.
Anderson, Thomas
    1981     *The War of the Dispossessed: Honduras and El Salvador 1969.* Lincoln:
             Univ. of Nebraska Press.
Annis, Sheldon
    1987     *God and Production in a Guatemalan Town.* Austin: Univ. of Texas Press.
Appadurai, Arjun
    1990     "Disjuncture and Difference in the Global Cultural Economy." In *Global
             Culture: Nationalism, Globalization, and Modernity,* ed. Mike Feather-
             stone. London: Sage.
Argueta, Mario
    1992     *La Historia de los sin Historia, 1900–1948.* Tegucigalpa: Editorial Guay-
             muras.
Ashcraft, Norman
    1973     *Colonialism and Underdevelopment: Processes of Political Economic Change
             in British Honduras.* New York: Teachers College Press.
Ashdown, Peter
    1978     "Antonio Soberanis and the Disturbances in Belize, 1934–1937." *Carib-
             bean Quarterly* 24:61–74.
    1979     "Race, Class, and the Unofficial Majority in British Honduras, 1890–
             1949." Ph.D. diss., Univ. of Sussex.
    1982     "The Belize Elite." *Belizean Studies* 10:10–36.
Banana Control Board
    1974     *Annual Report.* Big Creek, Belize.
    1975     *Annual Report.* Big Creek, Belize.
    1984     *Annual Report.* Big Creek, Belize.

Baron, James, and William Bielby
  1980    "Bringing the Firms Back in: Stratification, Segmentation, and the Orga-
         nization of Work." *American Sociological Review* 45:737–65.
Barrera, Mario
  1979    *Race and Class in the Southwest.* South Bend, Ind.: Univ. of Notre Dame
         Press.
Barth, Frederik
  1969    Introduction to *Ethnic Groups and Boundaries,* ed. F. Barth. Boston:
         Little, Brown.
Basch, Linda, Nina Glick-Schiller, and Cristina Blanc-Szanton
  1994    *Nations Unbound: Transnational Projects, Postcolonial Predicaments, and
         Deterritorialized Nation-States.* Langhorne, Pa.: Gordon and Breach.
*Beacon* (Belize City)
  1975a   "Strike Threatens Banana Industry." 8 Feb., p. 1.
  1975b   "DIU Wins Landslide Poll." 1 Mar., p. 1.
  1975c   "DIU Wins Three Year Contract." 7 June, p. 1.
Becerra, Longino
  1985    "The Early History of the Labor Movement." In *Honduras: Portrait of a
         Captive Nation,* ed. Nancy Peckenham and Annie Street, 95–101. New
         York: Praeger.
Beechey, Veronica
  1978    "Women and Production: A Critical Analysis of Some Sociological Theo-
         ries of Women's Work." In *Feminism and Materialism,* ed. Annette Kuhn
         and Ann Marie Wolpe, 155–97. Boston: Routledge and Kegan Paul.
Belize Chamber of Commerce
  1993    "Labour: Weak Unions, Outdated Conventions." *Chamber Update* 5, nos.
         2–3 (Feb./Mar.): 1–3.
*Belize Times* (Belize City)
  1964    "Banana Industry Expands in this Country." 7 May, p. 1.
  1979    "Union Calls for Independent Investigation of U.D.P. 'Arms' Charge." 26
         Aug., p  12.
*Belize Today.*
  1987    "The Immigration Issue." Jan.: 2–4.
Bentley, G. Carter
  1987    "Ethnicity and Practice." *Comparative Studies in Society and History*
         29:24–55.
Black, Clinton, ed.
  1984    *Jamaica's Banana Industry.* Kingston: Jamaica Banana Producers Associa-
         tion.
Blomberg, Lennart
  1993    "Work Force in the Banana Area of Belize." MS. Belmopan: United
         Nations High Commissioner for Refugees.

Bolland, O. Nigel

1973    "The Social Structure and Social Relations of the Settlement in the Bay of Honduras (Belize) in the 18th Century." *Journal of Caribbean History* 6:1–42.

1977    *The Formation of a Colonial Society: Belize, from Conquest to Crown Colony.* Baltimore: Johns Hopkins Univ. Press.

1981    "Systems of Domination After Slavery: The Control of Land and Labor in the British West Indies After 1838." *Comparative Studies in Society and History* 23:591–619.

1984    "Reply to William A. Green's 'The Perils of Comparative History.'" *Comparative Studies in Society and History* 23:591–619.

1986    *Belize: A New Nation in Central America.* Boulder, Colo.: Westview Press.

1988    *Colonialism and Resistance in Belize.* Belize City: Cubola.

1991    "Pluralism and the Politicization of Ethnicity in Belize." Paper presented at the sixteenth annual conference of the Caribbean Studies Association, Havana.

Bolland, O. Nigel, and Mark Moberg

1995    "Development and National Identity: Creolization, Immigration, and Ethnic Conflict in Belize." *International Journal of Comparative Race and Ethnic Studies* 2:1–18.

Bolland, O. Nigel, and Assad Shoman

1977    *Land in Belize: 1765–1871.* Mona, Jamaica: Univ. of the West Indies.

Bonacich, Edna

1972    "A Theory of Ethnic Antagonism: The Split Labor Market." *American Sociological Review* 37:547–59.

1976    "Advanced Capitalism and Black/White Relations in the United States: A Split Labor Market Interpretation." *American Sociological Review* 41:34–51.

1980    "Class Approaches to Ethnicity and Race." *Insurgent Sociologist* 10:9–23.

Bossen, Laurel

1982    "Plantations and Labor Force Discrimination in Guatemala." *Current Anthropology* 23:263–68.

Bourgois, Philippe

1988    "Conjugated Oppression: Class and Ethnicity Among Guaymi and Kuna Banana Workers." *American Ethnologist* 15:328–48.

1989    *Ethnicity at Work: Divided Labor on a Central American Banana Plantation.* Baltimore: Johns Hopkins Univ. Press.

Branigan, William

1989    "Crack, L.A.-style Gangs Trouble Torpid Belize." *Washington Post,* 19 Sept., A23.

Braverman, Harry

1974    *Labor and Monopoly Capital: The Degradation of Work in the Twentieth Century.* New York: Monthly Review Press.

Bridges, William
　　1988　"Developments in Labor Market Research: Recent Theory and Data."
　　　　　*Sociological Quarterly* 29:1–4.
Brintnall, Douglas
　　1979　"Race Relations in the Southeastern Highlands of Mesoamerica." *American Ethnologist* 6:638–52.
Brockett, Charles
　　1990　*Land, Power, and Poverty: Agrarian Transformation and Political Conflict in Central America.* Boulder, Colo.: Westview Press.
Brockmann, C. Thomas
　　1977　"Ethnic and Racial Relations in Northern Belize." *Ethnicity* 4:246–62.
Burawoy, Michael
　　1979　*Manufacturing Consent: Changes in the Labor Process Under Monopoly Capital.* Chicago: Univ. of Chicago Press.
Burdon, Sir John
　　1931　*Archives of British Honduras, Being Extracts and Précis from Records, with Maps.* London: Sifton, Praed.
Cain, Glenn
　　1976　"The Challenge of Segmented Labor Market Theories to Orthodox Theory: A Survey." *Journal of Economic Literature* 14:1215–57.
Cal, Angel
　　1991　"Rural Society and Economic Development: British Mercantile Capital in Nineteenth Century Belize." Ph.D. diss., Department of History, Univ. of Arizona.
Calvert, Peter
　　1976　"Guatemala and Belize." *Contemporary Review* 228:7- 12.
　　1985　*Guatemala: A Nation in Turmoil.* Boulder, Colo.: Westview Press.
Castells, Manuel
　　1975　"Immigrant Workers and Class Struggles in Advanced Capitalism: The Western European Experience." *Politics and Society* 5:33–66.
Catzim, Adele
　　1992　"Sewing the Threads of Dependency: Women in the Garment Industry Ten Years after Independence." In *Independence: Ten Years After. Fifth Annual Studies on Belize Conference.* Belize City: Society for the Promotion of Education and Research.
Central Bank of Belize
　　1991　*Tenth Annual Report and Accounts, 1991.* Belize City: Central Bank.
　　1992　*Eleventh Annual Report and Accounts, 1992.* Belize City: Central Bank.
Chaney, Elsa
　　1979　"The World Economy and Contemporary Migration." *International Migration Review* 13:204–12.

Chavez, Leo
   1994    "The Power of the Imagined Community: The Settlement of Undocu-
           mented Mexicans and Central Americans in the United States." *American
           Anthropologist* 96:52–73.
Commonwealth Development Corporation
   1983    *Banana Control Board Review.* Belmopan.
Cosminsky, Sheila
   1976    "Carib-Creole Relations in a Belizean Community." In *Frontier Adapta-
           tions in Lower Central America,* ed. M. W. Helms and Franklin O.
           Loveland. Philadelphia: Institute for the Study of Human Issues.
Crowe, Frederick
   1850    *The Gospel in Central America, Containing a Sketch of the Country.* Lon-
           don: Charles Gilpin.
Davies, Peter
   1990    *Fyffes and the Banana: A Centenary History, 1888–1988.* London: Athlone.
Dayley, Jon
   1979    *Belizean Creole: Grammar Handbook.* Brattleboro, Vt.: Experiment Press.
de Janvry, Alain
   1981    *The Agrarian Question and Reformism in Latin America.* Baltimore: Johns
           Hopkins Univ. Press.
Deere, Carmen Diana, P. Antrobus, L. Bolles, E. Melendez, P. Phillips, M. Rivera,
           and H. Safa.
   1990    *In the Shadows of the Sun: Caribbean Development Alternatives and U.S.
           Policy.* Boulder, Colo.: Westview Press.
Development Finance Corporation
   1977    *Labour and Immigration in Belize.* Belize City: DFC.
Dosal, Paul
   1993    *Doing Business with the Dictators: A Political History of United Fruit in
           Guatemala, 1899–1944.* Wilmington, Del.: Scholarly Resources.
Downie, Jack
   1959    *An Economic Policy for British Honduras.* Belize City: Government Print-
           ery.
Dunlop, W. R.
   N.d. [1920?]    "Report on the Economic and Natural Features of British Hon-
           duras in Relation to Agriculture, with Prospects for Development." Un-
           published report, Belize City.
Durham, William
   1979    *Scarcity and Survival in Central America.* Stanford, Calif.: Stanford Univ.
           Press.
Echeverri-Gent, Elisavinda
   1992    "Forgotten Workers: British West Indians and the Early Days of the

Banana Industry in Costa Rica and Honduras." *Journal of Latin American Studies* 24:275–308.

Evans, G.

1948    *Report of the British Guiana and British Honduras Settlement Commission*. London: His Majesty's Stationery Office.

Everitt, J.

1984    "The Recent Migrations of Belize, Central America." *International Migration Review* 18:319–25.

Falla, Ricardo

1994    *Massacres in the Jungle: Ixcán, Guatemala, 1975–1982*. Boulder, Colo.: Westview Press.

Fallas, Carlos

1975    *Mamita Yunai*. San José, Costa Rica: Lehman S.A.

Fernandez-Kelly, Maria Patricia

1983    "Mexican Border Industrialization, Female Labor Force Participation, and Migration." In *Women, Men, and the International Division of Labor*, ed. June Nash and Maria Patricia Fernandez-Kelly, 205–23. Albany: State Univ. of New York Press.

Fligstein, Neil, and Roberto Fernandez

1988    "Worker Power, Firm Power, and the Structure of Labor Markets." *Sociological Quarterly* 29:5–28.

Friedman, Milton

1962    *Capitalism and Freedom*. Chicago: Univ. of Chicago Press.

Gartman, David

1986    *Auto Slavery: The Labor Process in the American Automobile Industry, 1897–1950*. New Brunswick, N.J.: Rutgers Univ. Press.

Geertz, Clifford

1963    "The Integrative Revolution: Primordial Sentiments and Civil Politics in the New States." In *Old Societies and New States*, ed. C. Geertz, 105–57. New York: Free Press.

Glick-Schiller, Nina, L. Basch, and C. Blanc-Szanton, eds.

1992    *Towards a Transnational Perspective on Migration: Race, Class, Ethnicity, and Nationalism Reconsidered*. New York: New York Academy of Sciences.

Gmelch, George

1992    *Double Passage: The Lives of Caribbean Migrants Abroad and Back Home*. Ann Arbor: Univ. of Michigan Press.

*Gombay* (Belize City)

1979    Mar., p. 2.

Gonzalez, Nancie

1988    *Sojourners of the Caribbean: Ethnogenesis and Ethnohistory of the Garifuna*. Urbana: Univ. of Illinois Press.

Goodwin, Paul
    1992    *Latin America.* 5th ed. Guilford, Conn.: Dushkin.
Gordon, David, Richard Edwards, and Michael Reich
    1982    *Segmented Work, Divided Workers.* Cambridge: Cambridge Univ. Press.
Government of Belize
    1981    *State of Emergency (Essential Services) Regulations.* Statutory Instrument no. 31 of 1981. 3 Apr. Belmopan.
    1983    *Population Census 1980.* Belmopan: Central Statistical Unit.
    1991    *1991 Population Census: Major Findings.* Belmopan: Central Statistical Office.
    1992    *A Policy Statement on Refugees and Economic Migrants.* Mimeo. Belmopan: Ministry of Foreign Affairs.
Government of British Honduras
    1890–1903    *Blue Books.* Belize.
    1959    *Labour Ordinance.* Belize City.
Grant, Cedric
    1976    *The Making of Modern Belize: Politics, Society, and British Colonialism in Central America.* Cambridge: Cambridge Univ. Press.
Green, Susan
    1983    "Silicon Valley's Women Workers: A Theoretical Analysis of Sex-Segregation in the Electronics Industry Labor Market." In *Women, Men, and the International Division of Labor,* ed. June Nash and Maria Patricia Fernandez- Kelly. Albany: State Univ. of New York Press.
Green, William A.
    1984    "The Perils of Comparative History: Belize and the British Sugar Colonies after Slavery." *Comparative Studies in Society and History* 26:112–19.
Gregory, James
    1987    *The Mopan: Culture and Ethnicity in a Changing Belizean Community.* Columbia: Univ. of Missouri Museum of Anthropology.
Griffith, David
    1987    "Nonmarket Labor Processes in an Advanced Capitalist Economy." *American Anthropologist* 89:838–52.
    1993    *Jones's Minimal: Low Wage Labor in the United States.* Albany: State Univ. of New York Press.
Hall, Jerry
    1983    "The Place of Climatic Hazards in Food Scarcity: A Case Study of Belize." In *Interpretations of Calamity, from the Viewpoint of Human Ecology,* ed. K. Hewitt. Boston: Allen and Unwin.
Hamilton, Nora, and Norma Stoltz Chinchilla
    1991    "Central American Migration: A Framework for Analysis." *Latin American Research Review* 26:75–110.

Harpelle, Ronald
    1993    "The Social and Political Integration of West Indians in Costa Rica: 1930–1950." *Journal of Latin American Studies* 25:103–20.
Hartshorn, G., et al.
    1984    *Belize: A Country Environmental Profile.* Belize City: Robert Nicolait and Associates.
Hartz, Louis
    1955    *The Liberal Tradition in America.* New York: Harcourt, Brace and World.
Harvey, David
    1989    *The Condition of Postmodernity.* London: Basil Blackwell.
Helms, Mary
    1976    Introduction to *Frontier Adaptations in Lower Central America,* ed. M. W. Helms and Franklin O. Loveland. Philadelphia: Institute for the Study of Human Issues.
    1981    "Black Carib Domestic Organization in Historical Perspective: Traditional Origins of Contemporary Patterns." *Ethnology* 20:77–86.
*A History of Belize*
    1983    Belize City: Cubola.
Holt, Thomas C.
    1992    *The Problem of Freedom: Race, Labor and Politics in Jamaica and Britain.* Baltimore: Johns Hopkins Univ. Press.
Horowitz, Donald
    1985    *Ethnic Groups in Conflict.* Berkeley: Univ. of California Press.
Howard, Michael
    1977    *Political Change in a Mayan Village in Southern Belize.* Katunob—Occasional Publications in Mesoamerican Anthropology. Greeley: Univ. of Northern Colorado.
    1980    "Ethnicity and Economic Integration in Southern Belize." *Ethnicity* 7:119–36.
Hutson, Sir Eyre
    1925    *The Handbook of British Honduras.* London: Colonial Office.
James, Canute
    1993    "The Banana War." *African World* (Nov.): 23.
Kepner, Charles
    [1936] 1967    *Social Aspects of the Banana Industry.* New York: Columbia Univ. Press.
Kepner, Charles, and J. H. Soothill
    1935    *The Banana Empire: A Case Study of Economic Imperialism.* New York: Russell and Russell.
Kerns, Virginia
    1983    *Women and the Ancestors: Black Carib Kinship and Ritual.* Urbana: Univ. of Illinois Press.
Keyes, Charles
    1976    "Towards a New Formulation of the Concept of Ethnic Group." *Ethnicity* 3:202–13.

Kroshus Medina, Laurie

    1987    "Belize Citrus Politics: Dialectic of Strategy and Structure." Master's thesis, Department of Anthropology, Univ. of California, Los Angeles.

    1992a    "Immigration, Labor and Government Policy: Class Conflict and Alternative Paths Towards Development." In *Independence: Ten Years After.* Fifth Annual Studies on Belize Conference. SPEAReports 8. Belize City: Society for the Promotion of Education and Research.

    1992b    "Power and Development: The Political Economy of Identities in Belize." Ph.D. diss., Univ. of California, Los Angeles.

Laclau, Ernesto, and Chantal Mouffe

    1985    *Hegemony and Socialist Strategy: Towards a Radical Democratic Politics.* London: Verso.

Lapper, Richard, and James Painter

    1985    *Honduras: State for Sale.* London: Latin American Bureau.

Lash, S., and J. Urry

    1987    *The End of Organized Capitalism.* Madison: Univ. of Wisconsin Press.

Lewis, Gordon

    1969    *The Making of the Modern West Indies.* New York: Monthly Review.

MacCameron, Robert

    1983    *Bananas, Labor, and Politics in Honduras: 1954–1963.* Foreign and Comparative Studies/Latin American Series, No. 5. Syracuse, N.Y.: Maxwell School of Citizenship and Public Affairs, Syracuse Univ.

Manz, Beatriz

    1988    *Refugees of a Hidden War: The Aftermath of Counterinsurgency in Guatemala.* Albany: State Univ. of New York Press.

Marx, Karl

    [1847] 1977a    "The Poverty of Philosophy." In *Karl Marx: Selected Writings,* ed. D. McClellan. Oxford: Oxford Univ. Press.

    [1851] 1977b    "The Eighteenth Brumaire of Louis Bonaparte." In *Karl Marx: Selected Writings,* ed. D. McClellan. Oxford: Oxford Univ. Press.

    [1870] 1977c    "Letter to Meyer and Vogt." In *Karl Marx: Selected Writings,* ed. D. McClellan. Oxford: Oxford Univ. Press.

Marx, Karl, and Friedrich Engels

    [1848] 1977    "The Communist Manifesto." In *Karl Marx: Selected Writings,* ed. D. McClellan. Oxford: Oxford Univ. Press.

Massey, Douglas, Rafael Alarcón, Jorge Durand, and Humberto Gonzalez

    1987    *Return to Aztlan.* Berkeley: Univ. of California Press.

May, Stacy, and Galo Plaza

    1958    *The United Fruit Company in Latin America.* Washington, D.C.: National Planning Association.

McCann, Thomas

    1976    *An American Company: The Tragedy of United Fruit.* New York: Crown.

Miller, Robert

1989   "Segmentation and Gender Occupational Segregation Within an Industrial Labor Market: The Radio Manufacturing Industry in Philadelphia, 1926–1935." *Sociological Spectrum* 9:403–24.

Milliband, Ralph

1983   "State Power and Class Interests." *New Left Review* 138:57–68.

Mintz, Sidney

1974   "The Rural Proletariat and the Problem of Rural Proletarian Consciousness." *Journal of Peasant Studies* 1:291–325.

Moberg, Mark

1990   "Class Resistance and Class Hegemony: From Conflict to Co-optation in the Citrus Industry of Belize." *Ethnology* 29:189–208.

1991a   "Citrus and the State: Factionalism and Class Formation in Rural Belize." *American Ethnologist* 18:21–39.

1991b   "Marketing Policy and the Loss of Food Self-Sufficiency in Rural Belize." *Human Organization* 50:16–25.

1992a   *Citrus, Strategy, and Class: The Politics of Development in Southern Belize.* Iowa City: Univ. of Iowa Press.

1992b   "Structural Adjustment and Rural Development: Inferences from a Belizean Village." *Journal of Developing Areas* 27:1–20.

1992c   "Continuity Under Colonial Rule: The *Alcade* System and the Garifuna in Belize, 1858–1969." *Ethnohistory* 39: 1–19.

1994   "An Agency Model of the State: Contributions and Limitations of Institutional Economics." In *Anthropology and Institutional Economics,* ed. James Acheson. Lanham, Md.: Univ. Press of America.

Moberg, Mark, and J. Stephen Thomas

1993   "Class Segmentation and Divided Labor: Asian Workers in the Gulf of Mexico Seafood Industry." *Ethnology* 32:1–13.

Montgomery, Tommie Sue

1991   *Refugees in Belize, 1991.* Belmopan: Report to the United Nations High Commissioner for Refugees.

Nash, June

1985   "Segmentation of the Work Process in the International Division of Labor." In *The Americas in the New International Division of Labor,* ed. S. Sanderson. New York: Homes and Meier.

1994   "Global Integration and Subsistence Insecurity." *American Anthropologist* 96:7–30.

Nash, June, and M. Fernandez-Kelly, eds.

1983   *Women, Men, and the International Division of Labor.* Albany: State Univ. of New York Press.

*New Belize*

1979   "Banana . . . Banana . . . Banana!" Oct.: 12–15.

Omi, Michael, and Howard Winant
    1986    *Racial Formation in the United States.* New York: Routledge.

Ong, Aihwa
    1987    *Spirits of Resistance and Capitalist Discipline: Factory Women in Malaysia.* Albany: State Univ. of New York Press.

Paige, Jeffrey
    1975    *Agrarian Revolution: Social Movements and Export Agriculture in the Underdeveloped World.* New York: Free Press.

Painter, Michael
    1985    "Changing Relations of Production and Rural Development." *Journal of Anthropological Research* 40:271–92.

Palacio, Joseph
    1987    "A Rural/Urban Environment for Central American Immigrants in Belize." *Caribbean Quarterly* 33:29–41.
    1988    "Illegal Aliens in Belize: Findings from the 1984 Amnesty." In *When Borders Don't Divide: Labor Migration and Refugee Movements in the Americas,* ed. Patricia Pessar. New York: Center for Migration Studies.
    1990    *Socioeconomic Integration of Central American Immigrants in Belize.* Belize City: Society for the Promotion of Education and Research.
    1993    "Social and Cultural Implications of Recent Demographic Changes in Belize." *Belizean Studies* 21 (1): 3–12.

Pastor, Robert
    1985    "Introduction: The Policy Challenge." In *Migration and Development in the Caribbean,* ed. Robert Pastor. Boulder, Colo.: Westview Press.

Peckenham, Nancy, and Annie Street
    1985    "The Rolston Letter." In *Honduras: Portrait of a Captive Nation,* ed. N. Peckenham and A. Street. New York: Praeger.

Peña, Devon
    1988    "'Tortuosidad': Shop Floor Struggles of Female Maquiladora Workers." In *Women on the U.S.-Mexico Border: Responses to Change,* ed. Vicki L. Ruiz and Susan Tiano. Boston: Allen and Unwin.

Peoples' United Party (PUP)
    1989    *Belizeans First: PUP Manifesto, 1989–94.* Belize City.

Portes, Alejandro, and Robert Bach
    1985    *Latin Journey: Cuban and Mexican Immigrants in the U.S.* Berkeley: Univ. of California Press.

Portes, Alejandro, and John Walton
    1981    *Labor, Class, and the International System.* New York: Academic Press.

Purcell, Trevor
    1993    *Banana Fallout: Class, Color, and Culture Among West Indians in Costa Rica.* Los Angeles: UCLA Center for Afro-American Studies.

Radcliffe, Sarah
   1990    "Between Hearth and Labor Market: The Recruitment of Peasant Women in the Andes." *International Migration Review* 24:229–49.
Radio Belize
   1993    Evening news report. 15 Sept.
   1995    Evening news report. 17 July.
Reich, Michael
   1981    *Racial Inequality: A Political Economic Analysis.* Princeton, N.J.: Princeton Univ. Press.
Reich, Michael, Richard Edwards, and David Gordon
   1981    *The Segmentation of Labor in American Capitalism.* Cambridge: Cambridge Univ. Press.
Rout, Leslie
   1976    *The African Experience in Spanish America, 1502 to the Present Day.* London: Cambridge Univ. Press.
Rubenstein, Hymie
   1983    "Remittances and Rural Underdevelopment in the English-Speaking Caribbean." *Human Organization* 42:295–306.
Ruhl, J. Mark
   1983    "The Economy." In *Honduras: A Country Study,* ed. James D. Rudolph. Washington, D.C.: Department of the Army.
Sacks, Karen
   1988    *Caring by the Hour: Women, Work and Organizing at Duke Medical Center.* Urbana: Univ. of Illinois Press.
Safa, Helen
   1987    "Popular Culture, National Identity, and Race in the Caribbean." *New West Indian Guide* 61:115–26.
Sampson, H. C.
   1929    *Report on the Development of Agriculture in British Honduras.* London: H.M. Stationery Office.
Schwartz, Norman
   1987    "Colonization of Northern Guatemala: The Peten." *Journal of Anthropological Research* 43:163–83.
Scott, James
   1976    *The Moral Economy of the Peasant.* New Haven, Conn.: Yale Univ. Press.
   1985    *Weapons of the Weak: Everyday Forms of Peasant Resistance.* New Haven, Conn.: Yale Univ. Press.
Shaw, Kathryn
   1988    "Capitalizing on Success: The Belize Banana Growers Cooperative Society, Ltd." *Grassroots Development* 12:20–27.
Shoman, Assad
   1987a    *Party Politics in Belize: 1950–1986.* Belize City: Cubola.

1987b   "Double Jeopardy: Trade Union Relations with Party and State—The Case of the UGWU." In *Belize: Ethnicity and Development.* First Annual Studies on Belize Conference. Belize City: Society for the Promotion of Education and Research.

1988   "Reseña de la Industria Bananera en Belice." In *Cambio y Continuidad en la Economía Bananera,* ed. FLACSO. San José, Costa Rica: FLACSO.

1989   "La Inmigración Centroamericana en Belice: Un Choque Cultural." MS in the collection of Society for the Promotion of Education and Research, Belize City.

1994   *Thirteen Chapters in the History of Belize.* Belize City: Angelus Press.

1996   Personal communication with author. Letter dated 11 June.

Showalter, William Joseph

1913   "Countries of the Caribbean." *National Geographic* 24 (2): 227–50.

Smith, M. G.

[1965] 1974   *The Plural Society in the British West Indies.* Berkeley: Univ. of California Press.

Society for the Promotion of Education and Research (SPEAR)

1987   *Spearhead.* Belize City.

Sollors, Werner, ed.

1989   *The Invention of Ethnicity.* New York: Oxford Univ. Press.

Spillers, Hortense J., ed.

1991   *Comparative American Identities: Race, Sex and Nationality in the Modern Text.* New York: Routledge.

Stein, William

1984   "How Peasants Are Exploited: The Extraction of Unpaid Labor in Rural Peru." In *Research in Economic Anthropology,* ed. Barry Isaac. Greenwich, Conn.: JAL Press.

Stewart, Watt

1964   *Keith and Costa Rica.* Albuquerque: Univ. of New Mexico Press.

Stoler, Ann

1985   *Capitalism and Confrontation in Sumatra's Plantation Belt, 1870–1979.* New Haven, Conn.: Yale Univ. Press.

Stone, Michael

1990a   "Backabush: Settlement on the Belmopan Periphery and the Challenge to Rural Development in Belize." In *SPEAReports 6: Third Annual Studies on Belize Conference.* Belize City: Society for the Promotion of Education and Research.

1990b   *Report on the Valley of Peace Socio-Economic Survey.* Prepared for Belize Enterprise for Sustained Technology (BEST). Belmopan.

1994   "Caribbean Nation, Central American State: Ethnicity, Race, and National Formation in Belize, 1798–1990." Ph.D. diss., Department of Anthropology, Univ. of Texas, Austin.

Thomas, Robert
　1985　*Citizenship, Gender, and Work: The Social Organization of Industrial Agriculture*. Berkeley: Univ. of California Press.
Thorndike, Anthony
　1983　"The Conundrum of Belize: An Anatomy of a Dispute." *Social and Economic Studies* 32:65–102.
Topsey, Harriot
　1987　"The Ethnic War in Belize." In *Belize: Ethnicity and Development*. Belize City: Society for the Promotion of Education and Research.
Trimberger, Katherine
　1979　"World Systems Analysis: The Problem of Unequal Development." *Theory and Society* 8:127–37.
Trouillot, Michel-Rolph
　1988　*Peasants and Capital: Dominica in the World Economy*. Baltimore: Johns Hopkins Univ. Press.
ULG Consultants
　1975　*The Banana Industry in Belize*. London: Ministry of Overseas Development.
Vernon, Dylan
　1990　"Belize Exodus to the United States: For Better or for Worse." In *SPEAReports 4: Second Annual Studies on Belize Conference*. Belize City: Society for the Promotion of Education and Research.
Volk, Steve
　1981　"Honduras: On the Border of War." *NACLA: Report on the Americas* 15:2–37.
Waddell, D. A. G.
　1961　*British Honduras: A Historical and Contemporary Survey*. Oxford: Oxford Univ. Press.
Wilk, Richard
　1984　"Rural Settlement Change in Belize, 1970–1980: The Effects of Roads." *Belizean Studies* 12:1–9.
　1987　"The Kekchi and the Settlement of Toledo District." *Belizean Studies* 15:33–50.
　1991　*Household Ecology: Economic Change and Domestic Life among the Kekchi Maya of Belize*. Tucson: Univ. of Arizona Press.
Wilk, Richard, and Mac Chapin
　1990　*Ethnic Minorities in Belize: Mopan, Kekchi, and Garifuna*. Belize City: Society for the Promotion of Education and Research.
Williams, Brackette
　1989　"A Class Act: Anthropology and the Race to Nation Across Ethnic Terrain." *Annual Review of Anthropology* 18:401–44.

1991    *Stains on My Name, War in My Veins: Guyana and the Politics of Cultural Struggle.* Durham, N.C.: Duke Univ. Press.

Williams, Robert
1986    *Export Agriculture and the Crisis in Central America.* Chapel Hill: Univ. of North Carolina Press.

Wilson, Charles Morrow
1947    *Empire in Green and Gold: The Story of the American Banana Trade.* New York: Holt.

Wolf, Eric
1982    *Europe and the People Without History.* Berkeley: Univ. of California Press.

Worsley, Peter
1984    *The Three Worlds: Culture and World Development.* London: Weidenfeld and Nicolson.

Wouters, Myriam
1983    *Report on the Socioeconomic Survey of Dispersed Salvadoran Refugees Living in Belize.* Report to the United Nations High Commissioner for Refugees. San José, Costa Rica.

Wright, A C. S., D. H. Romney, R. H. Arbuckle, and V. E. Vial
1959    *Land in British Honduras: Report of the British Honduras Land Use Survey Team.* Colonial Research Publications No. 24. London: H.M. Stationery Office.

Young, Alma
1978    "Ethnic Politics in Belize." *Caribbean Review* 7:38–42.

# Index